This book is dedicated to
Changemakers everywhere working for
our highest aspirations and potential.

Reviews of
Change for the Audacious

A truly path breaking work. It will inspire and motivate the tens of thousands of individuals who are working to make positive change happen. Change agents dealing with societal challenges - whether working in large organisations or on their own - have now a treasure chest that will inspire and guide.

Georg Kell
Founding Executive Director UN Global Compact
Vice Chair Arabesque Partners

As the world's problems increase in complexity, leaders within the social sector are raising their sights from individual interventions to focusing more on multi-level interventions that support conditions for change within large scale systems. Steve Waddell's book provides a much needed resource for leaders of social change, with helpful frames and tools to support this challenging work.

John Kania
Managing Director
FSG

Change for the Audacious offers comprehensive yet understandable insight into what it will take for change makers to build a better world. It is a book meant for the courageous--those who would undertake their piece of the system change that orients business, economies, and other major systems towards greater sustainability and equity--that is towards building a world where all can flourish. Steve Waddell has taken his vast knowledge of systems and our planet, and given us a roadmap that can profoundly help us all as we undertake the system transformation that is needed in our world.

Sandra Waddock
Galligan Chair of Strategy
Carroll School Scholar of Corporate Responsibility
Professor of Management
Boston College

The Robert Wood Johnson Foundation is working with others to build a Culture of Health in America so that all who live here have an equal opportunity to be their healthiest. Our view is that health disparities between population groups, genders, income groups, ability groups, regions etc. are exacerbated by systems related to non-medical determinants of health. *Change for the Audacious* offers readers a road map for examining, reflecting and reimagining large scale systems changes so that the systems that impact peoples' lives can work better, work better together and ultimately lead to an equity rich society.

Dwayne C. Proctor, Ph. D.
Senior Adviser to the President
Director, Health Equity Portfolio
Robert Wood Johnson Foundation

Steve's passion for large systems change is unparalleled and in this book he has collected a broad range of methods, concept and tools that manifest that passion.

Dave Snowden
Chief Scientific Officer
Cognitive Edge

Guiding system change is easy to say and tough to do, but is essential in a world where systemic shifts increasingly impact our daily lives and survival prospects. Steve's book is not just a guide to action, but delivers the message that what seems impossible in theory can be done in practice through common sense, able brokering and an unreasonable ambition and appetite for work. UNEP's work in advancing a sustainable financial system is a great example of an attempt to blend all three in cohering and amplifying the many initiatives that have or currently do seek similar outcomes.

Simon Zadek
Co-chair
The Inquiry into the Design of a Sustainable Financial System
Visiting Professor and DSM Senior Fellow in Partnership and Sustainability
Singapore Management University

Dealing with issues like corruption clearly requires the depth of change in our societies, and the engagement of the number of people and organizations that *Change for the Audacious* refers to as Large Systems Change. The value of the book is that it both presents the change challenge in terms of the time and effort that it requires; and it also presents tools and frameworks that come from a range of experiences to help make the change happen. Reading it will be energizing and enabling for people fighting for a better world.

Peter Eigen
Founder and Chairman of the Advisory Council
Transparency International

It is now well established that the difficult problems facing the world are characterised by complexity. Much less clear is how we can work effectively with that complexity. Steve Waddell offers an interpretation which is tangible, practical and well written.

Professor Danny Burns
Participation Research Cluster Leader
Institute of Development Studies
University of Sussex

Tackling today's toughest challenges requires bringing people together across divides to produce innovative solutions. *Change for the Audacious* makes a valuable contribution to doing this with its large systems change perspective. It integrates Steve's own impressive experience with lessons from many leaders in this work to present a comprehensive approach with valuable frameworks, tools and insights.

Sandy Heierbacher
Director
National Coalition for Dialogue & Deliberation

Around the world, people are coming together in novel ways to challenge power and orthodoxy and to realise their transformational visions of a more just and sustainable future. Steve Waddell brings his unique experience from such movements across a range of contexts to provide profound insights into how change on a large scale actually happens. He offers practical approaches for how to more effectively engage with the complexity and unpredictability of the systems we seek to transform, whether local or global. Steve is both a lucid thinker and a committed practitioner at the forefront of helping us understand not only what we do, but how we can do it better.

Mike Taylor
Director
International Land Coalition secretariat at IFAD

Pick any given problem that philanthropy or the social sector aim to solve and you will find it sits within a larger system. Yet, while many of us acknowledge a systems approach can help us understand the root cause of a given issue and support us in maximizing the impact of limited resources, the leap to action can be daunting. Steve Waddell's *Change for the Audacious* puts forward a fresh and action-oriented approach to changing systems and scaling change that will prove enlightening and effective to change makers across the social sector. Inspiring and empowering, Waddell provides us with illuminating case examples and frameworks that provide the reader with the tools to get started on Large Systems Change (LSC).

Jamaica Maxwell,
Organizational Effectiveness,
The David and Lucile Packard Foundation

Addressing the many complex, "wicked" problems facing us today requires diverse collaboration, robust networks, new forms of leadership and making learning central for deep innovation. To do this, Change for the Audacious does an impressive job of pulling together a comprehensive summary of leading knowledge. Change makers at all levels of experience will find it provides valuable guidance.

Ajay Tejasvi Narasimhan
Convenor - Global Partnership on Leadership
World Bank

One of the most significant questions facing humans today is: how do we create the necessary large-scale change so that the future is sustainable, just, and healthy for people and the planet? This book has set out to deal with the capacity that humans need to address that question. This detailed and comprehensive volume will give readers a better understanding of what transformative change entails, but it also provides a plethora of tools and strategies to enhance social capacities for change. Moreover, Waddell draws on a rich set of case studies from around the world in order to explain how, when, and why to use these tools and strategies. The volume provides insights into how transformations occur – from the individual scale to broad systemic change. This book is an important companion for any person or organization that wants to initiate and navigate large-scale system change.

Per Olsson
Theme leader, Adaptive governance, networks and learning
Stockholm Resilience Centre

Steve Waddell has done it again – written a groundbreaking book on large systems change. In *Change for the Audacious*, Waddell not only provides a much needed meta-view of complex global systems but he marries his erudite understanding of these systems with useful concrete practices and distinctions for change leaders to use to transform them. This book is filled with case studies, key strategies and illustrative examples that researchers and activists alike will find essential for working more effectively with systems transformation.

Sean Esbjörn-Hargens PhD
Founder, MetaIntegral a global action network
Co-editor, Metatheory for the Twenty-first Century (Routledge, 2016)

The world of social media and networking offers much more tools and pathways than the past. So this book comes at the right time: It provides guidance from and for doer´s more than answers. The answers will have to be found out by each and every change agent herself applying the tools in the right way at the right time. Answers always depend on the context that we´re wanting to thrive in. That´s why the book ends with our role as an individual, working for transformation and deep change. And that´s why this book is a must read:

Because large systems change depends on many individuals making a difference. You can´t kiss a system, but you can embrace individuals.

Brigitta Villaronga
Head of Leadership Development
GIZ

This book provides a relevant and though provoking overview of the emerging field of large systems change. It makes a solid argument for the need to rethink how developed societies address change: rather than to optimise efficiency of existing structures, we need to rethink how societal systems are developing and should fundamentally change towards a sustainable future. By offering the tools and methods to explore such large system change this book moves beyond a strong argument and actually offers the reader a concrete starting point for advancing social change.

Prof. Dr. Derk A. Loorbach
Director - Dutch Research Institute for Transitions (Drift)
Professor of Socio-economic Transitions - Faculty of Social Science, both at
Erasmus University Rotterdam

Today's big change challenges require leaders in industry, government and social change networks working for collaborative impact with a firm understanding of complexity and transformation strategies. This book provides a unique resource for such leaders by pulling together knowledge and tools from a diversity of work and traditions to support strategic, collaborative impact.

Petra Kuenkel
Co-Founder, Executive Director
Collective Leadership Institute
Full Member - Club of Rome

Systemic approaches are critical to address the big change challenges facing us today. The Large Systems Change approach of this book, compiling the work and tools of so many change leaders, provides many examples and a valuable map of leading practice to support those working for transformation.

Mille Bojer
Christel Scholten
Directors
Reos Partners

About this book

We must and can do much better at addressing issues such as climate change, food security, health, education, environmental degradation, peace-building, water, equity, corruption, and wealth creation. This book is for people working on these types of issues, with the belief that we can create a future that is not just "sustainable", but also flourishing. This perspective means that the challenge is not just one of simple change, but of transformation – radical change in the way we perceive our world, create relationships and organize our societies. This is the implication of the United Nation's Sustainable Development Goals and other global efforts, and also innumerable efforts locally, nationally and regionally.

This book approaches these challenges as large systems change issues: issues requiring engagement of many, many people and organizations often globally; issues requiring deep innovation with shifts in mindsets and power structures; and issues that require capacity to work with complexity. Large systems change is presented as a new field of practice and knowledge; the book is not about a "method" or particular "approach"; rather it provides an overview of frameworks, methods and approaches to develop capacity to use the appropriate ones in particular contexts.

After introducing concepts of transformation and complexity, the book presents five case studies of large systems change. These cases and others are referenced throughout the remainder of the book to present large systems change strategy, organizing structures, steps in developing the necessary collective action, tools, and personal guidance for change practitioners.

About the Author

Steve Waddell's work over 30 years on large systems change has made him a thought leader and change agent at the local, national, regional and global levels. His work has covered a wide range of change challenges including many aspects of sustainability, youth development, poverty, health care, education, slavery, and finance. As an educator, community organizer globally, keynote speaker, consultant and project partner he has worked with the UN Global Compact, Gates Foundation, World Bank, Global Reporting Initiative, Ford Foundation, Humanity United, Civicus, International Youth Foundation, USAID, International Development and Research Centre, Impact Hubs, Robert Wood Johnson Foundation, the Forest Stewardship Council and many others.

In the 1980s in his hometown of Vancouver, Canada, Steve worked on systems change locally. From Boston over 25 years he has worked nationally and globally. Because he sees that change requires weaving together relationships in new ways, Steve focuses upon intersectoral (business-government-civil society), inter-organizational collaboration and networks to produce innovation, enhance impact, and build new capacity. Three key concepts are associated with his work: "societal learning and change," which is a deep change strategy to address chronic and complex issues; "global action networks", which are an emerging form of global governance that addresses issues requiring transformation; and "large systems change" which deals with profound shifts in individual orientations, organizational structures and societal institutions.

Dozens of publications include the books *Societal Learning and Change: Innovation with Multi-Stakeholder Strategies* (2005); *Global Action Networks: Creating our future together* (2011); and lead editor of a special issue of the Journal of Corporate Citizenship on large systems change (June 2015). Steve has a Ph.D. in sociology and an MBA.

Change
for the
Audacious:
a doer's guide

Steve Waddell

NetworkingAction Publishing, Boston, MA, USA

NetworkingAction Publishing
14 Upton St., #4,
Boston, MA 02118

Networkingaction.com

Waddell, Steve
        Change for the Audacious: a doer's guide. / Steve Waddell
Includes bibliographical references and index.
Large systems change. 2. Transformation. 3. Social change. I. Title

First edition 2016
ISBN: 978-0-692-65165-0 (paperback)
ISBN: 978-1-4951-9492-4 (ebook)
Library of Congress Control Number: 2016903509

Editorial Assistance: Bree Schuette and Rob Quinan
Cover design: Jim Hood, Hood Design
Interior design: Kusmin

Change for the Audacious:
a doer's guide

Large Systems Change for a Flourishing Future

On reading the book:

This book is designed for people who are working for transformation and large systems change. You can start at the beginning and work your way through if you wish. There is, of course, a logic in the structure to support this, starting from the foundation and the big picture and ending with personal guidance for change makers. However, since we know that people learn best when the topic is particularly relevant to them, feel free to jump in anywhere that particularly interests you.

The book is designed so you can quickly get the main ideas from headings, tables and figures…so feel free to skim. And remember: the tables and figures are not simply summary knowledge…they are ways to analyze current situations and guide your response. Footnotes are provided for those who want to dive more deeply into a particular question.

The core concept behind the book is "societal change systems" (SCSs), which are directly addressed in Chapter 6. This arises from looking at large systems change through a transformation, complexity, and systems thinking lens. The book is about making visible SCSs, and enhancing their power and your own change actions by seeing them within this context.

Finally, remember that all this should be treated only as guidance. Experimenting with riffs on these suggestions is part of advancing our knowledge and capacity.

Let me know what you find useful and what you'd change or add! Write me at: swaddell@networkingaction.net.

Contents

Large systems change is an emergent process, in contrast to a deliberative one. A valuable way to operationalize such a process is through theories of change. Collectively these form pathways to transformation that describe how societal change systems evolve over time to produce transformation. "Pathways" is a useful concept to understand how to move issues from a complex state to one that can be addressed through traditional complicated and simple approaches. It also explains why resilience is so important for transformation. Guidelines for designing resilience are presented.

Societal change systems comprise four distinct meta-strategies. Lacking a comprehensive understanding of these while tackling LSC is like working with a hand tied behind your back. Transformational change efforts always involve all four, but change facilitators tend to focus on just one. Understanding how the strategies interact and when to use each one greatly enhances the impact of any action. This is demonstrated by applying these four strategies to the Chapter 3 cases.

The collective strategies of initiatives addressing any change issue form societal change systems for that issue. These systems are all around us. However, we generally don't see them because our own predilections lead us to focus on particular parts. Without understanding the whole, you can actually undermine your efforts by undertaking poorly-informed action(s) on a part. This chapter presents the idea that these change systems can be developed with three approaches: societal learning and change, the systemic change matrix, and social movements. It also summarizes scaling approaches.

Historic organizing approaches cannot adequately address today's transformation change challenges, nor develop powerful societal change systems. In response to this gap, we are seeing the emergence of organizational innovations. Three are presented here: social (innovation) labs, communities of practice, and action networks. Collectively, these approaches power the emergence of societal change systems. There is a need for societal change system stewarding as a new organizing activity.

Those working on large systems change have developed ways to describe the process. Three of these approaches are presented here; each focuses on different development challenges. The Collective Leadership Compass emphasizes the dynamics of group formation to develop powerful collective leadership. The Systemic Change Process Map uses system dynamics mapping to describe the way key activities and tools interact as a system. Analysis of the development of Action Networks provides insight into on-going development processes and structures to realize breadth as well as depth. Creating a healthy array of these activities is a key to stewarding development of powerful societal change systems.

There are an overwhelming number of tools to support large systems change analysis and organizing events. Which methods and tools are appropriate for use at what times in the transformation process? How should they be used? This chapter aims to address these questions, with a particular focus on mapping approaches useful for seeing and developing various aspects of change initiatives and SCSs.

The real-life experiences of change agents can provide invaluable guidance to support you in your large systems change and societal change system development work. Five key qualities of successful change agents and four roles are discussed in this chapter.

Reflection is key to large systems change. Therefore, summary lessons are presented in the form of questions to ask yourself on your pathways toward large systems change through societal change systems.

List of Tables

List of Figures

Chapter 1

Transforming Our Approach to Change

Chapter Summary

A large change is needed in the way we approach change, if we are to successfully address modern challenges. This rethink comprises two core elements. One is to approach change in terms of a new field of knowledge, action, tools, strategy, and methods. This is referred to as Large Systems Change (LSC). An overview of LSC components is presented. The second element approaches change as a challenge to emerging societal change systems (SCSs); these systems comprise all change makers working on a particular issue. Both elements provide important insights for taking effective action.

We must and can do much better at addressing issues such as climate change, food security, health, peace-building, equity, and wealth creation. This book is for people working on these issues, with the belief that we can create a future that is not just "sustainable," but also flourishing.[1] This means that the challenge is not one of simple change, but of transformation – radical changes in the ways in which we perceive our world, create relationships, and organize our societies. This is the implication behind global efforts, such as the United Nation's Sustainable Development Goals, and also innumerable local, national, and regional efforts.

---

1   John Ehrenfeld has had a particular role in developing this line of thinking. Ehrenfeld, John, and Andrew Hoffman. 2013. *Flourishing: A frank conversation about sustainability*: Stanford University Press.

These big issues are addressed in this book with the perspective that we can influence the direction, but not the details, of transformational change. That direction hopefully reflects our highest aspirations. However, there are forces with great change power in their own right, such as climate change, population growth, and technological innovation. Change is an enduring constant that is accelerating in pace, breadth, and depth. To influence the direction of these forces and opportunities, we must develop our capacity for large systems change (LSC) and emerging societal change systems (SCSs). This book is about my LSC journey and those working in SCSs, with the goal of distilling insights and guidance for the journeys of all types of large systems change agents.

LSC challenges can be divided into those dominated by love and those inspired by fear. The love issues are ones that improve the world. Think of those working for gender equality, improving healthcare, and ending hunger. This love work is the work of time immemorial. It aims to support people and societies to reach their highest aspirations and potential by creating a space that provides for health and security, as well as the exploration of personal and collective possibilities.

Increasingly today, however, people work for transformational change out of fear of disaster and the collapse of our civilization. Think of those responding to climate change and plummeting bio-diversity. These issues are accompanied by a sense of urgency and a goal of making the outcome "less bad." It is essentially a conservative drive to preserve something that is valued.

Today, people increasingly recognize the interconnectedness of issues. Farming and water; health and domestic violence; education and economic well-being; equity and peace. Similarly, we see transformational energy based in love and fear increasingly coming together. This is expressed by many as sustainable development that produces a flourishing future reflecting social, economic and environmental concerns. We are struggling with the very deep implications of transformational change for core elements of life. The future *will* be different in very big ways; the change will be experienced as both loss and gain. How can we support the emergence of this desired future, given that there will be substantial losses?

Although superficially a blessing, the Chinese phrase "May you live in interesting times" is in fact a curse. Peace and constancy are highly valued, and interesting times are associated with disorderly change and the decline of civilization. It is easy to cast this as a conservative credo, emphasizing permanence and stability. But, can times of great change be interesting *because* they involve both real loss *and* the emergence of a flourishing future? The response depends in part on the questioner's position. Any change involves both destruction and creation. While air quality in China has plummeted, the country's economic well-being has sky-rocketed. Some mourn the demise of stability associated with the traditional family; however, many women and sexual minorities remember an oppressive patriarchy squelching self-expression and covering up domestic violence. These are the core types of contradictory views and outcomes associated with LSC.

The answer to whether loss and a flourishing future can be combined is also partly a question of imagination. Environmental questions are particularly challenging because of their scale and enduring impact. Sometimes I think the challenge we face is one of moving beyond Kubler-Ross's five stages of death and dying: denial, anger, bargaining, depression and acceptance.[2] The next stage is not the death of what we value, but a joyous recreation reflected in resilience thinkers who talk about developing:

> ...the capacity of a system, be it an individual, a forest, a city or an economy, to deal with change and continue to develop. It is about how humans and nature can use shocks and disturbances like a financial crisis or climate change to spur renewal and innovative thinking.[3]

The possibility is that after a shock the system is *more* robust, even taking into account the loss. We are struggling to bring forth a civilization that values and realizes bio-diversity and a clean climate, while ending hunger, providing universal health care and education globally, and supporting people in realizing their own aspirations.

So let's get serious about this, and develop the capacity to realize LSC for a flourishing future. This book aims to support the emergence of the knowledge, capacity and tools to do this, as LSC takes root. Of course, people are already working to realize this type of future, but as with any new approach, the emerging responses are not always obvious and are highly fragmented. The following pages provide an overview of what is currently known about how to undertake LSC action, provide some strategic and applied tools, and suggest where you can find out more. It draws on three decades of my work as a change leader, educator, consultant, and advisor. I began very locally, but for the last two decades, I have been dealing with issues from regional, national, and global perspectives.

The Challenge of Scale as Large Systems Change

Not all change is the same. This is the focus of Chapter 2, which explains why distinctions are important for effective action. Some action is about incremental change and doing more of the same; other actions are about reforming rules, not changing power structures. The depth and breadth of *transformational* change are today increasingly associated with calls to "scale" our change efforts. There are two dimensions to scale. One is "depth," which means change is radical and transformational. The other is "breadth," which means that huge numbers of people and organizations over very large geography are involved.

Depth and breadth are at the heart of the five cases that are the focus of Chapter 3. They clearly illustrate LSC with very different issues in very different geographical locations. They embody a "change sphere," which refers to "what" change makers focus on. The individual change sphere arises in the case of a Japanese-based global Buddhist group focused on "human revolution;" the technological change sphere

---

2   Kübler-Ross, Elisabeth. 2009. *On death and dying: What the dying have to teach doctors, nurses, clergy and their own families:* Taylor & Francis.

3   Stockholm Resilience Center. 2016. "What is resilience?". http://www.stockholmx-esilience.org/21/research/research-news/2-19-2015-what-is-resilience.html: Stockholm Resilience Centre.

Box 1A: The Two Core Ideas: Large Systems Change and Societal Change Systems

Large Systems Change (LSC) is a *complex process* to realize transformational change that involves depth (fundamental realignment of power structures, ways of making sense of the world, beliefs, priorities) and breadth (many people and organizations). LSC is supported by a great range of frameworks, strategies and tools.

Societal Change Systems (SCS) are composed of *change initiatives* (programs, projects, organizations) working for LSC with respect to a specific issue (e.g.: health equity, food security, climate change). Developing a powerful SCS is an important activity to effectively realize LSC.

looks at Germany's transition to sustainable energy; the institutional change sphere is illustrated by South Africa's apartheid struggle; marriage equality in the US is the focus of the meme and culture change sphere; and the natural environment sphere examines human evolution. The distinctions between change spheres are not simply interesting – they have large ramifications for action.

I have tackled scale while working locally and globally in perhaps the most power-laden institutional change sphere: the financial one. In the 1980s, as a member of a group that replaced the Board of Directors at the world's largest community-based credit union – VanCity Savings in Vancouver, Canada – and a Director of the provincial central bank and association of credit unions, I was inspired by what is possible. At that time, credit unions in Canada represented perhaps the largest cooperative financial sector in any nation, with approximately 25 percent of assets on deposit. In the United States, by contrast, the figure is closer to 2-3 percent. Banks and credit unions have very different underlying power logics. Banks are run based on one dollar one vote, whereas credit unions are run on one member (customer) one vote, regardless of a member's business or investment. Changing decisions within the financial system to be made predominantly on the one-person-one-vote concept is a transformational change of depth.

Canadian credit unions arose historically in response to two factors. One was that banks would not offer home mortgages to the average person; the second was a desire for those outside of the banks' geographic centers (mainly Toronto and wealthy English-speaking areas) to have local control of financial institutions. But, by 1980, the banks had a substantial share of the home mortgage market. At VanCity we renewed the credit union mandate by re-envisioning its role as a steward of the community's economic health. This led to a range of innovations in institutional change. All this was done with very high-profile elections covered extensively by the media, since VanCity is the province of British Columbia's largest banking institution. Fear-mongers claimed these elections would lead to capital flight based on concern about injecting populist dynamics into a financial institution's operations. The reality was that Board-turnover actually increased membership and assets.

While this was an inspirational experience, I also became aware of how provincial, national, and global laws and policies limited the range of actions for VanCity. For example, the VanCity Board discussed the implications of new agreements concerning capital requirements led by the Swiss-based Bank for International Settlement (BIS). Those agreements negotiated by global bankers limited the amount of money that credit unions could lend to members. This is one example of the challenge of scale in terms of breadth.

In the 1990s, one focus of mine was banks on the national level in the US, and their community relationships. Federal legislation was hugely important in these. Then in January 2008, I began a project called the Global Finance Initiative (GFI). It aimed to further investigate depth and breadth scales, by exploring how to integrate sustainability (social-environmental-economic) concerns into the global financial system. We began by interviewing system leaders and critics, asking, "Can we talk about a 'financial' system rather than separate insurance, banking, and investment industries?" "Absolutely not," we were told. "The risk profiles of each industry are very different." "And," we asked, "can we talk about 'global' finance rather than national finance (e.g., American, South African, French)?" Again we were told: "Absolutely not – finance is highly regulated on the national level and systems are very different." Eight months later, with the collapse of Lehman Brothers, everyone was suddenly talking about the "global finance" crisis.

The GFI experience illustrated that popular understanding of a system's boundaries and definition can quickly change. This presents unique opportunities to push transformation. However, without a clear vision of *how* the system can be really different, there is nothing to rally behind. In the case of finance, even the biggest, best-known critics, such as Joseph Stiglitz, were really only criticizing the margins with reform proposals, rather than offering transformational visions. No one was listening to proponents of ideas, such as alternative currency or radically different governance structures, in part because of a lack of a comprehensive alternative. Without a transformational vision, widely held and supported by a significant advocacy group and initiatives (i.e., a finance societal change system), there is no real chance of transformation getting onto the agenda.

Overcoming these challenges requires "emergent" approaches, supported operationally by "Theories of Change" and more broadly by creating transformation "pathways" as detailed in Chapter 4. That chapter provides historic and current illustrations of the underlying dynamic of moving issues from complex, unmanageable spaces into complicated and simple spaces in which new organizations can effectively address them. It also explores the importance of resilience, as a core ingredient, in emerging pathways.

Defining and advancing agendas like transformation of finance involves four archetypical change strategies, which are described in Chapter 5. The Forcing Change Strategy is reflected by powerful advocates who are ready to take to the streets and do even more; they are classically contrasted with those advocating a Co-Creation Strategy of collaboration based on love and respect. Those who have power in the current system, but want to support change, often develop a Supporting

Change Strategy; but at best, most with power adopt a Negotiating Change Strategy as a defensive move to limit change. All four strategies are part of the LSC dynamic. Their interactions, when well-developed, can greatly advance LSC.

The VanCity-national US banking-GFI experiences with scale taught me that changes made at the local level and in a local context are critical to crafting context-appropriate transformation. However, in our inter-connected, globalized world, the change system increasingly must have broad reach to realize transformation. It is not "global versus local" but "both-and." This breadth and depth of thinking and acting gradually led me to the idea of "societal change systems" (SCSs), explained in more detail in Chapter 6. Change initiatives surrounding most issues, including financial equity, collectively comprise a confusing, potentially overwhelming number of efforts by business, government, civil society, and multi-stakeholder groups. Some actors are working for radical change; others are actively resisting it. A societal change system or SCS embraces all these efforts around a particular issue. The idea of an SCS provides substantial power to enhance the effectiveness of change efforts. It leads to ways of visually describing relationships between change initiatives to develop synergies between efforts, to deal with duplication and conflict, and to address gaps that impede the ability to realize transformation.

Social movements are a 19th century innovation that remain critical for transformation. When I talk about SCSs, I'm including traditional social movements that pressure the status quo for change. However, I'm also talking about important new types of resilient, responsive, innovating structures that work for LSC, as described in Chapter 7. This includes social innovation labs, communities of practice, and action networks that categorically embrace collaborative strategies with the status quo. They include transformation agents comprised of multi-stakeholder networks addressing intractable issues with the sustained and entrepreneurial energy required to succeed. These structures are neither government, nor business, nor civil society, but rather are distinguished by their weaving together of the resources and competencies of all of these. They include hundreds of social labs, innumerable communities of practice, and a few dozen Global Action Networks like Transparency International, Forest Stewardship Council, the Global Compact, Principles for Responsible Investment, and the Global Fund to Fight AIDS, Tuberculosis and Malaria. These innovative approaches should not be thought of as *the* response to the issues they are tackling, but as important examples of what emerges to tackle the depth-breadth scale challenge.

Old Lenses

"Scale" is often referred to as a sort of great quest, as if responses to scale are not emerging all around us. A major problem is that people look at the issue through old lenses that can blind them to emergence and innovation. A good example is when people focus on inter-governmental organizations (IGOs, e.g.: United Nations, World Bank) and governments as though they are supposed to do the transforming. First of all, these institutions are, beyond anything else, bureaucracies. These organizations can do amazing things – just think of the incredible inventions of the welfare state and universal education – but they are inherently conservative organizations grounded in maintaining stability. They can be *part* of a transformational process and even have an important initiation and support role. Indeed, given their importance, their engagement is almost required. However, they cannot really be expected to *be* such a process. That requires a much broader range of players.

Old lenses include old assumptions about how to act. I remember organizing a webinar around 2002, when webinars were still rare. The call included a person in his mid-20s from Zimbabwe, and a senior Swedish diplomat in his 70s. The latter was stressing as absolutely critical the need for numerous face-to-face interactions before people could productively interact. The former challenged: "But, you should see what I'm doing with friends in India and Brazil. We are actually *doing* things together and supporting one another. We simply don't have the option of expensive face-to-face meetings." Our patterns of behavior and experiences limit our perceptions of what is possible. Thus, we have trouble perceiving innovative approaches.

Similarly, when I started looking at what I now call Global Action Networks as part of an investigation for the UN Secretary General on new governance forms, people within the networks thought of themselves as odd NGOs or weak IGOs. They were inspired and emboldened by the proposition that they are actually an organizational innovation: global networks, including business, government, and civil society organizations, forming around major change challenges. By thinking of themselves through the old lens, they undermined their innovation ability as they sought to become more like an NGO or IGO. Thinking of themselves as a new type of organization freed energy and imagination to innovate and evolve.

With respect to LSC, a particularly important blocking old lens is thinking in terms of "managing." Chapter 8 explores how transformational change processes develop – with "emerging," rather than managing or administering, being the key dynamic. Usually people with work experience in large organizations have learned and absorbed by osmosis a whole range of assumptions and behaviors that are problematic for realizing LSC. For example, LSC is not something to control, but rather to support its movement in the desired direction. It is usually not "driven," but "encouraged." It does not arise out of large bureaucracies, but rather through numerous initiatives in the spaces between bureaucracies; it is not so much about doing something to or for someone, but instead spurring participation in the collective discovery process that also involves personal change. LSC does not require leaders, as much as stewards. These new ways of acting are critical for LSC.

Chapter 8 presents three explicit processes for creating LSC. The Collective Leadership Compass, coupled with dialogue processes, produces powerful collective change teams. The Systemic Change Process Map provides a step-by-step process for teams to undertake effective transformational action. To greatly broaden that action, the development stages of Action Networks are described.

The LSC Field

We know what we know; we know something about what we don't know; and we don't know most of what we don't know. Yet, it is very common to turn to "experts" and encourage them to engage as though they know everything. Experts are paid well to play this role, since most people taking on complex challenges want a "solution." But, LSC is still a very young field of knowledge and action. Many experts adapt methodology from other experiences – often inappropriately. Others have developed expertise in particular approaches, such as: appreciative inquiry, social network analysis, scenario development, the U-process, and future search. They understandably tend to promote using their own particular approach or tool, even when better ones are available. Often, they simply don't know other tools that might be more appropriate. Knowing the full range is difficult if not impossible, new ones are continually evolving, and knowledge about them is highly fragmented.

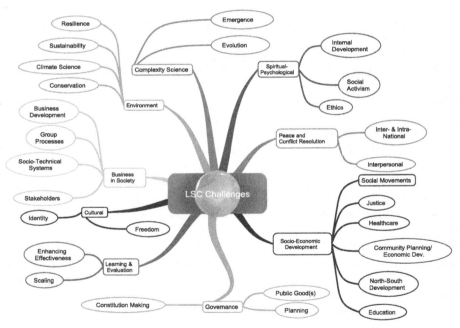

Figure 1A: Sources of LSC Knowledge[4]

4   This diagram was first presented in: Waddell, Steve. (2014). Addressing the world's critical issues as complex change challenges: The state-of-the-field. http://golden-forsustainability.com/what-golden-does/eco-system-industry-lab/: World Bank and GOLDEN Ecosystems Labs.

     The diagram and a version of its description here were presented in: Waddell, Steve, Sandra Waddock, Sarah Cornell, Domenico Dentoni, Milla McLachlan, and Greta Meszoely. 2015. "Large Systems Change: An Emerging Field of Transformation and Transitions." *Journal of Corporate Citizenship* (58):5-30.

Chapter 9 focuses on understanding the huge and confusing array of tools and methods that address LSC. It draws from the range of knowledge traditions relevant to LSC, supporting its development as a distinct knowledge and action field. Figure 1A, first developed when working with the World Bank, provides one way to understand what this book aims to support: the emerging "LSC field." Spend a few moments contemplating this figure – being able to grasp such diagrams takes time, and grasping them is important for LSC competency. Each of the arms of this diagram represents a knowledge tradition named in the rectangles that supplies different responses to the LSC field. The ovals represent particularly important LSC concepts that have arisen from the knowledge tradition. This mind-map is illustrative rather than comprehensive; you probably can add to it.

The Business in Society (BiS) and Socio-Economic Development (SED) knowledge traditions in Figure 1A have developed particularly rich approaches. Historically, the BiS tradition focuses on changes to enhance the performance of the corporation as the core stakeholder, emphasizing socio-technical systems, stakeholders, group processes, and business development. The SED tradition focuses on broader societal change to enhance justice, healthcare, education, and economic and community development.

Over time, these BiS and stakeholder perspectives have increasingly intersected as the perspective of corporations has broadened and the SED traditions have recognized the importance of corporations contributing to addressing their concerns. Both knowledge traditions have historically shared what might be described as an institutional-structural focus in their efforts to conceive change. Individuals' roles have often been framed, particularly within the BiS tradition, around the "leadership" concept, typically in a hierarchical heroic model. Group processes, as "teams" in BiS and "communities" in SED, have spurred a rich tradition that has grown into the shared concept of "multi-stakeholder convenings."

Approaches that start with learning and enhancing individual and group awareness have developed within what Figure 1A terms the Spiritual-Psychological (SP) tradition. Individuals' inner states of awareness and insight (as opposed to heroic leadership) are emphasized as central strategies to bring about change. These approaches focus on raising individuals' awareness so that they can work collaboratively on change. Historically, SP approaches have produced different types of intentional communities or communities of practice around living styles or particular practices.

Both institutional and individual interactions are foci of the Peace and Conflict Resolution knowledge traditions, which have received perhaps the most significant and concentrated attention as "complex change challenges" due to their obvious life-and-death issues. Again, dialogue stands out as a key method. Conflicts, such as with the apartheid regime in South Africa, the persistent Israel–Arab crisis, Northern Ireland's troubles, internecine guerilla activity in Colombia, and Central American violence, have produced an impressive array of methods relevant to LSC, from interpersonal strategies to post-conflict reconciliation commissions.

Box 1B: Transitions: An emerging science

In June 2009, the 1st International Conference on Sustainability Transitions took place in Amsterdam. While drawing predominantly Europeans, researchers also came from the US, Asia, and Australia, with about 100 papers being presented. The papers looked at sustainability problems in sectors such as energy, transport, water and food. These issues have turned the attention of scholars from various scientific communities to ways in which society can combine economic and social development with reducing environmental pressure. The success of the conference and its subsequent annual meetings confirm that Transitions is emerging as a new science.

Its emergence arises from the idea that, due to the specific characteristics of sustainability problems (ambiguous, complex), incremental change within prevailing systems will not suffice. There is a need for transformative change at the systems level, including major production and consumption changes that were conceptualized as "sustainability transitions." Transitions research is a new approach to sustainable development drawing on several inputs: complexity theory, integrated assessment, innovation studies, history, governance studies, and reflexive modernization.

Technical changes are seen within their institutional and social context, generating the notion of "socio-technical (s-t) systems," which are often stable and path dependent, and therefore difficult to change. Under certain conditions and over time, relationships within socio-technical systems can be reconfigured and replaced in a system innovation or transition process.

This book strongly identifies with this new tradition and aims to support its development. The field of large systems change is historically distinguished from Transitions Science by three factors. One is this book emphasizes societal change systems as a core concept in realizing LSC and transitions. Second is that this book goes beyond what are traditionally thought of as environmental – and even more broadly defined sustainability – issues, to include finance, health care, and peace making ones. Third is that this book underscores the need for individual human transformation, as well as the technological, institutional, and cultural changes that have been the focus of Transition Science founders. However, these distinctions appear to be diminishing.

See: http://www.transitionsnetwork.org

The Governance tradition and the need for effective government/governance has produced (in the political science field and beyond) notable LSC processes for national conversations around constitutional arrangements and strategies to advance agendas, such as regional planning. A top-down, "in control" government gives way to collaborative and deliberative governance concepts involving all organizational sectors. The collaborative governance approach contrasts with standard hierarchical government and the coercive power implied by mandate. "Experimentalist governance" more democratically integrates flexible processes than traditional top-down approaches. At an even broader cultural level, other methodologies have developed to support shifts in popular insights and values, often tapping a wide range of media and creative methods, such as Theater of the

Oppressed. Political, cultural, and socio-economic LSC strategies have produced a plethora of methods associated with community organizing, collaboration, and purposeful conflict generation, from protests to war.

The most impressive growth in LSC traditions over the first decades of the 21st century is associated with the Environmental tradition. It has developed concepts, such as "resilience" and "transitions," for a sustainable future. Concerns about environmental degradation originally brought biologists and natural scientists into the transformation fray; they gradually realized that addressing their concerns requires categorically addressing socio-economic and political concerns, not purely ecological ones. This tradition has led to holistic stakeholder strategies based around natural resource issues — ranging from the local level, such as land use and fisheries, to increasingly global strategies to combat harmful climate change.

Collectively, these knowledge traditions provide a rich LSC toolbox, as Chapter 9 describes. However, the breadth of these knowledge traditions and LSC audaciousness can easily overwhelm you. Chapter 10 provides some personal guidance, stressing the importance of humbleness and the value of "stewarding." LSC requires working with a much greater depth of collaboration than is supported by our current organizational and funding structures, and calls for creating new paths toward sustainable income generation for SCS stewards. Working with the whole requires working with an interdisciplinary engagement mindset (embracing different knowledge specialties), and also supporting mutually engaged, peer-like relationships amongst funders, problem-owners, methods leaders, capacity developers, and others engaged in change. Each has a different *role*, but the dynamics between them should not be power-based or linear, but rather peer-like and systemic. This all requires new capacities for SCS workers.

A Response

This book draws from many traditions to provide guidance, rather than answers, in addressing our big challenges. LSC issues are complex ones, and one clear imperative when dealing with complexity is that actions must be responsive to particular contexts. Since the mid-1990s, a wealth of knowledge has blossomed to address transformational challenges; these advancements provide a firm foundation for undertaking action. However, the connection is inadequate between macro visions and strategies and micro level actions and tools. This book responds to this situation. Given the immensity of the subject, the following chapters retain an overview flavor, while supplying references, to help readers identify where they can delve more deeply.

I draw from 30 years of my work around the world on a patchwork of issues. I have always asked the question: "How can the gap between our highest aspirations and potential and the current state be narrowed?" My life's work has been enriched by marvelous connections with people on similar quests and many of their contributions are integrated into this book. There are many whom I have not mentioned in my citations, but I hope these individuals will find a home within the LSC field.

The book concludes with the summary guidance questions in Chapter 11. Rather than "lessons," the aim is to emphasize the value of reflection and learning as a process to guide you in your LSC work.

This book works from the outside in. It starts with the big picture and ends with your role as an individual working for transformation. Each chapter has diagrams and tables that summarize key ideas. These are not presented simply as interesting and concise summaries. Instead, they are presented as analytic tools to assess and guide actions to more effectively address transformational complex change challenges. I hope that you find them useful to apply to the challenges you are tackling!

Chapter 2

Understanding Types of Change and Complexity

Chapter Summary

New language is important for new ways of acting. A new approach is required to support LSC and develop SCSs. So let's be clear on language. There are different types of change, and there is power in the language that distinguishes between them. Similarly, creating distinctions between simple-complicated-complex-chaotic challenges fosters a better understanding of various dynamics in change processes. The "complex adaptive systems" concept provides another important framework for developing effective action.

The arrival of Dr. Jim Yong Kim as President of the World Bank in 2012 suggested that the Bank was taking a new direction. He was the first President who was neither an economist nor a politician. He is an anthropologist and physician with two decades of international development experience. Previously, he served as President of Dartmouth College. Not long after Kim's appointment, in the spring of 2013, I met with Ed Campos from the Bank's Change, Knowledge and Learning Group. I successfully solicited his engagement with Ecosystems Labs, an initiative to investigate shifting the "ecosystem" of values, markets and policies – often referred to as an organization's operating or enabling environment – to support and nudge companies to become sustainable enterprises.[5] Towards the end of 2013, this led to the Bank funding a "Collective Action Platform" (CAP).

---

5   This was part of a larger initiative called GOLDEN that aimed to develop knowledge and action in support of pathways to sustainable enterprise.

CAP aimed to respond to the need for the Bank to develop new capacities. Traditional capacities focused on the core mission of addressing poverty through Bank lending, although the Bank did more than this. The core lending function had become less important with the growth of private investment and sovereign wealth funds. CAP aimed to support development of the Bank's large systems change (LSC) knowledge and capacity. But, the LSC term was still unclear. The project team, including Ceren Ozer and Joe Hsueh, immediately became entangled in basic language questions. What was meant by *collective action?* As a community organizer and trained sociologist, to me, it immediately summoned images of social movement traditions. Yes, important, but only a partial view of the array of approaches to the LSC challenge the platform was meant to address (see Chapter 6). Moreover, "collective action" in that tradition was very much about external acting and pressing others to change. Critical to my thoughts about LSC is also internal self-work to shift personal perspectives and understandings.

> ## Box 2A: Incremental Change Confusion
>
> Many people use the term "incremental change" to describe two very different types of change. One is change *within* the dominant system of power, relationships, beliefs, and environments. The other is change *of that system*. In *both* cases, "incremental" is often used synonymously with "evolutionary" to indicate that it happens over a relatively long period as opposed to "revolutionary" to indicate it happens over a very short period of time.
>
> This leads to fundamental confusion. In this book, the period of time is separated from the issue of whether the change is within or of the current system. "Incremental change" describes more of the same (change within a system), which can take place over a short or long period of time. See Table 2A for more explanation.

Three Types of Change

This led to questions about what to call the platform, as part of the project's investigation of key concepts, people, and organizations. My personal preference was for the term "transformation." This term had become central to my thinking while working with Global Action Networks (Chapter 7) and The Change Alliance colleagues. I was frustrated with the word "change" being used with several fundamentally different meanings. "Change management" had grown out of organizational development and business schools, and focuses on organizational change. We, on the other hand, were interested in societal change, which includes individual and organizational change. Our discussions refined Table 2A (that I had previously developed).

There are a few reasons to distinguish between these types of change. One is simply to foster more accurate conversations. Just as the Inuit have many ways to describe snow, people working with change need to sharpen their language. Another reason is to speed communication, by eliminating the need to always explain what type of change you mean. The types of change are not "good" or "bad," merely different. Distinguishing between them allows one to see relationships and develop insights. But, perhaps most importantly for me is that the distinction leads to potentially much greater sophistication and effectiveness in tool usage: aligning the type of desired change with the most effective tool. LSC incorporates three major types of change arising from very different core questions and goals. Framing these in terms of "learning types" can be helpful. "Learning" is a core change activity and has generally positive connotations. As well, each type of change reflects a very useful distinction between types of learning that grew out of Don Schon's and Chris Argyris' work,[6] and those following them. These types of change are appropriate for different challenges.

Table 2A: Types of Change[7]

	Incremental	Reform	Transformation
Learning Type	Single loop	Double loop	Triple loop
Core Question	How can we do more of the same? Are we doing things right?	What are the rules and structures? What are the rewards? Who should do what?	How do I make sense of this? What is our core purpose? How do we know what is best?
Purpose	To improve performance	To understand and change the system and its parts	To innovate and create previously unimagined possibilities
Power and relationships	Confirms existing rules	Opens rules up to revision	Opens issue to the creation of new ways of thinking and action
Core Dynamic	Replication	Reorganization	Transcendence
Archetypical Actions	Copying, duplicating, mimicking	Changing policy, adjusting, adapting	Visioning, experimenting, inventing
Logic Tools	Negotiating logic	Mediating logic	Envisioning logic

Single-loop learning and incremental change are most common. You have a goal, a set of assumptions, beliefs, and frameworks (Argyris refers to these as "governing variables"). You take action to realize the goal. Replication is commonly associated with this type of change. Think of a large retail chain, like Starbucks that wants to open a new cafe. It has a pretty clear idea and lots of experience about how to do this. Modest adjustments may need to be made at a particular location – Starbucks will have to negotiate with a different landlord, and perhaps there will be local preferences for certain types of coffee. But, the process is pretty straightforward. This is a type

6   Argyris, Chris. 1976. "Single-Loop and Double-Loop Models in Research on Decision Making." *Administrative Science Quarterly* 21(3):363-76.
7   Adapted from: Waddell, Steven. 2011. *Global Action Networks: Creating our future together.* Bocconi University on Management. Hampshire, UK: Palgrave-Macmillan. and Waddock, Sandra, Greta M. Meszoely, Steve Waddell, and Domenico Dentoni. 2015. "The complexity of wicked problems in large scale change." *Journal of Organizational Change Management* 28(6):993-1012.

of change that many funders want applied to pilot projects. Unfortunately, this "roll-out" strategy does not work well with social change issues, because context greatly impacts success – they are "complex" rather than "complicated," as will be explained.

Double-loop learning and reform change are associated with "policy reform" and "adaptation," as archetypes of this sort of change. Here, governing variables are reassessed. Experience suggests some of the assumptions are no longer valid – maybe there have been changes in the operating/enabling environment, such as a technological change. For example, increasing threats of floods in the Thames estuary led to barriers being erected to protect London (as a climate change adaptation measure). The invention of cell phones presented a

Box 2B: LSC and Types of Change

Large Systems Change is a process that realizes transformation through incremental, reform and transformative change.

In some cases, the change process includes a clear transformative intention. In many cases, however, it does not. In both, a key activity is experimenting (planned and explicit, or haphazard and implicit) with how to do something in a profoundly transformative way. As the number of successful experiments increases, they eventually create a "tipping point" where their new way of doing something becomes the new normal. This is supported by reform changes, such as new legislation or policies. After this, expansion of the new normal is more like incremental change than an experiment. This is also discussed in in Chapters 3 (the German energy case) and 5.

big change in interpersonal communication. New companies arose, and traditional ones had their business model challenged. This required changes to laws and regulations to mediate the change process. But, in both examples, the basic structure of laws, regulators, companies, and stakeholder roles did not change. It was a question of organizing them differently.

Triple loop learning is something others have added to Argyris' learning types.[8] It is the space of pure invention, rather than replication or mere adaptation. Thomas Kuhn, who popularized the term "paradigm shift,"[9] described this as a product of an increasing number of observations that contradict prevailing beliefs. At a certain point, the contradictions become so great that the fundamental understanding of reality changes. Kuhn's analysis arose from the physical sciences. For example, at one point, the dominant belief was that the world was flat. However, numerous contradictory observations arose. Christopher Columbus noticed that as ships moved over the horizon, the bottom disappeared first – whereas, if the world were flat, the ships would be expected to simply disappear as a whole into a dot on the horizon. Columbus' voyages did not "prove" the world was round.

---

8   Tosey, Paul, Max Visser, and Mark NK Saunders. 2012. "The origins and conceptualizations of 'triple-loop' learning: A critical review." *Management Learning* 43(3):291-307.

9   Kuhn, Thomas. 1962. *The Structure of Scientific Revolutions*. Chicago, IL: The University of Chicago Press.

However, they added to accumulating data. At a certain point, the competing belief that the earth was round better explained observations, such as those from the first around-the-world (1519-22) expedition of Magellan (who actually did not make it, since he was killed in the Philippines).

Transformation deals with a paradigmatic scale of change. It reflects the "depth" dimension of LSC as a fundamental shift in how people understand their reality. Transformation reflects the "breadth" dimension of LSC through which a novel insight or invention spreads to the point that it becomes a widely-held new perspective or innovation. A transformational change, in the way that I use the term, does not imply that no one ever thought of the invention before – some individuals claimed the world was round even in Columbus' day. A transformational change, however, is associated with the widespread adoption of innovations (physical and/or ways of thinking) that leads to large shifts in power structures and organizations. Conceiving of the world as round birthed the Portuguese and Spanish empires in the New World, led to the collapse of the Middle Eastern spice route, and supported what is referred to as the Copernican revolution, in which the earth was seen as revolving around the sun. In turn, this caused fundamental philosophical, religious and cosmological impacts.

Box 2C: The Incremental Change Trap

Single-loop learning and incremental change characterize most collaborations with business around the environment. Sometimes, this is appropriate. More often, however, it is simply inadequate. Behind incremental change is the implicit assumption is that values, production processes, products, and markets are all fine. It is simply a question of making them "greener" from a technical perspective. In a project with the Port Authority of Los Angles and its shippers, action researcher Hilary Bradbury realized the inherent weakness in this approach. It did nothing for the rewards mechanisms and pay structures, for example, that drive unsustainable action (double loop questions). And it certainly did nothing about asking whether consumption of goods or their importation (rather than local production) was part of the problem (triple loop questions). To answer these deeper questions requires generative dialogue processes that incorporate personal concerns and deeper group purpose (Chapter 3, Individual Change Sphere). "The entire paradigm of achievement needed to come into question if we were to truly embrace a sustainable paradigm. It is, frankly, not an easy thing to countenance," writes Bradbury.[1]

Some believe that with sufficient number of incremental changes (as opposed to transformational experiments distinguished in Box 2A), transformation can be realized. The more likely path is that people engaging in incremental changes finally realize they are not getting to the change needed, and will opt to shift to reform or transformational change.

---

1   Bradbury, Hilary. 2015. "The Integrating (Feminine) Reach of Action Research: A Nonet for Epistemological Voice." Pp. 573-82 in *The Sage Handbook of Action Research*, edited by Hilary Bradbury. Los Angeles, USA: Sage.

Contradictions that lead to transformation do not arise simply from the scientific sources that Kuhn identified. Karl Marx wrote about revolution and meant transformation, in terms of this book's language. He focused on economic contradictions with simultaneous growth in enormous wealth and poverty (something that is occurring today in the US with increasing inequity in wealth distribution).[10] There are forces other than contradictions that give rise to transformation. Consider technologically-driven transformations: in developing country agriculture markets, cell-phones have eliminated middle-men knowledge gaps, since farmers can easily learn market prices. Transformations also occur due to shifts in fundamental beliefs and values. Consider the transformation of governing systems from the era of kings and emperors to the classic democratic state model grounded in fundamental individual rights. There are also environmentally-driven transformations. Today, this is associated with climate change; with the Mayans, it was associated with over-farming and deforestation that led to their civilization's collapse.[11]

Today, we are experiencing a really big transformation associated with "sustainability." Our systems were built on the fundamental assumption that nature is infinite and that humans do not have a fundamental transformative impact on the planet. Contradictions, however, are arising with increasing frequency.

Transformation can arise out of trends that occur without human design or at least without human intention. Transformation can also be consciously driven by humans, such as the drive to increase life expectancy and to promote human rights.

Box 2D: An Experiment in Forestry

Transformation experiments are initiatives to do something that has not previously been done, or is very uncommon. They are not like total quality improvement approaches that simply build on past practices for incremental change. Rather, transformation experiments incorporate new fundamental organizing principles.

On the west coast of Vancouver Island (Pacific Canada), Iisaak is an example of a transformational experiment. Its mission statement is "to apply innovative approaches to the management and conservation of coastal temperate rainforests while maximizing opportunities for current and future generations and to be a successful Central Region First Nations (aboriginal; "Indians") business that improves quality of life through the creation and promotion of social, cultural, economic and ecological benefits through the application of cultural beliefs."[1]

Iisaak arose from the largest civil disobedience in Canadian history, resulting in the arrests of more than 800

1 Iisaak Forest Resources Ltd. 2009. "Sustainable Forest Management Plan." http://bit.ly/1JMh0Ej p. 8

---

10 Marx, Karl. 1859/1973. "A Contribution to the Critique of Political Economy." in *Dynamics of Social Change: A Reader in Marxist Social Science*, edited by H. & Goldway Selsam, D. New York: International Publishers.
11 Diamond, Jared. 2005. *Collapse: How societies choose to fail or succeed*: Penguin.

people for blocking logging operations. People were fighting over forest management practices that denuded vast swaths of mountains and cut down primordial forests. One unusual aspect of Iisaak is that it was founded in 1998 as a joint venture between the Nuu-chah-nulth Central Region First Nations community and a very large traditional forest company. This reflected a new principle that the people most closely affected by resource management decisions should be responsible for making these decisions. This principle was also reflected in a shift from provincial government controlled forest management to joint management with the Nuu-chah-nulth.

Iisaak also led to experimentation with principles arising from a new ecosystem-based approach. With that approach, the primary objective is to sustain a region's productivity and natural diversity. Watersheds become a key management unit and the guideline is to mimic natural disturbance regimes.

In 2005, the Nuu-chah-nulth took over full company ownership, in part because of changes in the traditional forest company's ownership and in part to reflect completion of a transfer of knowledge and skills. However, since the principles of Iisaak are not yet the new normal, it remains a relatively isolated experiment.

In either case, transformation is not simply a series of linear events or responses. The process is messy. We can see some quite old transformations that are still incomplete. Only following the collapse of the Berlin Wall was the democratic governance transformation of Europe completed (and still not in Russia). In many parts of the world, this transformation is still hotly contested, and may never occur.

Of course, the exciting part of these transformations is that they allow re-imagining possibilities and inventing new ways of being together. Methods and strategies to support transformation must do two things. First, they must open up minds and spaces to get beyond current assumptions to imagine new ways of organizing and doing. This is often difficult, since assumptions are deeply embedded. Second, it is important to experiment with new possibilities. More prosaically, we can see this happening with things such as the rise of "prosumers" in electricity systems. In the traditional model, utilities generate and distribute electricity to consumers. With decentralized renewable energy generation, consumers become producers when they return surplus wind or solar energy to the grid. This forces a basic transformation in the energy system and topples the dominant role of utilities. In 2014 E.ON, at one time Germany's largest utility, announced that it would sell off its generating capacity (Chapter 3).

The relationship between the three types of learning is important, as illustrated by the energy example. Incremental change has its own independent logic. However, reform change leads to – indeed, supports – incremental change. Think of legislative reforms supporting cell phone network construction, which fostered incremental development of cell phone use. This followed many experiments to develop these networks. Transformation is usually associated with multiple experiments that, when sufficiently successful and numerous, lead to reform (see Box 2B). Many prosumer experiments are underway, and regulators are at various stages of responding to them. There is significant resistance, confusion and open engagement in experiments by many traditional utilities.

The evolving prosumer model provides a good example of a key transformation dynamic: transcending. The evolving electricity system does not do away with the generation-transmission-distribution-consumption that is core in the traditional electricity production system. However, the new model integrates prosumers into a new production system – one in which utilities will be very different types of entities. However, core utility functions are still necessary, since not everyone will be an electricity generator. The ability to transcend – go beyond various perspectives and incorporate them into a new shared one – is core transformation work. In the late '80s, there was a large battle over whether population growth in developing countries, or consumption in developed countries, was the main threat to the natural environment. The views were integrated into the transcending "environmental footprint" concept.

I'd like to return to the World Bank project to further explore transformation. There was some discomfort with replacing "collective action" with "transformation," since the latter was perceived as being popularized with a wide range of meanings. So what other term could we use? Having just written an article using the "wicked problems" framework, that term sprang to my mind as a possibility. The origins of the term are associated with a 1967 and 1973 article in which "…[t]he adjective 'wicked' is supposed to describe the mischievous and even evil quality of these problems, where proposed 'solutions' often turn out to be worse than the symptoms."[12] The authors, who came from architecture and planning backgrounds, discussed how to "tame" these problems.

There are two other terms from academia that have similar meanings. Russell Ackoff, an early systems expert, coined the equally unscientific sounding term "messes" to describe "systems of problems" in which systems are a whole (e.g., a city) are traditionally divided into inter-related parts (e.g., streets, stores, and inhabitants) to address a problem. He commented:

> In the Machine Age, messy problematic situations were approached analytically. They were broken down into simpler discrete problems that were often believed to be capable of being solved independently of one another. We are learning that such a procedure not only usually fails to solve the individual problems that are involved, but often intensifies the mess. The solution to a mess can seldom be obtained by independently solving each of the problems of which it is composed.[13]

The other academic term, associated with a 1983 article, is "meta-problems," which are "systems of problems" rather than discrete ones. These problems are

---

12   Churchman, C. West. 1967. "Guest Editorial: Wicked Problems." *Management Science* 14(4):B141-B42. p. B-141.
13   Ackoff, Russell L. 1997. "Systems, messes and interactive planning." *The Societal Engagement of Social Science* 3(1997):417-38. P. 428

beyond the capacity of any single organization to address.[14] With a psychology and organizational studies background, Eric Trist wrote about "problem domains" of multiple stakeholder organizations and "referent organizations" that have key roles in organizing domains to address the problem. These are associated with something recently popularized in the US by FSG's collective impact work with "backbone organizations."[15]

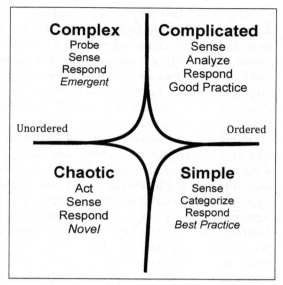

Figure 2A: The Cynefin Framework

However, for the World Bank project, we decided to settle upon the term "complex challenges" as a transcending framework that incorporates the advocacy tradition associated with collective action, the need for internal self-work and multi-stakeholder co-creation. "Challenges" gave a good focus, and the "complex" framework provides a rich knowledge vein to understand critical dynamics. It is explained in part by a learning-and-action relationship. Perhaps most importantly, a focus on complex challenges highlights the distinction between the Bank's traditional "complicated" activities to address its poverty-alleviation mission, and "complex" activities that are also required.

Simple-Complicated-Complex-Chaos

The differences between complicated and complex are well-illustrated by David Snowden's cynefin framework that distinguishes between the four types of challenges in Figure 2A.[16] In terms of change, the four quadrants refer to four different situations requiring distinct strategies. One core concept behind this diagram is "order," characterized by complicated and simple. In an ordered world, variables and their relationships are definable. In the "unordered" world of complex and chaotic, not all variables and relationships can be identified – there is a constant state of change that produces unanticipated outcomes.

14   Trist, E. 1983. "Referent Organizations and the Development of Inter-Organizational Domains." *Human Relations* 36(3):269-84.
15   Kania, John, and Mark Kramer. 2011. "Collective Impact." *Stanford Social Innovation Review* Winter:36-41.
16   Snowden, David J., and Mary E. Boone. 2007. "A Leader's Framework for Decision Making." *Harvard Business Review* 85(11):68-76.

An example of a *simple* change challenge is repairing a city water main. It is like incremental change. It depends upon known technology that has been applied many times before and requires a relatively small number of people and organizations to handle it: usually a city department or its contracted services. In this world, action follows a sense (learn about water flowing where it should not) – categorize (understand if it is a water main break) – respond (put into action the oft-repeated solution). This is where simple bureaucracies excel. Given limited parameters, best practices can be developed.

In complicated situations, people deal with difficult questions that require answers. However, there are identifiable answers. For example, sending a person to the moon required building innovative machinery. However, the challenge was essentially a definable physical science one in which modeling and testing could produce likely successful solutions. It also required developing a large network of organizations and people to answer the questions and develop necessary infrastructure. In complicated situations, there are important unknowns. Therefore, each situation is in some ways different. This quality makes good, rather than best, practices the goal. Given the unknowns, categorizing based on historic precedents is often not possible. Complicated situations depend on analyzing and learning about how to build and put together the pieces of the puzzle. Repetitive experiments and testing are possible since key variables can be controlled.

Complex situations, in contrast, are dominated by unknown unknowns in which controlled experiments are usually impossible. Many key variables, and how they interact, are only discovered as they are experienced. Patterns emerge and change. Think of the efforts to develop sustainable approaches to fisheries. At one time, state-of-the-art approaches involved managing species, such as whales, cod, and salmon. Then, interdependencies with other variables, such as other species and the broader ecosystem, were found to be critical. The state-of-the-art shifted to a much broader goal of healthy oceans with a focus on specific geographies. But, this only refers to the physical side of the challenge. Many problems resulted from rapidly changing technologies and the size of boats, burgeoning populations, and extrapolating historic practices in unsustainable ways. The socio-economic-political issues are immense, and everything is continually shifting. In these dynamic and complex situations, the action logic begins with trying multiple inventions. This involves probing via experiments; sensing patterns in reactions; and responding by supporting the application of inventions that appear most beneficial. Action is focused on creating patterns. In these situations, context is everything, since small variables can have an enormous impact on outcomes. "Rolling out" responses in the incremental change tradition cannot be done in detail. It is more about sharing methods and "stances," vis-à-vis the challenge.

The term "complex adaptive systems" (CAS) is now popularly used to describe complex challenges. Let's apply this to agriculture and food production. First, let's consider the word "system:"[17]

---

17   Ackoff, Russell L. 1971. "Towards a system of systems concepts." *Management Science* 17(11):661-71.

- A system comprises **inter-related elements**. "Complex" suggests among other things that there are lots and lots of elements. Elements include: water, vendors, soil quality, farmers, and packagers.
- As a system, the **behavior of these elements depends on other elements** – if there is lots of water, there will be the possibility of growing different types of crops that in turn will have customer, farmer, and processor implications.
- This means that the **whole is greater than the sum of the parts** – the traditional scientific analysis of dividing up the whole to look at parts can lead to learning something about the parts that represent sub-systems (e.g., farmers), but a very different understanding arises from how the parts interact.

Now, let's consider the implications of the "complex" concept:
- The system has so many parts of such a range in variety that it is **impossible to predict** how they will interact when there is an intervention. This is where unintended consequences come in. The "butterfly effect" describes how a very modest change can lead to transformative outcomes.
- There is **no single control mechanism** governing system behavior. The many interacting parts and the system, as a whole, have a decentralized logic. Again, think of the food system. Although producer groups and large businesses may attempt to exert a monopoly influence, in fact, many factors, such as the natural environment and broader culture and values, are always influencing what is possible for these enterprises.
- **Interactions are non-linear.** That is to say, equations like A leads to B which leads to C are rarely if ever true – there are simply too many variables that affect C. Think of shifts in consumer preferences for certain foods. This does not simply mean that prices for that food will go up; some who traditionally ate that item will shift preferences; more of this crop will be planted, which usually means less of something else will be planted. There are **no "root"** causes in complex systems: poverty, for example, is the product of a complex interaction of numerous factors.
- **Context is important.** One example is that proximity is important: the closer you are to a factor – say you have a cousin who is low-income – the more likely you are to know other low income people and feel that poverty is an issue requiring a response. Another example is the importance of the history behind an issue: during the Greek debt crisis, it was important to remind Greeks of their historic fiscal irresponsibility, and to also remind Germans that after World War II they had loans forgiven. Context again emphasizes the inappropriateness of "rolling-out" solutions based on a particular success story.
- The general dynamic of complexity is **emergence**. Some associate CAS with "evolution." Factors combine in new, unpredictable ways to produce innovative outcomes. Or, alternatively, something might have always existed (e.g., the world is round), but it is just now being "seen" and its implications (interactions with other elements) are now understood to produce new possibilities. Emergence occurs as variables come together with increasing regularity until

in some cases they form new and relatively stable patterns. A new order (structures, industries, and leadership groups) arises, which is often disruptive. In complex issues, pre-determined solutions rarely work. Addressing climate change is an example of a complex issue where people are trying to "emerge" solutions. A carbon tax is a logical option, but it is not viable for complex political reasons. The Kyoto Accord was another failed attempt to develop a response. Some see the "emergence" of solutions with renewable energy as production price declines. However, the lesson is that **experimentation with multiple options and learning** is critical.

The "adaptive" concept of CAS points out that:

- New patterns are always emerging, and there is **no equilibrium** – or, it might be said there is **always equilibrium,** except sometimes the phenomenon is much more ephemeral than at other times. Egyptian civilization lasted thousands of years without significant transformations; our civilization, on the other hand, is characterized by rapid transformations. The system is *always* adapting to changes in the natural environment, plus what people and organizations are doing.

- "Successful" adaptation depends on the quality of **resilience and learning systems** to support quick responses to shifts in system elements. In the food system, this is expressed, for example, with the ability to respond to increased concerns about genetically modified organisms, antibiotics, and pesticides.

Box 2E: "Nudging" as an LSC Strategy

The complex adaptive systems perspective has important implications for LSC strategies. Given the many unknown and moving parts, a core LSC concept is "to nudge" the system in a certain direction. This contrasts with engineering input-output planning models that assume there are not significant unknowns and that production can be controlled. In LSC, a more humble strategy is required, supporting system movement in a certain direction.

For example, in 2014, the UNEP formed an *Inquiry into the Design of a Sustainable Finance System*. In the fall of 2015, it produced a report.[1] This all represented a very audacious change nudge. Will this approach support transformation or simply incremental change? Simon Zadek, Inquiry co-director, explained a lot of conversation was about just that. And, as with any complex change, the answer is…complex. "When the macro conditions are right, small-scale change creates learning effects that create more change," said Simon. He also points to lack of certainty about factors necessary to spur transformation. The Inquiry can be seen as an important, but insufficient factor on its own. There may be other aligning factors that are difficult to assess. Timing is everything.

---

1   UNEP. 2015. "The Financial System We Need - The UNEP Inquiry Report - Aligning the financial system with sustainable development." UNEP.

Chaotic situations, the fourth cynefin type, are the most difficult ones to address. Perhaps the best example is disasters associated with earthquakes and wars. Each situation is unique. The best that can be done is to put away reserves that can cushion the impact of these disasters. Although very high level patterns can be identified with disasters, the unknowns are so great that rational action is highly problematic. Think of the Syrian War: there has been a continual reconfiguration of interests and alliances with ever-shifting military actions. Families have constantly reassessed whether to stay or leave – and the answer of what they might leave for has been constantly changing. Very specific – novel – actions are formulated in chaotic circumstances, based on innumerable factors, such as the physical environment, family composition, religious beliefs, and ethnic identities.

These four cynefin situations can have a flow between them. For example, out of chaos, patterns may gradually emerge to move a situation to complex. If enough stability and definable knowns are identified, the situation may become complicated; in turn, many complicated activities are successfully divided into parts that can be routinized with bureaucracies. However,

Box 2F: The Global Compact as Skunk Works

In the late 1990s, many UN members pressed Secretary-General Kofi Annan for major UN reforms. Partly in response, the UN Global Compact (UNGC) was born as a multi-stakeholder, UN-led skunk works to develop a new way to engage with businesses in supporting UN principles on labor, the environment, human rights, and transparency. Integrating business relationships more directly into the UN would have been very difficult for a host of bureaucratic and historic reasons. Moreover, doing so would have simply expanded problematic bureaucratic procedures that were the reason behind reform pressures.

Instead, the UNGC was established as a "skunk works": group operating with a party (the UN) with its legitimacy, but where the organization's limiting rules are suspended, and the group had a high degree of autonomy to invent new approaches. This Some approaches could subsequently be integrated into the UN itself to support its internal reform. For example, the UNGC could establish formal relationships with businesses, without the approval of all nation states (as a more direct integration into the UN system would have required).

As skunk works, the UNGC undertook "experiments" that flowed back to the UN. For example, it:

- developed guidelines for the entire UN system;
- organized innovative encounters between governments and the private sector (now part of the annual UN General Assembly opening);
- mobilized, through its 90 country networks, businesses to partner with UN entities on the ground on humanitarian and development priorities; and
- mobilized business for COP21 and advocated policy changes - in particular, pricing carbon.

for the major challenges, such as poverty, the over-arching dynamic will always be complex.

Implications

This analysis raises questions about how we approach complex issues. The World Bank, owned by member states, is a bureaucracy with the mission to *end extreme poverty within a generation and boost shared prosperity*. Its contradiction is, of course, that it has an organizational form that is particularly good at simple and complicated challenges, but is pretty poor, on its own, at addressing complex ones. It depends on policies and procedures that are developed from experience to make loans and support activities, such as infrastructure and bureaucracy development. Historically it (the World Bank) has been very limited in its ability to create innovative spaces, since it has been restricted to acting through other governments – it could not do much of anything without their consent. It is good at incremental change and reform; on its own, it is simply incapable of realizing its transformation mission.

There are many reasons to question the real potential of an organization, like the World Bank, to support transformation. It can actually undermine complex change efforts, by demanding that projects be defined to a degree of detailed outcome specificity and at a scale that undermines the ability to undertake action appropriate for complex challenges. Such an organization can, however, play a critical role in partnering with others to develop the societal change system (SCS) necessary to address complex challenges. Partnering in this case does not mean simple contracting or consulting, but rather deep collaboration to support context-specific and appropriate actions to address complex challenges. Collaboration plays an important role in reform and transformation. It requires enormous capacity-development to shift to this role. For the Bank, this work could be facilitated by something like collaborative skunk works (see Box 2F) with other organizations that would access the Bank's legitimacy and networks, but would not have to follow its rules and procedures. These innovative partnering spaces are critical to transformation.

Chapter 3

What Has to Change:
Five Change Spheres, Five Cases of Large Systems Change Work

Chapter Summary

Let's dive into some examples of large systems change and their societal change systems. The examples reflect different starting points that different change makers emphasize: individual, technological, institutional, memes, or the natural environment. All of them are fine, but each one has its own logic that leads to different strategies and tools. This is explored through five case studies of large systems change: the global strategy for individual "human revolution" of the Soka Gakkai International (SGI); national technological transformation arising from Germany's actions to support renewable energy; national institutional change with South Africa's journey beyond apartheid; memes change sparked by the same sex marriage struggle in the United States; and environmental change from the perspective of human evolution.

When we were putting together the June 2015 special issue of the *Journal of Corporate Citizenship* on large systems change (LSC), we noted that contributors focused on different change objects. These included: organizations, electricity systems, global networks, production chains, leadership capacities, and health care. We accepted these articles, because they all dealt with LSC questions and complexity. However, they all seemed to be writing about a piece of the total range of what needs to change. "Is there," we as editors asked, "any good way to describe the totality of the objects of change in a way that is comprehensive and yet not overly simplistic? That is to say a way that would visually convey the range of what has to change so that it would provide insights and a springboard to guide action?"

Figure 3A is what we can up with. We call it the change spheres diagram. It proposes five different points of departure or focus for most people engaged in

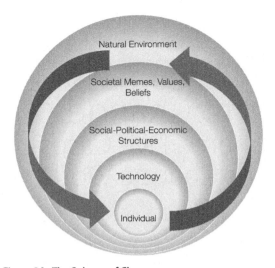

Figure 3A: The Spheres of Change

change efforts. Some, such as Otto Scharmer who has developed the well-known "U-Process"[18], start with the individual and their awareness and assumptions. Some focus on technology, such as the rise of the Information Age and connectivity, as key transformation drivers. Social-politi-cal-economic structures are the traditional focus of revolutionaries and many development organiza-tions, such as the World Bank. Culture, memes, and underlying patterns of consciousness – the DNA of broader societies and civiliza-tions – are often the initiating focus of anthropologists and social movements, such as ones focused on racial justice. And over the past 30 years, in particular with the rise of sustainability concerns, the natural environment is the focus of still others.

The arrows in the Figure aim to convey that there is great interaction between these change spheres. Scharmer, for example, deals extensively with technolog-ical and structural change with prototyping, although his point of departure is individual awareness. Institutions and structures both "have" memes and cultures, and are the product of the broader societal culture within which they function. Societal memes are memes that can transcend individuals and institutions, since they are so widely held.

This change presentation will simply overwhelm many…but this book is about change for the audacious. With audaciousness goes humbleness in understanding that any one person, initiative, project, or program will make only a modest contri-bution. However, the diagram aims to support understanding about the position of any one change effort and the *relationships* between them, which is very helpful for successfully developing change initiatives.

This diagram provides a better understanding of the question of "scale." With respect to the breadth dimension of scale, in addition to people and organiza-tions, the natural environment brings in flora, fauna, and nature, as additional factors. The understanding of "depth" is detailed to include the transformation of all spheres: it is hard to imagine transformed individuals without eventually transformed societal memes, since the transformed individual would exist within a hostile meme environment. And there is the added dimension of time. Moving

---

18   Scharmer, C Otto. 2009. *Theory U: Learning from the future as it emerges*: Ber-rett-Koehler Publishers.

from the individual to the natural environment involves ever greater periods of time to realize transformation. Of course, there are exceptions to this general time assertion: volcanoes and asteroids have quickly transformed the natural environment in the past. Revolutions can arguably quickly change structures, although most would say that the periods spent incubating revolutions and putting new structures into place with firm foundations takes considerable time.

The diagram also makes the point that a range of starting points is valid, rather than asserting that one is more important that the other: they can all be sources of transformation. For the transformation practitioner, the diagram raises questions about the relationship between spheres of change focus, and how to maneuver with them all in mind. For example, most governmental agencies supporting change, particularly development ones, such as the World Bank, focus on the institutional sphere. However, a recent effort by the World Bank, GIZ (the German government's development agency) and others to support Universal Health Coverage in several countries started with individual transformation leadership. This approach suggests this type of leadership is a critical element in realizing change within the institutional sphere and that it needs to be addressed early on...without denying the importance of the institutional sphere. These different approaches reflect different change theories.

Perhaps the most helpful insight from the Figure, for the transformation practitioner, is that it suggests there are five realms in which transformation dynamics, challenges, and opportunities are significantly different – and therefore, calls for different interventions and strategies. Let's look at each a bit more deeply from this perspective with some relevant case studies. For each case the events are presented, followed by discussion about it from a LSC perspective.

The Individual Sphere: The Sokka Gakkai International (SGI)

Generic sphere description: Individuals' awareness, unrecognized assumptions, and mindsets are the focus of many change practitioners. Transformation requires: broadening awareness to understand more about the experience of others; recognizing assumptions that prevent inventive approaches or that support conclusions that are out of alignment with observable and experiential life (such as stereotypes); and shifting mental models about how people and issues do and can relate.

Particularly relevant change knowledge traditions: spiritual, religious, psychological, and dialogic.

Some key change sphere dynamics: moving through fields of conversation, presencing, and deepening and broadening awareness.

Some key change sphere activities: dialogue, meditation (silent, chanting, and dancing, etc.), and retreats.

The Case Events

It was the end of June, 2015, and along with four of my Buddha-buddies, I was planning the next meetings for our neighborhood District. It was Sunday morning and we were at the SGI Boston Community Center. We had just finished a 30-minute *gongyo*: chanting brief sections of the Lotus Sutra in archaic Japanese, and for longer periods, "Nam-myoho-renge-kyo," which literally means "devotion to the Mystic Law of the Lotus Sutra." I was feeling energetic, as I typically do after gongyo. We did our brief "hellos." I added to mine "Let's just take a moment to appreciate what a great week it's been. We had the Supreme Court support same-sex marriage and the national health plan, and I'm so impressed with the way the families of those massacred in North Carolina publicly announced 'forgiveness.'" On this last point, I was referring to a massacre (carried out by a white supremacist) in a black church, which had followed an incredible series of police brutality incidents towards black Americans.

Whoa! That last point on forgiveness created sparks of reaction and anger that I hadn't anticipated! I'd assumed others would also be positively impressed, given our Buddhist orientation. But, one buddy was definitely angered by the families' statements, and two others were cautious, at best. I was, all of a sudden, very conscious of being the one white person in the group. I thought, "What don't I know?" I felt pretty ignorant as one of them pointed to the families' statements as directed to dampen any chance of riots – not that that was a bad thing to aim for, but I simply hadn't thought of the pressure that had likely been placed upon the families to make these statements.

We started a discussion about our range of views, and decided it would be a great topic to integrate into our next District discussion meeting. There are usually about a dozen people who come to these 90-minute meetings that rotate being study meetings focused on a particular SGI writing, a meeting devoted to chanting, and a discussion meeting connecting our current life challenges with some Buddhist insights. I teamed up to organize the discussion with my Buddha-buddy who had felt anger at my initial statement.

As well, the angered Buddha-buddy was doing a radio talk show that evening. "So," she asked, "how about coming on the show with me, and we can talk about this some more?" "Sure," I said, wondering what I had gotten myself into, but convinced I'd better explore it some more. We had a wonderful on-air hour together. She had calmed down, and took great leadership in the discussion, as we explored the core idea and our different reactions. I was impressed with how she brought in an audio clip of the renowned Buddhist Jack Kornfield (not of the SGI tradition) in which he talked about how the concept of forgiveness had looked into the psychological definition of forgiveness: "a conscious, deliberate decision to release feelings of resentment or vengeance toward a person or group who has harmed you, regardless of whether they actually deserve your forgiveness."[19]

My buddy particularly focused on the need to pay more attention to the horror of the event and what to do about it; she saw forgiveness as coming too soon, and believed that it cut off needed discussion. Me, I was imagining that the families had been deeply immersed in the topic of "forgiveness" in their church – one of the

---

19   Greater Good Science Center. "What Is Forgiveness?". http://greatergood.berkeley.edu/
     topic/forgiveness/definition: Greater Good Science Center, University of Berkeley.

most prominent and oldest African-American ones – given the string of atrocities nationwide over the previous few months, and that "forgiveness" had arisen from those discussions.

The dialogue continued a few weeks later in our discussion meeting with about a dozen people, predominantly African American, but also white and Asian. We again started with chanting, and then had an "experience" from a member. These are personal stories about the application of Buddhist principles to daily life. My buddy and I then led a discussion on forgiveness, connecting it to a monthly message from SGI President Daisaku Ikea, who quoted our lineage's founder: "Whatever happens…you must not despair. Be firm in your approach, and if things should not go as you wish…then determine to be more contented than ever." The word "contented" provoked a lot of discussion given SGI's action-orientation. We concluded that it might have just been an awkward translation. We tied the quote to the subsequent part of the message that included, "There is absolutely no obstacle you cannot overcome."

Our dialogue revealed, in part, that people had very different ideas about the meaning of "forgiveness" – we were using the word with different definitions. Some thought of it as glossing over the seriousness of an event, or excusing the perpetrator. Others thought of it as a personal reconciliation with reality and a release of feelings of vengeance. Others thought it inferred absolving people of their crimes. Some agreed that it was a question of timing – forgiveness, in this case, had followed the event too closely.

I felt vulnerable and unsure of my language – talking about "African-Americans" and "blacks" as categories made me uncomfortable as a white person – particularly

Box 3A: A Personal Transformation

"Transformation" can involve relatively modest, but significant, changes. In SGI, members share "experiences" of the human revolution as encouragement. Here's an excerpt from member Boston Snowden's first encounter with chanting by his mother and a group of other women:

"I heard the sound of Nam-myoho-renge-kyo emanating from my mom's room. Initially, I was shocked and somewhat freaked out. When the women left, I went into my mom's room and saw the Gohonzon[1] enshrined in a shirt box. My mom said to me, 'Boston, our life is gonna get a lot better with this Gohonzon!' I immediately saw a change in her. The neighbors in the apartment upstairs were loud, and my mom would often curse them out. When she began changing, however, she actually went upstairs and addressed the neighbor in a nice way. She told me 'I was so happy I handled it differently. It's because of this (chanting). I'm changing.'"[2]

---

1 A scroll inscribed with Chinese and Sanskrit characters with Nam-myoho-renge-kyo. SGI members receive their own Gohonzon that they enshrine in their homes and which they focus on when they chant.

2 Snowden, B. (2015). The Family of My Dreams. Living Buddhism. Santa Monica, CA, USA, Soka Gakkai International. 19: 22-23.

with black Americans whose world I could never experience. I felt myself fighting inhibitions about speaking because of fears about possibly offending by using the wrong words or demonstrating ignorance. I felt myself opening up to being guided, learning, and hearing and feeling to bring others' experiences and perspectives more into myself. I hoped others would trust my good intentions and accept my clumsiness and ignorance when I spoke. At the end of the process, we had new potential as a group: we could talk with each other about issues we had previously avoided, because they had seemed peripheral to our group, or we had simply not had the trust and language to be able to previously have the conversation.

This dialogue fits within SGI's "human revolution" focus (Buddhists do not believe in "God," and instead emphasize the role of personal development). The SGI is a Buddhist tradition arising from a 13th century Japanese founder, with a global following of approximately 13 million participants in 192 countries. Human revolution "is the work of transforming our lives at the very core. It involves identifying and challenging those things which inhibit the full expression of our positive potential and humanity."[20] It is associated with the pathway to realizing our Buddha-nature: breaking through our "lesser selves" bound by ego to our "greater selves," where we realize the happiness associated with caring for and taking actions with others. Individuals' human revolution leads to relative happiness and absolute happiness. Relative happiness concerns things in our environment that might make us happy (e.g., a secure income, and a loving spouse); absolute happiness, on the other hand, involves drawing on our own inner resources so that we establish a resilient state of life which is not swayed by anything. By supporting each other to realize happiness, we will realize the ultimate goal of *kozen rufu*, often referred to as "world peace." As SGI President Daisaku Ikeda notes, 'Kosen-rufu does not mean the end point or terminus of a flow, but it is the flow itself, the very pulse of living Buddhism within society.'"[21]

This goal is similar to other Buddhist traditions. However, the SGI has developed a distinctive approach to support it. One is chanting, rather than meditation – I've done both extensively, and found that the latter leaves me peaceful and more aligned with my Buddha-nature, but withdrawn from people. Chanting leaves me feeling aligned, energized, and connected. SGI members chant individually and in groups, morning and evening.

SGI does not have "temples" or any form of "clergy." Activities are instead organized around "community centers" and neighborhood districts. The community centers host a range of education and cultural activities, including large group chanting. Neighborhood meetings, with a strict 90-minute duration, are organized around monthly cycles: study meetings at which texts are analyzed; tozo meetings for extended periods of chanting, and discussion meetings (such as the meeting I described). People share their experiences in implementing the practice and provide support and suggestions; cultural presentations, such as music, poems, and skits,

---

20   SGI. 2015. "Human Revolution." http://www.sgi.org/about-us/buddhism-in-daily-life/human-revolution.html: Soka Gakkai International.
21   http://www.sgi.org/about-us/buddhism-in-daily-life/kosen-rufu.html

are also regular features. The monthly regional meeting at the community center includes a video message from Tokyo, usually from the cherished leader President Ikeda who has received literally hundreds of honorary degrees from universities around the world and other honors. I am always impressed by the racial and cultural diversity (a true distinction), the high profile of youth, the self-organizing of voluntary leaders, and the great dispersion of leadership amongst geographic units and a range of sub-groups (men's group, women's group, academic division, and gay-lesbian-transgender, etc.).

The Case Discussion

Broadening and deepening awareness is a basic dynamic of personal transformation. In this case, I broadened my awareness by learning what a wider range of people thought and felt. We collectively deepened our awareness through the dialogue of sharing experiences and creating a new collective meaning that arose around the idea of forgiveness and racism. It was not about reaching "consensus," although we did come much closer through the process. It was about sharing, exchanging, and strengthening our relationships and ability to "be" and "act" together via greater awareness and insight. I experienced this in a safe location, with a Buddhist group. This is so much more challenging between people who have literally been at war shooting each other, battling one another across picket lines, or otherwise holding deep convictions about someone as "the enemy."

This dialogue movement is nicely summed up with the four fields of conversation.[22] Habitually, we are in the "talking nice" world of managing transactions, such as in a store, simply getting along with intermittent contact, such as passing on the street, or having more lengthy conversations about the weather or, more lengthy exchanges that convey information, such as about work or what we did last weekend. In the example, this was the friendly good mornings at the beginning of our discussion meeting.

Debate involves taking positions with the idea that there is a "right" or "wrong" to be identified, a winner and a loser. This is what I felt at our planning meeting from the reactions to my initial comments. The general dynamic is to move from something claimed as a reality, to support a conclusion. "It's obvious that X is true, and therefore Y." This dominates most political conversations as people try to make points vis-à-vis one another. It can be useful to uncover relevant objective evidence, such as in the US legal process with "findings of evidence." Debate is an important academic scientific process to evolve a consensus around "the preponderance of evidence." This is a field of rules, in which anger commonly surfaces as an expression of frustration with what one claims is simply contrary to what another person perceives.

Reflective dialogue is dominated by curiosity – a desire to explore and deepen understanding. We moved into this field in the radio show and in subsequent discussion meetings. People are willing to recognize their assumptions and rules,

---

22   This is attributed to Otto Scharmer in Isaacs, William. 1999. *Dialogue and the art of thinking together.* New York, NY: Currency Doubleday. P. 261

and challenge them. There is not a drive for agreement or consensus. Diversity is something to investigate, rather than fight over. This is a field of consultation, and sharing views to be understood. It is about hypothesis building. There is a trusting environment that supports personal revelations. People make themselves vulnerable about expressing their fears and experiences to deepen interpersonal connections and meanings. This was the dominant dynamic in the discussion meeting.

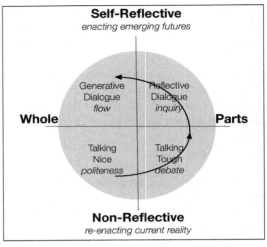

Figure 3B: Four Fields of Conversation[23]

To enter into generative dialogue, people empty themselves of expectations and allow the new to emerge. In this example, I felt newness emerging as a totally new appreciation of the amount of violence that the black American community lives with, compared with the white community. By "violence," I mean the physical violence of guns and fighting. I also mean violence in terms of being dismissed, shunned, or feared simply because of race. I intellectually *understood* racial profiling before, but I came to understand and feel it in an entirely new way. This generative space is rare, but is usually critical to transformation. A challenge is to not just develop it, but to have it continually develop into reference points supporting the transformation process. Although in the SGI example we did not get to a specific action in response to a new understanding, it is something I carry with me in my relationships now with fellow SGI members.

In the generative dialogue field, people move into a space of awareness of the whole. Interaction rules are lightly held or recreated, to support collective consciousness emerging. Flow and synchronicity are common: one person vocalizes what others are also feeling. Radically different views can be shared. Often a sort of synthesis or transcendence of views emerges into which they are transformed into another way of looking at a topic. Essentially, this dialogic framework is the theory behind SGI: create spaces that give rise to generative dialogue and relationships that support "human revolution." These changes take time and support, and SGI's activities and structures sustain individuals' efforts to realize human revolution.

These dialogic processes are often associated with small groups. However, there is no reason these cannot happen with very large, even global groups growing out of face-to-face encounters. This has happened around slavery, for example. More recently, in the 1980s, we saw this type of process occur with environmental

23   Isaacs, William. 1999. *Dialogue and the art of thinking together*. New York, NY: Currency Doubleday. P. 261

Box 3B: Dialogue and Transformation

"Dialogue starts from the courageous willingness to know and be known by others. It is the painstaking and persistent effort to remove all obstacles that obscure our common humanity.

Genuine dialogue is a ceaseless and profound spiritual exertion that seeks to effect a fundamental human transformation in both ourselves and others. Dialogue challenges us to confront and transform the destructive impulses inherent in human life. ...earnestly believe that the energy generated by this courageous effort can break the chains of resignation and apathy that bind the human hear, unleashing renewed confidence and vision for the future."

Source: Ikeda, Daisaku. 2007. "Civil Society Peace Forum at New York's Cooper Union Focuses on Abolishing Nuclear Weapons". http://www.joseitoda.org/reports/070908c.html: Soka Gakkai International.

impact over the positions of "the problem is Northern countries' consumption" versus "the problem is Southern countries' population growth." This produced a transcendent understanding that is technically represented by the environmental footprint concept: the impact a person, organization, or country has on the environment.

The general directional dynamic for this individual sphere was nicely summed up in the book entitled, *Leading from the Emerging Future - from Ego-system to Eco-system Economies,* by Katrin Kaufer and Otto Scharmer. They described big individual transformation as "...from an ego-system awareness that cares about the well-being of oneself to an eco-system awareness that cares about the well-being of all, including oneself."[24] This process involves developing meaningful exchanges with others, fostering dialogue fields.

Scharmer also emphasizes the importance of "presencing." "Presencing happens when our perception begins to connect to the source of our emerging future. The boundaries between three types of presence collapse: the presence of the past (the current state), the presence of the future (the emerging field of the future), and the presence of one's authentic Self."[25] This is a very personal process, and requires periods of introspection and deep personal reflection about how one "is" vis-à-vis others and nature, as well as one's highest aspirations and potential. It is a directioning and centering process. Some find individual retreats critical to support this. Presencing is never "completed," but rather is an essential quality to bring into daily life. There are many traditions supporting this. SGI focuses on chanting; some practices focus on silent meditation; others upon prayer; some like the Whirling Dervishes and the Shakers integrate dance. Other activities associated with "art" can also be used.

---

24   Scharmer, Otto, and Katrin Kaufer. 2013. *Leading from the Emerging Future: From Ego-System to Eco-System Economies.* San Francisco, CA, USA: Berrett-Koehler Publishers, Inc. location 53

25   Scharmer, C Otto. 2009. *Theory U: Learning from the future as it emerges:* Berrett-Koehler Publishers. P. 165

The Technology Change Sphere: The German Energy Transition

Generic sphere description: Technological invention and its widespread application (innovation) often have a transformative impact. The media has had a huge impact on accountability processes; electricity has revolutionized daily life. Today, Massive Open On-line Courses (MOOCs) are beginning to up-end traditional education structures. Although there is a tremendous focus on how to develop innovative technology, the bigger LSC challenge is about how to integrate it into society.

Particularly relevant change knowledge traditions: technological invention in the physical sciences, technological innovation systems (TIS), business innovation, and transitions.

Some key change sphere dynamics: development phases, multi-actor development, and co-evolution.

Some key change sphere activities: Problem-focused scenarios, commissions of inquiry, multi-stakeholder working groups

The Case

In 1980, the Institute for Applied Ecology (Öko-Institut) produced a book based on problem-focused scenarios and forecasting (see Chapter 9 for methodologies) that extrapolated energy trends; the methodologies are central to the work of the International Panel on Climate Change today when it forecasts the impact of greenhouse gases. Öko-Institut's book introduced the term Energiewende, as a call to completely abandon nuclear and petroleum energy. Translated as "energy transition," the term today is associated with Germany's pathway to a dramatic reductions in carbon emissions through changes in fuel sources, energy efficiency, and energy conservation. For many, a key part of this process is the democratization of energy through radical energy production decentralization.

Along with Denmark, Germany is commonly cited as one of the countries that has had the most success in making the energy transition. In 2002, the German Parliament unanimously ratified the Kyoto Protocol, which included a commitment by Germany to reduce its emissions to 21% less than 1990 levels between 2008 and 2012. By 2008, it had already reduced emissions 22.4%. Driven by climate change concerns, in 2007, the German government set greenhouse gas reduction targets at 40% by 2020 (compared with 1990 levels); by 2014, it achieved a 27% reduction.

Energiewende has strong public support. In 2014, 92% of Germans said that they support increasing the development and use of alternative sources; the same percentage say they support enforced expansion of renewable energy; 65% state that they would like to produce their own electricity.[26]

Energiewende is addressing the challenge of transforming an energy production model that is more than a century old – and all the entrenched interests associated with it. The model developed by industrialized countries has consisted of energy generation-transmission (long-distance)-distribution (short-dis-

---

26   http://strom-report.de/renewable-energy/

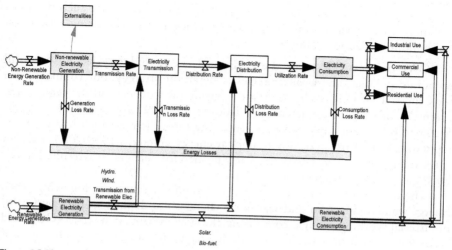

Figure 3C: The Energy Production System: A system dynamic map (see p. 170)

tance)-consumption, as illustrated in the top of Figure 3C. Renewable energy, illustrated in the lower part of the same Figure, implies dramatic technological innovations that drive the need for policy, finance, organizational, and consumer changes. This need for change was further heightened by the German government's decision to eliminate the 17% of nuclear-generated electricity (following the 1986 Chernobyl (Soviet Union) nuclear disaster).

The Öko-Institut report provided an intellectual and popular framework for energy transition. This was followed by pilots and option testing. For example, a large-scale wind power testing program launched by the German government in the 1980s provided an important empirical basis for the approach taken. "This program simulated a fee-in tariff in the form of fixed subsidies per kilowatt hour of wind power fed in, thus encouraging trust and renewable energies, and served as the basis for the feed-in act initiative."[27] In Germany most legislative initiatives come from Ministries. However, the Bundestag (the German parliament) itself took active leadership in defining the 1991 "Electricity Feed-In Act," which established the German strategy with two key elements:

1. **The Feed-In Tariff (FIT):** Utilities are required to purchase electricity from renewable energy sources at minimum prices higher than the real economic value of electricity. In the 1991 Act, prices were linked to retail prices. Companies were obliged to accept renewable energy preferences in transmission.

2. **Consumption Reduction:** The financial burden resulting from FIT was distributed between consumers. However, large energy-intensive industries were exempted. This means that households and small enterprises primarily pay the added cost. These higher costs resulted in downward pressure on

---

27   Bruns, Elke, Dörte Ohlhorst, Bernd Wenzel, and Johann Köppel. 2010. *Renewable Energies in Germany's Electricity Market: A biography of the innovation process:* Springer Science & Business Media. p. 58.

energy consumption. There is also an extensive provision for such things as more energy efficient buildings, with municipalities also taking action (via building codes, for example).

Over the next few years, the traditional energy industry led unsuccessful economic, political, and legal strategies to derail the strategy; one company even took the step of unilaterally cutting the legally prescribed tariff for renewables. From the side of renewable energy advocates, the 1991 Act was seen as insufficient to reach renewable energy targets. The Green Party, which had made its reputation in part in opposition to nuclear energy, entered a 1998-2005 coalition government. In the late 1990s, the Party pushed for changes that resulted in the 2000 German Renewable Energy Act (succeeding the 1991 Act).

The basic framework was adjusted and reinforced over the following years. Energiewende's direction and legislative changes are defined in part by (inter) ministerial working groups, comprising the government, industry, NGOs, and academic participants. The focus includes regulating and defining the roles of others in the transition.

The 2011 Fukushima disaster reinforced the commitment to rid the country of nuclear energy by speeding up its phase out. Seven reactors were immediately closed. During the next several years, adjustments were made to pricing and industry exemptions were narrowed. Major adjustments through 2015 include:

- Requiring companies to give renewable energy preference in transmission;
- Accelerating targets for renewable energy production and nuclear phase-out;
- Guaranteeing renewable energy producers a fixed price for 20 years, with prices linked to production costs;
- Applying caps to renewable energy expansion;
- Reducing every year or two the price per kilowatt hour for energy from a particular technology for new energy production, to reflect cost reductions as technology advances; only the most efficient forms will get full support; and
- Supporting a range of renewables (e.g., solar, wind, and biomass) at the same time as differentiated pricing that adapts to technological standards.

The European Union and global actors influence Energiewende policy. In the 1990s, the EU strongly promoted energy

> **Box 3C: Change as Open-Heart Surgery**
>
> Much could go wrong (with **Energiewende**). Wholesale electricity prices will be 70% higher by 2025, the Karlsruhe Institute of Technology predicts. Germany must build or upgrade 8,300km (5,157 miles) of transmission lines (not including connections to offshore wind farms). Intermittent wind and solar power creates a need for backup generators, while playing havoc with business models that justify investing in them. Hans-Peter Keitel, president of the Federation of German Industry, likens **Energiewende** to "open-heart surgery."
>
> *Source:* 2012. The Economist, July 28. Pp. 45-46

market liberalization, influencing the municipal scope of action. Germany danced around accusations that Energiewende supported collusion in contravening EU policies. On the global level, German citizen groups and NGOs have been supported by programs, such as Agenda 21, a non-binding product of the 1992 Rio Earth Summit. Agenda 21 goals legitimize action, and its structure has evolved into an influential organizing network. Furthermore, municipalities play a central role in Agenda 21 implementation, since many commitments require local action. In 2005, the EU launched its emissions trading platform, further supporting the transition.

The German legislative changes represent the government's intention to create a market. Its strategy implied reorienting policy from demand to supply, and shifting from centralized to distributed generation. This implies a huge change for an industry with long-term investment horizons, a predictable and stable business environment, and huge companies with associated bureaucracies. The elephants would have to learn to dance – or disappear. In September 2011, the German engineering giant Siemens announced a total withdrawal from the nuclear industry. In 2014, Germany's top utility E.ON said it would get out of its traditional coal and nuclear power businesses entirely, to focus on clean energy, power grids, and energy efficiency services. Behind these notable announcements was a complexity of action.

Local governments play an unusual role in the German energy transition, since distribution historically has been managed by utilities under the strict control of local governments. In the 1990s, two notable changes with respect to local government occurred. One is that in response to "liberalization" and financial pressures, many transferred grid ownership or management to private companies. However, German local governments remain key players and many local governments are aiming to reach renewable energy self-sufficiency. The second change, arising not from Energiewende, but from broader reform, was a strengthening of local democratization. Provisions were made for citizen referenda to vote on particular proposals. In addition, direct elections of mayors were introduced and provided a new platform for debate about energy action.

By 2013, approximately 10% of energy produced by public utilities came from renewables.[28] The ability of local governments to take action is constricted by financial issues and political will. Three examples illustrate varying local government strategies:

- In **Berlin**, utility ownership ended up with a Swedish state-owned company, Vattenfall. The Green Party and the NGO Powershift criticized both the company's pursuit of coal-fired energy and its subsequent biomass plant proposal. In general, the city government has been criticized as too passive. The Berlin region has ranked last in energy transition. In response in 2011, NGOs created a coalition and agenda that aims for 100% renewable energy

---

28   Schmid, Eva, Brigitte Knopf, and Anna Pechan. 2016. "Putting an energy system transformation into practice: The case of the German Energiewende." *Energy Research & Social Science* 11:263-75.

and a democratically-controlled energy system with a Board directly elected by citizens. A second proposal is for control via a cooperative. In 2013, even though the majority of voters favored re-municipalization, the referendum failed due to low voter participation. The renewal of the concession to Vattenfall is under continuing debate. One large issue is the price that private companies claim they are worth, and the cost of investment they claim is necessary to renew grid operations that they have failed to invest in.

- An impressive contrast is **Lüchow-Dannenberg**, which is comprised of 27 very small municipalities with a total population of only 50,000. In 1997, a working group on climate protection and energy set an ambitious target of meeting 100% of electricity needs with renewable energy. The district was motivated in part by the need to remedy high regional unemployment, and in part, by being a prospective site for final nuclear storage. It has become a model for reducing electricity consumption and going renewable. Four years ahead of its goal, on May 1, 2011, Lüchow-Dannenberg reached its goal with a diverse technology mix.

- The electric utility SWM is owned by the municipality of **Munich**. By 2025, Munich aims to be the first city of more than a million residents to realize 100% renewable energy use. By May 2015, green energy fed into the grid equaled the consumption of all private households and the electrically powered public transport system.

A different energy issue presented itself to Torgelow, a community of 10,000, on September 24, 2014. Various government agencies and representatives, companies, associations, and the public were invited to become involved in identifying a suitable corridor for a new transmission line, which was to be 500 to 1,000 meters wide. New legislation supports developing transmission infrastructure to transport wind-generated energy from the north of Germany to the south. (However, these power lines will be needed much more for new coal plants built near the sea, than for offshore wind.) The legislation included defining a consultation process with various formats of events, ranging from citizens' conferences to information markets, to discussion evenings in which locals have the opportunity to get together in small groups. The goal is for locals to learn about envisaged projects, to voice their concerns, and to discuss possible solutions - preferably before the formal process of involving the public begins. Mediation services will also be available as needed to supplement this dialogue.[29]

The shift to renewables has been accompanied by a rise in totally new players. In the face of lethargic response by traditional utilities to the changing business environment, institutional and strategic investors (such as pension funds) stepped in to develop capital-intensive and large-scale energy generation projects. These comprise large-scale wind and solar energy parks/farms and biomass generation.

---

29   BMWI. 2015. "Public Dialogue." http://www.bmwi.de/EN/Topics/Energy/Grids-and-grid-expansion/public-dialogue.html: Federal Ministry for Economic Affairs and Energy.

By 2013, they owned 41.5% of all renewable capacities, compared with only 8.5% for traditional utilities.[30]

Another major change with the shift to renewables is the development of small producers and "prosumers:" people who are principally consumers, but also produce (usually wind or solar) surplus electricity that is then sold back to the distribution grid. A 2016 report explains:

> Such local actors owned 46% of the installed renewable generation capacities in 2012, consisting of individual citizens and farmers (25%), cooperatives and other forms of citizen organizations (9%), jointly referred to as citizen participation in the narrow sense, and minority or interregional citizen participation models (12%), known as citizen participation in the wider sense. Cooperatives have experienced a boom in the energy sector, increasing from 35 in the year 2005 to 635 involved in electricity and heat generation by 2013.[31]

This represents an enormous change in the structure of the electricity generation business, as well as its broader activities. Considering the amount of capital investment and the organizational development involved, it has all happened in a very short period of time. It has also significantly shifted German energy industry dynamics, towards a much more decentralized structure with diverse ownership forms. Rather than investor-dominated interests, forms, like coops and local utilities, are much more user-responsive.

While subsidy costs for Energiewende have been criticized by many, energy costs as a percentage of household expenditures have remained constant at approximately 2 percent since 1990.[32] Moreover, since 1970, conventional baseload technologies, such as nuclear and black coal, have received more than twice the subsidies of renewables. The accumulated amount given to renewables only overtook brown coal in 2013.[33]

Nevertheless, Energiewende represents an enormous investment in developing new renewable energy technologies: some say solar has been Germany's gift to the world. The direction is still being challenged, however. In March, 2014, the CEOs of Europe's largest energy companies moved to slow down the deployment of mainly decentralized renewable power through EU rule changes. The EU made bidding rather than FIT the key pricing system, determining that FIT pricing was a subsidy to companies. EU commissioners claim renewable energy is now mature enough to compete: in 2000, the price of a photovoltaic module was more than €5 ($5) per watt; by 2015 that figure had dropped to €0.57 ($0.64) per watt, reflecting the

30   Schmid, Eva, Brigitte Knopf, and Anna Pechan. 2016. "Putting an energy system transformation into practice: The case of the German Energiewende." *Energy Research & Social Science* 11:263-75.
31   Ibid. p. 266
32   Pang, John, Chris Vlahoplus, John Sterling, and Bob Gibson. 2014. "Germany's Energiewende." *Public Utilities Fortnightly* 152(11):14.
33   Greenpeace Energy eG. 2015. "Was Strom wirklich kostet." http://www.foes.de/pdf/2015-01-Was-Strom-wirklich-kostet-kurz.pdf: Greenpeace Germany.

impact of intense R&D and scaling. However, doubts remain about whether the tipping point has been reached, and there are continued protests pointing to the very substantial subsidies traditional energy has received for many years. There are calls to include risks and externalities in pricing, which would greatly benefit renewables and accelerate their implementation. There also remains the technological challenge of fluctuations in the supply of renewable energy, and problems with storing it.

The Case Discussion

Bringing carbon footprints within sustainable limits involves enormous technological change from carbon-based fuel sources to renewable ones; and this requires transformation. Energiewende is a complex process, because the end-points are unclear from two perspectives. One is, with reference to the electricity system, what does a carbon-sustainable energy system actually look like? There are myriad possible structures and technologies, which is typical of a complex issue. Second is the question, "What are the pathways to the various options?" Again, there are numerous options. Moreover, innovations can cut both ways: promoting natural gas as a bridge to sustainable energy, for example, is just as likely be a carbon-fueled system trap that prevents the move to renewables.

However, the transition is more appropriately referred to as socio-technical change, given its impact on industrial structures as well. Socio-technological transformations are not easy. The German approach is not just about changing the energy source, as would be represented by big companies harvesting solar energy in the Sahara with transmission via cables to Germany. Energiewende is also about displacing large companies, like Siemens and E.ON, with a decentralized, resilient, energy independent system. One analyst commented that socio-technological transformation is a "…long-term process (40-50 years); while breakthroughs may be relatively fast (e.g. 10 years), the preceding innovation journeys through which new socio-technical systems gradually emerge usually take much longer (20-30 years)."[34]

The German energy case illustrates the importance of public support for change, the development of new technologies, and business models and action mechanisms to create a change system.

Public Support

Public support for Energiewende remains strong. In 2014, 92% of Germans said that they support increasing the development and use of alternative sources.[35]

The driving concerns for German support are three-fold: the desire for energy security, concerns about nuclear energy, and climate change. Because oil and gas were never produced in Germany in quantity, decreasing dependence upon them was a goal that gained steam with the 1973 oil crisis. To address the security concern, until the 1980s, German energy policy emphasized nuclear generation. Problems with the disposal of nuclear waste, the 1979 Harrisburg Incident in the US, and the 1987 Chernobyl Disaster coalesced opposition to nuclear energy.

---

34   Grin, John, Jan Rotmans, and Johan Schot. 2010. *Transitions to sustainable development: new directions in the study of long term transformative change*: Routledge. P. 11
35   http://strom-report.de/renewable-energy/

The 2011 Fukushima Accident abruptly reversed growing support for the nuclear option. These coincided with rising concerns about climate change.[36]

Reviewing public attitudes, a comparative multi-national study concluded that:

> In Germany, there was hardly any opposition to wind projects because the framework favored civil and local shareholding, while simultaneously also promoting increased involvement in decision-making.[37]

Another comparative analysis concluded that

> …an approach that focuses on implementing as much wind power as possible, relying on technocratic reasoning and hierarchical policies is in practice the least successful, whereas collaborative perspectives with more emphasis on local issues and less on the interests of the conventional energy sector were particularly dominant in the most successful case, North-Rhine Westphalia.[38]

The change process depends on three types of social acceptance:
- Socio-political acceptance (of technologies and/or of policies that effectively support innovation) by key stakeholders, the public, and policy makers;
- Community acceptance (of facilities, of the investors, owners, and managers) by residents, local authorities, and local stakeholders;
- Market acceptance (of investments in facilities, and of prices or tariffs) by consumers, by investors, and within companies.[39]

Socio-political acceptance was supported by emerging structures. When the federal government support for renewables waned following a government change and the 2008 financial crisis, it weakened the transition program. However, there were limits to what could be done because of strong support from other levels of government, and because, by then there was an increasingly large and vocal group of small renewable energy producers. "Though a huge project, it (Energiewende) is far from being just a top–down process. In some ways, it resembles a huge citizen initiative, a bottom–up movement," two analysts commented.[40]

---

36 Hake, Jürgen-Friedrich, Wolfgang Fischer, Sandra Venghaus, and Christoph Weck-enbrock. 2015. "The German Energiewende – History and status quo." *Energy* 92, Part 3:532-46.
37 Wolsink, Maarten. 2010. "Contested environmental policy infrastructure: Socio-political acceptance of renewable energy, water, and waste facilities." *Environmental Impact Assessment Review* 30(5):302-11.
38 Wolsink, Maarten, and Sylvia Breukers. 2010. "Contrasting the core beliefs regarding the effective implementation of wind power. An international study of stakeholder perspectives." *Journal of environmental planning and management* 53(5):535-58. P. 535
39 Wolsink, Maarten. 2010. "Contested environmental policy infrastructure: Socio-political acceptance of renewable energy, water, and waste facilities." *Environmental Impact Assessment Review* 30(5):302-11.
40 Lauber, Volkmar, and Moritz Buschmann. 2013. "Germany: Challenges of a Full Transition to Renewable Energy." Pp. 295-313 in *Renewable Energy Governance:* Springer. P. 211

Technological and Business Innovation

The technical concerns of transition are about sustainability, security, and affordability. Germany has long been a technology leader and prides itself on its engineering competency. Therefore, although developing renewables represented a significant challenge in terms of utilities' business models, the technological challenge was one that was approached by a skilled establishment. In 2015, an observer commented on the scale of change: "The tenet of all power capacities being fully under System Operator (SO) command is growing obsolete with every new wind turbine or PV panel coming on line."[41]

The basic dynamic in socio-technical change is one of invention (identifying an option) and innovation (popularizing it). This transition is associated with developing a "technological innovation system" (TIS), which refers to the whole process from R&D to continuous improvement over the course of industrial mass production. This includes improving efficiency, developing new patents, new materials, new designs, setting up an equipment industry for producing generation technologies, and developing a knowledge system to accompany it. These are *complex* from several standpoints. For a start, there is a need for significant experimentation to identify technologies, and these experiments do not follow traditional management planning charts with deliverables on day X. Inventions cannot be predicted. The problems with solar energy storage exemplify the need to find transformative technological breakthroughs built on new ways of approaching the problem, rather than simply improving existing practices. Secondly, the innovation system is complex because of its socio-technical nature that requires new relationships exemplified by the rise of prosumers.

Taking the scientific products of the first phase of ideas about possibilities leads to the second phase of pilot projects. This is necessary to apply theoretical

Box 3D: Building Support through a Learning Journey

A group of US utility and renewable energy executives toured Germany in 2014 to investigate Energiewende. This mixed stakeholder participation reflects a key quality of the learning journey methodology (Chapter 9): by bringing together advocates for change and incumbents, there is greater opportunity for fostering generative dialogue and creating new relationships. They reached the following conclusions:

- The utility business model changed rapidly, and incumbents weren't nimble enough. Since 2007, the eight largest European utilities have lost a combined total of 300 billion euros of market capitalization. New entrants have taken new renewable market opportunities and market share.
- Large amounts of renewable energy have been successfully integrated into

---

41   Verbruggen, Aviel, Rosaria Di Nucci, Manfred Fischedick, Reinhard Haas, Frede Hvelplund, Volkmar Lauber, Arturo Lorenzoni, Lutz Mez, Lars J Nilsson, and Pablo del Rio Gonzalez. 2015. "Europe's electricity regime: restoration or thorough transition." *International Journal of Sustainable Energy Planning and Management* 5:57-68.

insights and understand limits and potential. The large socio-technical innovation phase then follows. This is the large-scale application that requires changing policies and regulations, financing, infrastructure, consumer behavior, marketing, finding ways to finance this transformation, and managing changes in power structures, such as the displacement of traditional carbon fuel suppliers.

People working on these huge transitions have identified three inter-related levels of change, comprising a TIS:

1. *Regimes* are the policies, regulations, rules, and structures that support one technology system versus another. Historically, in electricity, this means those who support the traditional centralized carbon fuel-based system versus those in favor of the renewable energy one. Both what the latter regime will look like and how to get there are large questions involving huge power interests, roles, policies, and structures. This is the essence of the German activities.

2. *Landscapes* refer to the larger environment of "hard" features, such as geographical dispositions to new technologies (e.g., wind generation requires wind), and "soft" features like broad economic conditions (it is easier to change in a robust market), political realities (who is in power and what is their attitude), and social attitudes (is climate change even seen as an issue).

3. *Niches* are spaces in which innovation application is being tried.   Typically, these are protected from the broader operating environment with such things as subsidies and waivers of traditional regulation.[42] In the German case, niches were developed in solar, biomass, and wind that resulted in important political constituencies of their own.

> the distribution and transmission grids.
> - The pricing strategy to place costs largely on consumers (to protect industry and reduce consumer energy consumption) was largely successful. Although consumer electricity prices doubled from 1991-2013, electricity, as a household expenditure, remained steady at 2 percent.
> - The 1980 Öko-Institut Energiewende report provided the basis for today's direction, and has been successfully followed up with continued strong public support and a general conviction that a competitive advantage will emerge from early adoption. Buttressing this support are climate change, energy independence. and anti-nuclear concerns.
>
> *Source:* Pang, John, Chris Vlahoplus, John Sterling, and Bob Gibson. 2014. "Germany's Energiewende." *Public Utilities Fortnightly* 152(11):14.

This framework provides a useful way to analyze the technological transformation challenge and its evolution for strategic action. Niches can be thought of as large-scale experiments. They comprise new technologies that aim to identify

---

42   Geels, Frank W. 2005. "Processes and patterns in transitions and system innovations: refining the co-evolutionary multi-level perspective." *Technological Forecasting and Social Change* 72(6):681-96.

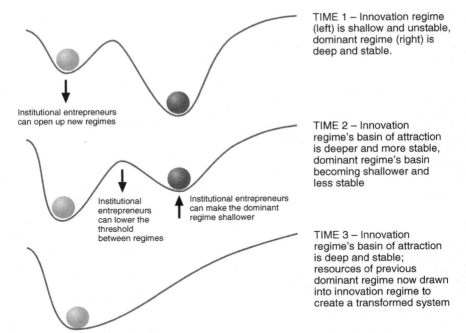

TIME 1 – Innovation regime (left) is shallow and unstable, dominant regime (right) is deep and stable.

Institutional entrepreneurs can open up new regimes

TIME 2 – Innovation regime's basin of attraction is deeper and more stable, dominant regime's basin becoming shallower and less stable

Institutional entrepreneurs can lower the threshold between regimes

Institutional entrepreneurs can make the dominant regime shallower

TIME 3 – Innovation regime's basin of attraction is deep and stable; resources of previous dominant regime now drawn into innovation regime to create a transformed system

Figure 3D: Stages of Technological Change: Cross-scale dynamics of social (systemic) innovations and the role of institutional entrepreneurs.

the type of regime that will support traditional regime displacement, and grow from a niche to the dominant actor. This is popularly associated with the process of realizing a tipping point. Through its FIT pricing and distribution policies, the government aimed to protect renewable energy development to the point of it becoming competitive with tradition energy sources.

This description draws heavily from the work of a large number of people that produced Figure 3D.[43] Particularly important in this process are change agents, "institutional entrepreneurs" whose "…role is to question the institutional context, frame it for those working at more microscales, identify those inventions with potential to tip systems and sell these to institutional decision-makers when the opportunity arises."[44] These are individuals, and increasingly organizations, that play critical roles in

43   Westley, Frances, Per Olsson, Carl Folke, Thomas Homer-Dixon, Harrie Vredenburg, Derk Loorbach, John Thompson, Måns Nilsson, Eric Lambin, and Jan Sendzimir. 2011. "Tipping toward sustainability: emerging pathways of transformation." *AMBIO* 40(7):762-80.
       See also: Geels, Frank W. 2010. "Ontologies, socio-technical transitions (to sustainability), and the multi-level perspective." *Research Policy* 39:495-510.
       Grin, John, Jan Rotmans, and Johan Schot. 2010. *Transitions to sustainable development: new directions in the study of long term transformative change*: Routledge.
44   Westley, Frances, Per Olsson, Carl Folke, Thomas Homer-Dixon, Harrie Vredenburg, Derk Loorbach, John Thompson, Måns Nilsson, Eric Lambin, and Jan Sendzimir. 2011. "Tipping toward sustainability: emerging pathways of transformation." *AMBIO* 40(7):762-80.

Box 3E: The Challenge of Shifting Regimes

Not many alternative producers in technologies also have the capacity to do the lobbying and policy-designing that would help them crack current patterns. The old regime – the incumbents – fight the hardest and has the most resources. The WBGU report "World in Transition" made a very important distinction within the niche: pioneers find new solutions and change agents seek to help scale or multiply them (regime change) – the latter could be advocates, the media, or risk-liking investors, etc. I think it is helpful to differentiate these players – in particular, as here lies the link to what a change system needs with an ecosystem approach to resolving wicked problems.

Source: Maja Goepel, Wuppertal Institute for Climate, Environment and Energy - personal correspondence.

developing the change system (as Chapter 6 explains in greater detail). They include new renewable energy participants, those advocating for change, and those writing supportive legislation.

This description suggests a linear process from academic insight to new regime realization. However, the process is actually quite non-linear. There are many trials and errors involved, and at various times, there is great potential for disruption. Although the German example is outstanding for the constancy of public support (in the face of substantial opposition from incumbent businesses), the United States is another extreme where support for electricity system transformation has ebbed and flowed along with factors, like the financial crisis, fracking, and who is leading the government.

Factors, such as the ownership structures of power companies, are also important in the generation of new business models. In Germany, there was no national oil industry (although coal had been important). Employment in renewables grew quickly to surpass the traditional energy sector, creating new interests. Private citizen investment and ownership made a big difference. Private citizens and farmers own almost half of the country's renewable energy generation capacity. In addition, the role of municipalities in the electricity system is unusual. This provided for responsiveness to local pressure for change at the political level that could result in much more direct action than when private owners are involved. Also politically important was that the Green Party was strong in Germany and proved an effective political agent to support the transition; the weakening of the energy transition commitment after 2013 was associated with the Party's electoral set-back and dissatisfaction with high energy prices. These factors emphasize that socio-techno system innovation is required, not just technological changes.

Action Mechanisms as a Change System

Another way to look at the transition is in terms of developing a robust "change system." This consists of all types of organizations: academic, governmental, NGOs, and businesses, as well as, individuals, networks, and collaborations. Looking at global initiatives to support electricity transition, an investigation that I led identified five foci of change thought of as "change sub-systems" that collectively form a change system:

1. **Policy Change Sub-system:** The concern of this sub-system is appropriate government direction. This comprises governmental bodies, including regulators and legislators at the local, national, regional, and global levels. Other stakeholders engage in co-producing rules and policies. In Germany, this involved, in particular, the local and federal governments. Although there was significant policy debate, compared with other countries, the German case stands out as one of particularly strong and sustained action.

2. **Innovation Change Sub-system:** This sub-system produces new technologies. Its initiating leadership is scientists and research organizations, and it involves prototyping government agencies, NGOs, and companies that are developing new technologies and innovations. Scaling innovations is part of the service provider change sub-system (below), the distinction being that different stakeholders and competencies are then engaged. Germany took a lead in developing solar technology, in particular.

3. **Finance Change Sub-system:** This sub-system is about innovating and influencing financial markets and tools to enhance the flow of capital to sustainable electricity production. This includes both public and private sector capital. The financing issue in Germany was significantly simplified through government action around FIT and cross-subsidization with a 20-year guarantee to address investors' concerns about potential risk.

4. **Service Provider Change Sub-system:** This refers to change initiatives forming an emerging electricity provision infrastructure. Historically, the infrastructure was referred to as "electric utilities," both public and private. Some technological innovations imply significant disruptions in this sub-system, such as decentralized generation. This raises substantial business model issues. This was particularly important for developing prosumers and a decentralized model; a new range of actors (co-ops, individuals, and small businesses) became important.

5. **Consumer Change Sub-System:** This change sub-system is about demand for electricity and how it is used: how to influence it and the scale of consumers' changing role in the emerging service provider system. Strategically, it is useful to divide it into commercial and retail consumers. Important players in this sub-system are organizations promoting 100% renewables and government actions that promote conservation.

To develop an effective change system requires robust change mechanisms. "Mechanism" means processes to transform one context (organizations and power relationships based on one set of assumptions (sustainability is not a consideration)) into another in a different context to accommodate different assumptions (sustainability is critical). Even with the right technology and public support, transformation is often frustrated by entrenched elites. Germany demonstrates a resilient society with respect to energy strategy compared with most countries. It has mechanisms reflecting public support and technological possibilities.

The German political system represents one mechanism. It has successfully initiated and refined a direction for more than 30 years. The steadiness of the steering is remarkable. There are many ways the system has proven to be resilient. One is with the election process and the formation of coalition governments; another is with the willingness of the Bundestag (the parliament) to take direct leadership in crafting legislation when the traditional ministry process was proving to be insufficiently responsive. Also notable are party organizations: unlike a country like the US that is ossified into a two-party system, Germany (like most countries) has developed a Green Party that acts as an influential renewable energy advocate.

A second mechanism is organizational variety within the traditional energy system. There is an incredible diversity in German structures associated with energy. As well as traditional market-owned utilities, public utilities, co-ops and producer associations all play a role. When the traditional market-owned utilities failed to be sufficiently responsive, other organizational forms were used to lead the transformation.

It is also important to note that Germany has never had an indigenous lobby group supporting oil and gas, since it produces none. The questions were commercial to the extent that electric utilities were challenged to shift their business model, which they generally failed to do with respect to generation, but were more successful in terms of transmission and distribution. Today, an additional mechanism supporting renewables is producers who represent a new economic lobby group.

Summary Energiewende Discussion

The overall electricity innovation process is indeed a very big one, taking place over 40-50 years, given investment horizons, organizational structures, and physical infrastructure. However, in other industries, there are technological innovations that have much shorter impact periods, in part, because they involve a much smaller threat to invested interests (e.g., carbon fuel suppliers, and huge financial investments in traditional generating capacity), and also because they are consumer-level rather than industry-level innovations. There are many examples associated with information technology. Internet access, for example, has fundamentally changed the power relationships in some industries, such as publishing and taxis, in much less time.

Reviewing the Energiewende process, three analysts commented that:

> They (the major challenges) are not of technical nature. A deep implication of this insight is that a greater awareness for values, worldviews, takes on democracy and other normative aspects is imperative when contemplating or debating on the future of the German energy system. However, this insight is equally valid for energy transitions around the globe. Yet, as

long as they are conceived as engineering endeavors conflicting values will remain the elephant in the room.[45]

The degree of commitment to the Energiewende scale of experimentation is a big deterrent factor in many countries. Displacing traditional energy interests and companies is a significant challenge. Even in Germany, there is still the possibility of a stalemate with the old energy sector maintaining a significant role. Tipping points are not always obvious or clear-cut. Energiewende still could fail technologically, such as with power burn-outs, or socio-economically, such as with the cost differential between renewables and traditional generation becoming too great, particularly if other countries continue with the latter.[46] However, Germany has demonstrated the capacity and commitment for very large-scale experimentation. It has "proven" an alternative, and policy action has now fallen into the incremental change mode.

The Social-Economic-Political Institution Sphere: South Africa and Apartheid

Generic sphere description: Institutions and organizations that define and maintain social, economic, and political structures are the focus of this change sphere. They are the formal and informal processes for determining leadership and undertaking decisions in particular with respect to government structures, business organizations, and civil society ones, ranging from labor unions and churches to NGOs. Classic examples of transformation in this sphere are the French, Russian and Chinese Revolutions; the American one is much less so, since the economic-social structures underwent a relatively modest change. A historical strategy involving modest numbers of people is the development of intentional communities. A major 20th century example was the rise of the welfare state. Today, a new emerging strategy is developing around the concept of "social innovation labs" and multi-stakeholder processes.

Particularly relevant change knowledge traditions: experimentalist governance, business in society, social innovation labs, social movements, and revolutions.

Some key change sphere dynamics: increasing consciousness of gross inequality/injustice for a large percentage of the population; heightened tensions and confrontations with the broadening action and participation of masses versus increasing suppression by the status quo until a cathartic transformation; declining support for the status quo by outsiders.

Some key change sphere activities: Reflexive Interventionist/Multi-Agent-based Scenarios, demonstrations, boycotts, multi-stakeholder dialogues

---

45   Schmid, Eva, Brigitte Knopf, and Anna Pechan. 2016. "Putting an energy system transformation into practice: The case of the German Energiewende." Energy Research & Social Science 11:263-75. P. 272

46   Hake, Jürgen-Friedrich, Wolfgang Fischer, Sandra Venghaus, and Christoph Weckenbrock. 2015. "The German Energiewende – History and status quo." *Energy* 92, Part 3:532-46.

The Case

(How) can South Africans reconcile 'the black demand for majority rule (with) white concerns stemming from this demand?' How can the redistribution of resources and opportunities occur without the destruction of the economy? How can South Africa protect the rights of its white citizens without entrenching the privileges of old? [47]

The 1990 release of Nelson Mandela from prison is undoubtedly a watershed moment in South African history. Preceding and following events provide fertile ground for thinking about the transformation of social-economic-political structures, given that apartheid was so heavily institutionalized in daily South African life.

The 1948 elections were another watershed moment, with the National Party (NP) beginning its government control that would only end with the ending of apartheid itself. However, this particular change re-enforced earlier developments, such as the 1913 Land Act that regulated black acquisition of land. The development of a full-fledged racist state was associated with many tactics. Laws severely restricted the movement of blacks by requiring the possession of passbooks to identify bearers, their race, residence, and employment. Races were forced to live in separate areas. More than 80% of the country was allocated to its 16% (1980) white population. "Banning" outlawed publications, organizations, or assemblies and restricted individuals' interactions. Blacks could not participate in the national government. Access to public facilities was divided by race. Inter-racial marriage was prohibited. All of this was backed up by the legal, police, and military apparatus of the state. This included torture and gross violence. For example, in the 1960 Sharpeville Massacre, police fired on a group of unarmed blacks demonstrating against the Pass Laws, killing 67 and wounding more than 180. By 1961, most resistance leaders had either left the country or were in prison. Mandela's long imprisonment began in 1963.

Internal resistance advanced with the formation of the Congress Alliance in the early 1950s, as a non-racial coalition of organizations opposed to apartheid. The African National Congress (ANC) held political leadership of the Alliance, which included the South African Communist Party (SACP) and the South African Congress of Trade Unions (SACTU), representing the country's powerful mining workers. The Alliance produced a coherent opposition, and in 1955, the Freedom Charter. It was a statement of core principles developed through wide engagement, including door-to-door canvassing. The Charter was a social-political-economic statement. It included pledges "to strive together, sparing neither strength nor courage, until the democratic changes here set out have been won" and that "every man and woman shall have the right to vote for and to stand as a candidate for all bodies which make laws." The Charter also stipulated that "(T)he mineral wealth beneath the soil, the Banks and

---

47   Ndebele, Njabulo Simakahle. 1999. *Of lions and rabbits: Thoughts on democracy and reconciliation*. P 5 cited in Alexander, Neville. 2002. *An Ordinary Country: Issues in the Transition from Apartheid to Democracy in South Africa*. Scottsville, South Africa: University of Natal Press. P. 119

monopoly industry shall be transferred to the ownership of the people as a whole."[48]
While this last goal might sound radical to those living in Western capitalist countries today, at the time, this was a position reflected in many countries' party positions.

Resistance comprised a four pillar strategy: mass struggle at home, under-
ground struggle, armed struggle, and international isolation of the governing
regime. Mass mobilization took many forms, including: demonstrations, strikes
and boycotts. In 1976, thousands of black children in Soweto (outside of Johan-
nesburg) demonstrated against a requirement that the Afrikaans language be their
primary medium of instruction (as opposed to their mother tongues). Police fired
tear gas and bullets. A 1985 campaign aimed to make local townships ungovern-
able: people refused to pay fees to local authorities for utilities and other services;
attempts to cut off service provoked illegal hook-ups; and attempts to evict delin-
quents were met with mass opposition.

The international community was also deeply involved in South Africa.
Its role was highly influenced by global Cold War dynamics. The Soviet Union
provided support and training, as well as an ideological framework for SACP and
SACTU participants in particular. The West, in particular the United States and
the British governments, for years supported, albeit with increasing criticism, the
South African government. They and NGOs also provided financial and training
support for anti-apartheid groups, most notably those associated with the ANC.

The United Nations provided a stage for the international fight. Following the
1960 massacre, the Security Council for the first time demanded an end to racial
separation and discrimination. However, the West also supported South Africa
in the UN, such as opposing a 1974 motion to expel South Africa. In 1977, the
UN voted for a mandatory arms embargo. There never was an economic embargo
because of opposition by Western trading partners, although in the late 1980s, the
United States, the United Kingdom, and 23 other countries passed trade sanctions.

Many cities, individuals, and organizations became involved in supporting
disinvestment from South Africa. Cultural and sporting ties were increasingly
restricted. Churches and their networks – particularly the Anglican Church, with
the leadership of Nobel Peace Prize winner Desmond Tutu – played important
internal and external opposition roles. However, the Dutch Reformed Church of
South Africa strongly supported apartheid as "God's will."

The South African government mounted campaigns of its own in the West.
This included comparisons with the battle in Northern Ireland, the role of blacks
in the US, and increasingly after the Civil Rights Movement, references to the
treatment of Native Americans.

Economically, the 1980s were difficult for South Africa. Merchandise trade,
as a percentage of GDP, hit a high in 1980 of 56%; it quickly fell to 32% in 1989.
GDP growth was very problematic, cresting at 6.6% in 1980 with the following
years (up to 1990) averaging only 1.75%.

---

48   Congress Alliance. 1955. "The Freedom Charter." http://www.anc.org.za/show.
      php?id=72: African National Congress.

Beginning in 1982, Mandela and the South African government began secret negotiations. Mandela explained that he did not consult with others in the ANC because they would have killed the initiative, and there are times when a leader has to move out ahead of the flock.[49] When de Klerk took over from Botha as President in 1989, an intense negotiations process began and some restrictions were lifted (such as ending the ban of the ANC in 1990). A process to develop the way forward began in December 1991 with the *Convention for a Democratic South Africa* (CODESA), with wide representation, but some boycotts by black organizations. Other events included:

- 1992: whites-only referendum with landslide victory for the "yes" side, with more than 68% of the voters voting for a continuation of reforms and negotiations;
- 1992: CODESA breaks down after a massacre and rolling actions, followed by another massacre;
- 1992: NP-ANC negotiators agree to a "sunset clause" for a coalition (NP-ANC) government for five years following a democratic election and concessions, such as:
- recognizing all existing property rights; and
- guaranteeing continued employment for apartheid era civil servants.
- 1993: the Multiparty Negotiating Forum begins with all parties initially participating;
- 1993: violence on both sides, withdrawal of some process participants; US and British diplomats get involved;
- 1993, Nov. 18: interim Constitution agreed upon;
- 1994, April 27: elections with ANC winning 62%, NP 20%; a joint national unity government was formed;
- 1995: final constitution agreed upon.

The timing of all these events must be understood within the global context, most notably the rise of Gorbachev, perestroika and glasnost in 1986, and the ensuing 1989 collapse of the Soviet Union. This spelled an end of access to Soviet military and training resources, and perhaps even more crucially the delegitimizing of ideology and the "victory" of capitalism as an ideology. In *An Ordinary Country*, Alexander Neville comments that "...as a result, the leverage in the Congress Alliance of the SACP generally and of its left wing in particular was reduced, so that the moderate centrist elements in the leadership of the ANC could rapidly become decisive."[50] This also lowered the fears of whites.

This historic moment made capitalism, particularly as practiced by the United States, a victor. This gave it significant weight in international institutions – the World Bank and associated financial institutions being particularly influential in South Africa. The European social democratic model's distinctions and strengths appeared to be marginalized. The era was the high-water point of the "Washington

49   Alexander, Neville. 2002. *An Ordinary Country: Issues in the Transition from Apartheid to Democracy in South Africa.* Scottsville, South Africa: University of Natal Press. P. 53
50   Ibid. P. 45

Consensus" and enthrallment with globalization. The idea of small nation states being able to go their own way was associated with, at the time, negative models of Cuba, Myanmar, and China (before its economic emergence). This meant there was a large vacuum in terms of real alternative visions for social and economic approaches, which in the end strongly favored isomorphic capitalist model pressures to adopt the status quo (if South Africa were to regain a place in the international community).

Over this period, scenario development as a method (see Chapter 9) played an extensive role.[51] The method was introduced by Shell and its associates, who were leaders in its application within the business sphere. Scenarios in corporate settings assume the corporation will not be able to determine its favored future; rather, the purpose is to support corporate resilience in responding to a range of possible futures.[52] Of course, the situation is quite different with nation states that do have a significant ability to determine their desired future. In South Africa, there were several social contract scenarios business-financed scenarios, as well as some labor and social democratic ones.

Perhaps the most famous of these is the Mont Fleur scenarios, sponsored by the Institute for Social Development, developed by 25 people over four weekends. In classic scenario fashion, four alternative futures were envisioned and colorfully labeled, in terms of flight:

- Icarus as the Greek who flew too close to the sun, melting the wax of his wings, and tumbling into the sea as an analogy for trying to do too much too quickly;
- Ostrich told as the story of a non-representative white government, sticking its head in the sand;
- Lame duck anticipated as a prolonged transition under a weak government that, because it purports to respond to all, satisfies none;
- Flight of the Flamingoes describes a successful transition with which everyone in the society rises slowly and together.

The scenarios were publicized to spur public discussion. However, the 1955 Freedom Charter and its economic vision of a strategy that included nationalization of mines and financial institutions was still alive for many in the South African struggle. Socially, there was also deep concern about the need to end the huge housing and human services deficit and inequitable access to public services. In addition, there was a need to somehow address the violent history and ongoing ill-will between whites and blacks.

Many of these goals were woven into a 1994 project called, the *Reconstruction and Development Program* (RDP). While radicals found much to criticize about it, it was clearly a socio-democratic attempt to make a clear break with the country's economic and social traditions. Bond comments that, "There were mutually supportive means within the RDP to 'decommodify' (remove from the market) and

---

51   Bond, Patrick. 2014. *Elite transition: From apartheid to neoliberalism in South Africa.* London, UK: Pluto Press.

52   For an excellent and brief look at scenarios see: Wilkinson, Angela. 2009. "Scenarios Practices: In Search of Theory." *Journal of Futures Studies* 13(3):107-14.

'destratify' (make universal) basic needs goods, in addition to other radical reforms."[53] However, by 1996, the RDP was replaced by the *Growth, Employment and Redistribution* policy statement (GEAR), that fit within a very neo-liberal orthodoxy that gutted socio-democratic aspects aimed at great quality of life equity. Basically, the issue became one of how to integrate some blacks into leadership via key social, political, and economic organizations. GEAR was passed into law with little debate over a few weeks.[54]

The result can be seen today. From an RDP commitment to 30% land redistribution by 2000 (very attainable, considering 6% was sold on average per annum), there has been no significant redistribution. The GINI coefficient[55] indicates that income inequality has become worse since the 1994 elections. The World Bank estimated the coefficient at approximately 0.57 in 1995, and the OECD estimated in 2013 at about 0.70; it was ranked as the fourth most unequal income country in the world in 2009.[56] The 2013 OECD report estimates that the coefficient amongst blacks *increased* from 0.55 to 0.62 between 1993 and 2008,[57] describing the economic ascendance of a few blacks who left the vast majority behind.

Mending the divide caused by the history of racist violence was the task of the *Truth and Reconciliation Commission* (TRC), inspired by an earlier Chilean strategy. In contrast with the Nuremberg Trials following World War II, the TRC was a court-like restorative justice strategy. Formed in 1996, it was restricted to gross *legal* violations during the apartheid era. Its Chair, Desmond Tutu, observed that its concern was legal, rather than moral. Hearings were held for people who committed such violations to come forward and confess their crimes. The focus was on individuals and their actions, avoiding the real master-minds, strategists and theoreticians behind apartheid.[58] Surveys of South Africans show they do not see the TRC as having done much in terms of "reconciliation." However, James Gibson found in a study of 3,700 South Africans that "...those who accept the 'truth' about the country's apartheid past are more likely to hold reconciled racial attitudes. Racial reconciliation also depends to a considerable degree on interracial contact..." In other words, people who had meaningful relationships across race lines – clearly an indicator of low-racism – were more reconciled. However, there

53   Bond, Patrick. 2014. *Elite transition: From apartheid to neoliberalism in South Africa.* London, UK: Pluto Press. Loc, 1669/9634

54   Gumede, William Mervin. 2007. *Thabo Mbeki and the Battle for the Soul of the ANC*: Zebra, Marais, Hein. 2001. *South Africa: Limits to change: The political economy of transition*: Palgrave Macmillan.

55   A coefficient of 0 describes total equality; 1 describes maximal inequality.

56   http://www.chartbookofeconomicinequality.com/inequality-by-country/south-africa/, http://www.hsrc.ac.za/en/review/hsrc-review-november-2014/limitations-of-gini-index; accessed

57   OECD. 2013. "OECD Economic Surveys: SOUTH AFRICA." Paris, France: OECD.

58   Alexander, Neville. 2002. *An Ordinary Country: Issues in the Transition from Apartheid to Democracy in South Africa.* Scottsville, South Africa: University of Natal Press.

were significant racial differences: among blacks, truth does not lead to reconciliation; reconciliation also does not lead to truth. This is likely an outcome of blacks
being apartheid victims.[59]

The Case Discussion

This description of the South African "miracle" includes tactics undoubtedly
developed to a significant degree by some, to obfuscate and muddle through as
a way to manage hard-line apartheid supporters amongst whites and left-wing
radicals. This arose from self-interest and fear about alienating the white business
elite to produce options nicely described by the Mont Fleur Icarus scenario. In
hindsight, rather than the flight of the flamingos being the enacted scenario, it
was more like the lame duck scenario, with a narrow black and traditional white
elite being key beneficiaries. In the end, the very remarkable accomplishment was
realizing universal suffrage without mass violence or a great cost of human life
and civil war. This was associated with highly visible, symbolic racial reconciliation
gestures and integration, such as with the 1995 World Rugby (a white's only sport)
Cup final when Mandela created a bridge by wearing the Springbok team jersey.

The 1994 election reflects a significant change in terms of moving to a
non-racist "logic" in political structures, with basic power structure rules changing
and a traditionally excluded group taking control. However, there are many reasons
to associate it with something between transformation and the reform processes
that in many Western countries produced ever-expanding enfranchisement from
wealthy land-owning males down to women and universal suffrage. The actual
processes and structures themselves did not change, although racial rules did.

The approach reflected scenario planner Clem Sunter's comment that "In the
mid-1980s, there was still a political belief that one side could impose the future
on the other side. I think we have been vindicated by saying it had to be negotiations."[60] While he may not have consciously distinguished between transcending
and visioning strategies from negotiations and mediation strategies (see Chapter
2), the former seems to have played a modest role. In fact, it was close-knit negotiations that took the day against a backdrop of armed violence and attempts by both
blacks and whites to torpedo the change process. Discussions were characterized
by agreements around the major issue of universal enfranchisement; the negotiations were narrowly around how to get there. Advancing social and economic
restructuring required this political shift. However, the potential for broader
social-economic transformation was limited by decisions, such as guaranteeing
continuing land rights and the tenure of civil servants. The potential for a different
option continues to be debated. However, it will never be known. The results
today though appear to confirm the short-term benefits the route developed with

---

59   Gibson, James L. 2004. "Does Truth Lead to Reconciliation? Testing the Causal
     Assumptions of the South African Truth and Reconciliation Process." *American
     Journal of Political Science* 48(2):201-17.
60   Bond, Patrick. 2014. *Elite transition: From apartheid to neoliberalism in South Africa.*
     London, UK: Pluto Press. Location 1089/9634.

Box 3F: The Role of Scenario Development

From the historic perspective of strategy and tool development, the South African case is particularly important in providing a testing group for important tools that continue to be advanced in many ways: scenario development, multi-stakeholder forums, restorative justice processes, and the hard work of deeply democratic grassroots organizing. Scenario developer for the Mont Fleur process, Adam Kahane, commented:

> "(T)he Mont Fleur process made some contribution to this much-better-than-it-might-otherwise-have-turned-out result. The more significant lesson, however, is not in the scenario stories themselves. The process itself is typical of one of the most important innovations of South Africa's transition: the multi-stakeholder dialogue forum. From 1990 onwards, South Africans created – in parallel with the formal negotiating structures – hundreds of such informal forums." [1]

Bond[2] takes a highly critical view of the scenarios offering several critiques: meaningful participation was largely restricted to traditional and opposition elites. Participation was restricted to a very small number of people; they always avoided the really hard issues; and they were supported by inadequate traditional analysis. However, the intense scenario development process did provide a good forum for deepening relationships between traditional white and other leaders. In essence, rather than being a tool to support democratization and debate, Bond sees it as a tool to develop new elites who identified "solutions," and then used various media and other strategies to promote their findings. One observer concluded that there is a need to broaden participation in developing scenarios, if the method is to be useful in such situations.

---

1 http://www.montfleur.co.za/about/scenarios.html
2 Bond, Patrick. 2014. Elite transition: From apartheid to neoliberalism in South Africa. London, UK: Pluto Press.

---

very modest transitionary violence and loss of life, and condemn the route taken in longer inequality terms.

Alexander says, "ANC never a revolutionary organization...even at height of 1986 uprising ANC President Oliver Tambo said the ANC's main objective was not a military victory, but to force Pretoria to the negotiating table...lack of revolutionary overthrow in favor of negotiated compromise favored continuity as vehicles to obstruct real change continued in place...there was no 'smashing of the machinery of the old state' as required in true revolution."[61] Whites believed their own propaganda about the ANC being a "communist" and "terrorist" organization. And, in the end, there was a huge "aspiration gap." Corporations, for example, often embrace diversity, because of risk analysis and public relations, rather than a desire for true social change.

---

61   Alexander, Neville. 2002. *An Ordinary Country: Issues in the Transition from Apartheid to Democracy in South Africa*. Scottsville, South Africa: University of Natal Press. P. 46

Box 3G: South Africa: More like Mexico than the US?

The American revolution is considered "conservative" because it only focused on the political system, and left the social-economic systems intact since it was working well, with the marked exception of the role of slavery which required war to address. This reflects the South African approach and the approach tried unsuccessfully in Mexico in the second half of the 19th century, as T.R. Fehrenbach explains in a magisterial work:

> The Reform never attempted to cope with the caste-class system. The liberals misread the social landscape throughout the century because they were intellectuals wrapped up in institutional reform. What they had done by 1857 and reconfirmed in blood by 1867 was to bring about the institutional democratic revolution as it had taken place in France and North America – separating Church and state, abolishing legal class privileges and making men theoretically equal before the law…and permitting the choice of popular government.

> This had been a wholesale adoption of the programs of Anglo-Saxon and French liberals. As the antithesis of custodianship by Church, crown, class or even the state, it threw men back on private institutions. This was deliberate; the Mexican liberals did not believe in strong or activist government, and they were no more hostile to the idea of private wealth or private opportunity than the famers of the United States Constitution, which they had taken as a model. This fact had allowed a mass migration of landowners and rich men into liberal ranks… The social faith and hope of the liberals was in fact rooted in the concept of private property. Its ownership and free use was expected to make the citizen truly free from institutions and confining corporations, and to bring about economic and social progress. But this was an alien ideology, born of alien societies, and it could not work in Mexico as in the United States or even France.[1]

The Reform was followed by the violent 1910-20 Mexican revolution that finally broke open the social-economic system.

---

1 Fehrenbach, Theodore Reed. 2014. *Fire & blood: a history of Mexico*: Open Road Media. P. 444

The South African transition to a post-apartheid society is informed by an analysis of other revolutions. The reason for whites' fears and hopes of the more radical were also heavily influenced by the recent fall of the Berlin Wall. Of the four ANC strategies mentioned earlier, this led to a renewed emphasis (after 1985) on isolating the South African apartheid community.

The importance of context and the international environment for real social-political-economic structural transformation is confirmed by Theda Skocpol's comparative study of the French, Russian and Chinese Revolutions. She paints a picture of a crisis developing when the countries' monarchical regimes could not compete economically with others externally, and were simultaneously squeezed by internally increasing class dissention. Crucial factors that she identified in success were (1) a revolutionary ideology, (2) the simple existence of exploitation, and (3) the acuteness of relative deprivation. However, those countries underwent a thorough and bloody smashing of the old state machinery.[62]

Various analysts of revolution have identified causes and development stages. Karl Marx, perhaps most famously, pointed out the contradictions between the presence of enormous wealth and productive power alongside great poverty, leading to dissatisfaction and the (r)evolution of capitalism into socialism.[63] Martin Malia focuses on what he calls "Great Revolutions," and concludes that there is no necessary connection between economic change and a change in the governing system (economic development issues are a necessary, but not sufficient cause of revolution). Instead, he emphasizes the importance of political crisis (the governance system becoming ineffective in decision-making) and a challenging ideology that has broad (cross-social group) attraction.[64] Cronin Brinton points to movement from hope and moderation, to a reign of terror, that ultimately ends in some sort of dictatorship (noting, however, that the American Revolution did not follow this pattern). [65] Indeed, the South African revolution more closely resembles the conservative one of the Americans, rather than the more radical French, Russian and Chinese situations.

The Memes Change Sphere: Marriage Equality for Same-sex couples in the United States[66]

Generic sphere description: This sphere focuses on changes in attitudes, beliefs, and behaviors that produce transformative outcomes. Memes are the stories, words, norms, and symbols that guide behavior and action – and provide frameworks for evaluating and "making sense" of what we hear, see, and experience. They include religious, scientific, and philosophical beliefs. They are "habits of mind" and deeply held collective understandings learned inside and outside of formal learning structures. The term "memes" arose as a short-hand metaphor for genes to describe cultural evolution, and was introduced by biologist Richard Dawkins in 1976. He described them as "units of cultural transmission which propagate themselves."[67] The gene-meme metaphor usage has greatly diminished due to a range of inadequacies. Today, rather than think of memes as replicators, they are

---

62   Skocpol, Theda. 1979. *States and social revolutions: A comparative analysis of France, Russia and China*: Cambridge University Press. P. 47
63   Marx, Karl. 1859/1973. "A Contribution to the Critique of Political Economy." in *Dynamics of Social Change: A Reader in Marxist Social Science*, edited by H. & Goldway Selsam, D. New York: International Publishers.
64   Malia, Martin. 2008. *History's Locomotives: Revolutions and the Making of the Modern World*. New Haven, CT, USA: Yale University Press.
65   Brinton, Crane. 1938. *The anatomy of revolution*. New York, USA: Vintage Books.
66   This draws from many sources. Thanks in particular to Gary Buseck, Legal Director, GLAD and Josh Friedes, formerly Advocacy Director, FTMC – Massachusetts and Executive Director, Equal Rights Washington.
67   Dawkins, Richard. 1976. *The Selfish Gene*. New York, USA: Oxford University Press.

thought of as important for understanding how culture is transmitted through words, symbols, and ceremonies.[68]

Once learned, memes are difficult to unlearn or change, because people and societies associate them with their core identities. Transformation involves radical redefinition and associations with historic ideas, symbols, and stories; acceptable behaviors, norms, and beliefs are also changed. Classic transformation memes include: smoking, and individual/human rights (slavery and women's rights, etc.). "Economic growth" as a meme is now common under pressure from various angles, including the "degrowth movement."

Particularly relevant change knowledge traditions: experimentalist governance, business in society, community development, peace-building, social movements, and social evolution and change.

Some key change sphere dynamics: transmission by inference, contagion, adaptation, increasing diversity, enhanced ability for societies to integrate increasing diversity, experimentation with and diffusion into various aspects of life, and societal learning and evolution.

Some key change sphere activities: campaigns, gatherings, story-telling, and social movement building.

The Case

In 1996, President Bill Clinton, generally considered progressive, signed into law the Defense of Marriage Act (DOMA) that defined (for federal purposes) marriage as being between one man and one woman. At that time, only a quarter of American supported marriage rights for same-sex couples. But, 19 years later, the US Supreme Court declared that the Constitution of the United States provides same- sex couples with a right to the institution of marriage; about 60% of Americans agreed.[69] One resulting story is legal change. However, the deeper story is one of cultural change – one of the quickest about faces on a deeply and widely held conviction and cultural standard. Political and cultural change are obviously intertwined, but most observers say that the former would not have happened without the latter. How did it happen?

I was a participant in this story as a gay man. In 1983, living in my native Canada with my "partner," as we then called each other, I successfully asked my employer for the same benefits for my partner as provided to married people. In that part of Canada (British Columbia), common-law tradition considers couples married after two years of co-habitation. A couple of years later, when someone doing research asked how I obtained the benefits, I discovered that I was the first known person to have done so (my employer was a labor union with a strong justice orientation). More than a decade later, after having moved to the US and having lived with another (American) man for five years, I was almost forced to leave the

68   Waddock, Sandra. 2015. "Reflections: Intellectual Shamans, Sensemaking, and Memes in Large System Change." *Journal of Change Management.*
69   Gallup. 2015. "Gay and Lesbian Rights." Gallup.

country, because I could not marry as a straight couple could to gain citizenship. In the late 1990s, I became active with the grassroots movement organization, Freedom to Marry.

When the City of Boston created a civil partnership registry in the late 1990s that extended some rights, we registered. When Vermont law provided for civil unions in 2000, we became civil unionized. In 2004, when our state of Massachusetts became the first US jurisdiction to provide for marriage equality, we got married. However, we were still without access to more than 1000 benefits provided for married people under federal law.[70] In 2013, in the wake of the Supreme Court's *Windsor*

> ## Box 3H: Language
>
> Language and memes are closely interwoven, points out Gary Buseck, Legal Director, Gay and Lesbian Advocates and Defenders (GLAD). "We at GLAD are very determined never to say 'same-sex marriage' or 'gay marriage,'" he explains. "What we won was marriage; not some new kind of marriage. Our opponents talked of 'same-sex marriage' as some new entity that had no historical basis; we said we should have access – like all other citizens – to the institution of marriage. It is an easy shorthand and talking about marriage equality or marriage for same-sex couples is more cumbersome, but we have always thought that the language choice is important."

decision telling the federal government that it must treat all state-authorized marriages equally, we successfully applied for three years of tax refunds that previously only opposite sex married couples could receive, and we are now taxed just like other married couples.

Our 2004 marriage happened in two steps. Anxious to get access to my husband's (yes, it *was* uncomfortable to call him that at first for me, too) health benefits, in July, we were married at a restaurant table over dinner by a friend who was a judge. In October, we were married at an event with friends and family at the MIT faculty club. This was clearly part of the process of public legitimization for us and my own theory of change analogous to pebbles being dropped into water causing ripples. It was the first marriage between a same-sex couple at the faculty club, as a conversation with its staff (proud to be hosting us) revealed. The people invited talked with others about it, since for most it was their first time attending a marriage between a same-sex couple. I remember one person telling a story about shopping for a wedding gift, with the elderly clerk assuming a mixed-sex couple's marriage; when told it was for a same-sex couple, apparently without missing a beat, she brought up some appropriate gift suggestions.

Most gays and lesbians were as astonished as anyone else by the speed of change. Many in their 40s and older commented that, as recently as a few years prior to 2015, they had not expected to see national, federal recognition of same-sex relationships in their lifetimes. In fact, in the 1990s and during the first

---

70   This affected how we filed income taxes, rights to federal pension and other social programs, and every time we crossed state lines our marriage became dubious.

decade of the 21st century, many disdained marriage as a sell-out to tradition and patriarchy, and opposed marriage equality as "assimilationist." The issues were deeply personal and emotional, involving the rights of children and parents, as well as potential spouses.

In 1960, every American state had laws that criminalized some form of same-sex sexual intimacy; homosexuality was described as a "mental disorder" by the American Psychiatric Association; homosexuals were commonly the brunt of jokes; an ultimate negative epithet was to call someone a faggot or a fairy or a "bull-dyke." A deep reservoir of animus was fed by political, cultural, and religious traditions.

Although there had been tentative, yet important, steps towards gay rights over the previous two decades, gay liberation is popularly seen to have started in the US with the 1969 riots at a New York gay bar, the Stonewall Inn. Rather than submit to police harassment, the lesbian-gay-bisexual-transgender (LGBT) community fought back. Over the next two decades, the LGBT community focused on gaining acceptance and basic rights, and over-turning anti-gay legislation. In 1979, between 75,000 and 125,000 individuals participated in the first national LGBT march on Washington, DC.

The 1980s AIDS epidemic profoundly affected the gay community. The disease was so commonly transmitted through anal intercourse, in particular, that it was originally called the "gay plague." As well as killing a generation of leaders and other gay men, it forced many "out of the closet" – both those with the disease and their friends who associated with them. However, President Regan would not even speak about the disease. The lack of government further propelled public action by the LGBT community and its supporters, and gave enormous momentum to building a powerful LGBT rights movement.

The LGBT marriage campaign was a sub-set, but closely connected to, the need to more broadly change the "gay meme." There could hardly be gay marriage acceptance without the acceptance of LGBT individuals' sexual orientation. In 1987, a Harvard-educated researcher in neuropsychiatry and a Harvard-educated expert on public persuasion tactics and social marketing wrote a strategy entitled, *The Overhauling of Straight America*.

> The first order of business, "they wrote" is desensitization of the American public concerning gays and gay rights. To desensitize the public is to help it view homosexuality with indifference instead of with keen emotion. Ideally, we would have straights register differences in sexual preference the way they register different tastes for ice cream or sports games: she likes strawberry and I like vanilla; he follows baseball and I follow football. No big deal.[71]

Their program consisted of eight main points:
1. Talk about gays and gayness as loudly and as often as possible;

---

71   Markshal K. Kirk, and Erastes Pill. 1987. "The Overhauling Of Straight America: Waging Peace, Part Two." *Guide Magazine* (November):7-14. P. 7

2. Portray gays as victims, not as aggressive challengers;
3. Give protectors (of gays) a just cause;
4. Make gays look good (pillars of society);
5. Make the victimizers look bad;
6. Solicit funds: the buck stops here;
7. Get on the air, or, You Can't Get There from Here; and
8. Start with print (as opposed to electronic media)[72]

While not formally adopted by the emerging movement or organizations, together, these foreshadowed the emerging marriage campaign.

The LGBT community was disproportionately represented in the entertainment and media communities, although even in that relatively accepting community, people remained deeply in the closet because of fear of what openness could do to their reputations. The first major popular breakthrough came in 1971 with an episode of the highly popular *All in the Family*, which became the first sitcom (and among the most popular of TV shows) to depict a homosexual character. It even went so far as to challenge stereotypes by presenting an effeminate straight male and a former National Football League player who was gay. Sporadic gay-positive movies followed, and the 1993 Broadway hit *Angels in America* placed the AIDS epidemic and gay life front and center. In *1997, mainstream Time magazine put comedienne Ellen DeGeneres on its cover with a bold title in red ink stating, "Yep, I'm Gay."* In 1998, *Will and Grace* became the first television sitcom to feature a gay man as its lead character; it had a large audience. Popular culture continued to produce positive role models with hits like *Brokeback Mountain* (2005); and in 2012, *Marvel Comics* gave one of its superheroes a homosexual wedding. The top-rated sitcom *Modern Family* placed a gay couple with a child firmly in a positive family setting.

The popular culture shift was having a big impact on business, too. LGBT employees formed workplace groups, increasingly with company support. In 1994, IKEA placed its first ad featuring two men as a couple. By 2013, two-thirds of Fortune 500 companies provided at least some domestic partner benefits, and major brand-name businesses publicly signed on in support of gay marriage legal briefs.

Local and national LGBT organizations were springing up to advance gay rights. They wrapped themselves in Americana tradition, even in their names, such as the Human Rights Campaign founded in 1980 to raise money and lobby for general LGBT issues. The Freedom to Marry Coalition of Massachusetts (FTMC) began in 1993 as a grass-roots volunteer organization that worked with other LGBT organizations to spearhead social change. This included lobbying, but focused more on outreach by speaking to hundreds of community groups, houses of worship, and gatherings in individual homes around the state. In 2001, as the marriage issue grew in importance, a coalition of gay organizations in Massachusetts (including the FTMC) formed MassEquality to take leadership on marriage equality strategy and coordination.

In the early years, funding was always difficult for the FTMC, and it depended on individual modest donations and "events," such as a Valentine's Day dance and

---

72   Ibid.

auction. Obtaining even $25,000 from the Gill Foundation (which focused on LGBT issues) was very difficult. Funders usually saw marriage as unobtainable. Moreover, they wanted inappropriate outputs for the social change stage, and they set an unrealistic timeframe. Nevertheless, significant progress was noted in Massachusetts when no legislators who supported gay marriage were defeated electorally, and attempts to change the state constitution to prohibit marriage equality were firmly defeated.

With growing success, funding from individual donors increased significantly. The FTMC hired staff and became a significant funder of the Religious Coalition for the Freedom to Marry, which grew into an association of 1,000 ordained clergy in Massachusetts representing 23 faith traditions. However, in late 2003, an intense political campaign heated up. Leaders of MassEquality organizations, with the strong support of the FTMC, agreed to make MassEquality the lead staffed professional arm and to hold the FTMC as the grassroots, social change arm. MassEquality itself underwent a significant change from a coalition to an organization with a board made up of those who would "give or get (from other donors)" $50,000. This led to a dramatic increase in the professionalization of the campaign in terms of polling and media outreach. The "handover" from the FTMC and other organizations comprising MassEquality was not without friction. A strategic operations committee formed for these organizations to provide MassEquality with their input and share plans.

Building and maintaining the unity of the LGBT community required on-going work. Different segments of the community had different and strong opinions about whether marriage equality should be a major priority, as well as about the timing and form of actions. The transgender community literally negotiated priorities with those pushing for marriage equality, resulting in an agreement that marriage equality would be followed by making transgender issues a priority (and it has been, also with significant success). Gary Buseck, Legal Director, GLAD, recalls tension arising when liti-

Box 31: American Legal Jurisdiction

The issue of gay rights and marriage in the US represents a complicated intertwining of federal and state rights. Marriage, as a legal act, is a function of the states, and traditionally, states automatically recognize marriages performed in other states (but this, too, became a battlefield). Access to more than 1000 federal benefits is tied to marriage. Many relevant issues, ranging from adoption to hospital visitation rights, are the subjects of state law. This created a mess of issues for those married in one state, when traveling to others where their marriages were not recognized.

Each state, as well as the federal government, has constitutions that were playgrounds for change to prohibit marriage between same-sex couples; the federal one, being much more difficult to change, never was a serious focus. Some states' constitutions are much easier to change than others are. When a state and federal constitution are in conflict, the federal one prevails.

gators in California tried to advance their case to the Supreme Court earlier than others thought appropriate; going too soon and receiving a negative ruling would make future cases more difficult.

Religious organizations were perhaps the most important opponents of LGBT rights, including marriage. They claimed LGBT practice was immoral and contrary to God's wishes. During the 1992-2012 period, nearly 60% of the population rated religion as "very important" in their lives, and a quarter identified with evangelical Christianity, the home base of the equal marriage rights movement's core opponents. However, debates in churches and their national meetings over marriage equality began in the late 1980s. In 1997, the FTMC spearheaded the formation of the Religious Freedom to Marry Coalition in Massachusetts, demonstrating that religions were not monolithic on this issue. The Coalition was made up of more than 1000 clergy, congregations, and organizations from 23 faith traditions.[73] Similar religious groups formed elsewhere. Although coalition members performed same-sex marriages, one key issues was to distinguish for the public between civil (government) marriages with accompanying legal rights and religious marriages, which on their own bore no legal rights.

Debating whether to focus on their own congregants or externally, the Massachusetts clergy decided in favor of the latter by organizing faith prayer breakfasts, speaking at inter-faith events, and writing and signing a declaration in support of marriage equality. Josh Friedes, former FTMC Advocacy Director, commented that he always carried around a copy of the clergy declaration in support of marriage equality: "You'd just watch legislators, fascinated with who signed. And media couldn't believe that there was this support."

Marriage equality was a legal, as well as a cultural, issue. The courts, elections, and votes to change constitutions and laws provided key mobilization opportunities for both sides. As early as 1970, in Minnesota, the first claim for the right to marry a spouse of the same- sex was filed in court; it was dismissed by the US Supreme Court without even an oral argument. In 1983, Harvard Law student Evan Wolfson, who later became the leader of the Freedom to Marry Coalition, wrote a thesis advancing marriage equality.

Nationally, the legal issues were coordinated by a loose group, referred to as "The Roundtable." Key leaders included: the American Civil Liberties Union, the National Center for Lesbian Rights, Gay and Lesbian Advocates and Defenders (GLAD), and Lambda Legal. They developed a strategy to first aim for marriage as a right under state constitutions, then federally challenge DOMA, and finally aim to secure marriage as a federal constitutional right. They carefully analyzed jurisdictions by their laws, constitutions, legislators, public, and judges to identify which ones would be the most favorable arenas.

---

73   Those who are LGBT usually went through deeply difficult personal transformation processes to reconcile the traditional dominant view of being LGBT as contrary to religious teachings and their own sexual orientation. See: Creed, WE Douglas, Rich DeJordy, and Jaco Lok. 2010. "Being the change: Resolving institutional contradiction through identity work." *Academy of Management Journal* 53(6):1336-64.

However, the marriage equality side also believed it was critical to win hearts and minds between elections. LGBT individuals increasingly had more conversations with parents, relatives, neighbors, and strangers in sidewalk campaigns. Their campaign focus shifted from emphasizing the LGBT community as a wronged minority that deserved rights associated with marriage, to being about families, love, and an abiding commitment that deserved the social institution of marriage. Gay couples, as families, often with children who suffered legally from a lack of recognition, were themes. The strategy change became even more pronounced when a 2004 poll revealed that knowing a gay person made you 65% more likely to support marriage equality — and having a conversation with a gay person about marriage raised the figure to 80%. The proportion of Americans who reported knowing someone who was gay increased from 25% in 1985 to 74% in 2000,[74] and to 88% in 2015.[75] The first point of the Harvard graduates nine-point strategy — *Talk about gays and gayness as loudly and as often as possible* — was central.

The media also played a central role. In 2013, the journalist Dennis Leap observed:

> The media love it (the marriage equality issue): Images of same-sex couples lustfully embracing are popping up everywhere on television, the internet, and magazine covers. Gallons of ink and tons of paper are being used to publish newspaper stories on marriage for homosexual couples. Try as you may, you can't get away from the issue. [76]

LGBT advocates built on American civil rights traditions, with a particular reference to the movement in the 1950s-60s that sought to improve legal protections for black Americans. It was only in 1967 that the federal Supreme Court declared unconstitutional laws prohibiting inter-racial marriage. While comparisons seemed obvious to the LGBT community, it was often badly received within the black community where anti-gay sentiment and religious fundamentalism remain higher than in America, as a whole. Moreover, many black Americans perceived LGBT community members as privileged, because of their comparatively greater wealth, and, for many, connections to power-holders through family and social networks.

However, key legal victories piled up. A 1999 decision by the Supreme Court of Vermont held that excluding same-sex couples from marriage violated the state constitution, prompting the legislature to create "civil unions" as marriages in all-but-name; a 2003 watershed ruling of the Massachusetts Supreme Judicial Court made marriage between same-sex couples legal for the first time in an

---

74   Klarman, Michael J. 2013. "How Marriage Came to Be." *Harvard Magazine* (March-April):30-35.

75   PewResearchCenter. 2015. "Section 2: Knowing Gays and Lesbians, Religious Conflicts, Beliefs about Homosexuality." http://www.people-press.org/2015/06/08/section-2-knowing-gays-and-lesbians-religious-conflicts-beliefs-about-homosexuality/: People-press.org.

76   Leap, Dennis. 2013. "The Shrewd Strategy Behind Same-Sex 'Marriage.'" in *The Trumpet*: Philadelphia Church of God.

American jurisdiction; in 2012, for the first time, voters (in four states) supported marriage equality – after 32 votes had been lost around the country.

Around 2004, there were several defeats in the courts. Also, opponents continually rallied their side to change state constitutions to ban marriage equality with great success. By 2012, 31 of 50 state constitutions had been amended to prohibit same- sex unions. In 2008, California voters chose to change their constitution to make marriage between same-sex couples illegal (by a 52% to 48% vote).

In 2013, the federal Supreme Court, on a technicality, ruled on a case that in effect had made same-sex marriages legal in California. The case was presented by two famous lawyers, without initial support from The Roundtable organizations who opposed advancing the case as being "too soon." Also, in the same year, that

Box 3J: Campaign Changes to Integrate Insightful Polling[1]

Throughout the legal maneuvering, the ring of activity spread out from courts, to the legislatures, and on to public opinion. The latter was the critical forum, since the other two greatly resisted acting without public support. In 2009, in the state of Maine, voters overturned their legislators' decision to provide marriage equality. Within weeks, Freedom to Marry (a national organization) helped assemble a coalition of state-based gay groups, polling experts, and academic researchers to centralize and share information so that each campaign didn't have to start from scratch for each new battle.

What came out of this tightly coordinated effort was the key to dismantling anti-gay myths from the last 40 years. For decades, gay advocates had framed their arguments in terms of equal rights and government benefits, often using confrontational ("We're here, we're queer, get used to it") and demanding rhetoric ("We deserve equal rights now!"). Third Way, a centrist think tank working in coalition with Freedom to Marry, began to unpack exactly how straight people reacted to these tactics. The group found that when straight people were asked what marriage meant to them, they spoke of love, commitment, and responsibility. But when asked why they thought gay people wanted to marry, they cited rights and benefits. Tapping into anti-gay stereotypes, they suggested gay people wanted marriage for selfish reasons, whereas they themselves wanted to express love and commitment.

The gay rights coalition's response was the "Why Marriage Matters" campaign. Its message was "love, commitment, and family," with no mention of rights or benefits. On the surface, it looks like any garden-variety public education campaign, a little vague, a little sappy. But, this message was the result of several years and millions of dollars of research. It signaled a sea change in the way gay advocates pled their case. It invited straight people to empathize with gay people, to reassure the majority that gay people wanted the same things that they did, and to shift focus from minority rights to points of commonality.

---

1 How Gay Marriage Finally Won at the Polls. Nov. 7. Retrieved Aug. 15, 2015, from http://www.slate.com/articles/news_and_politics/politics/2012/11/gay_marriage_in_maryland_and_maine_the_inside_strategy.html

court overturned DOMA's definition of marriage as being between a man and woman as unconstitutional. This resulted in federal government recognition of same- sex marriages if they were recognized by a state. This ruling opened a flood-gate of challenges to state constitutions that banned marriage equality as being in conflict with the federal constitution. Almost all of these challenges were successful, and by October 2014, marriage between same-sex couples was legal in 35 states.

The one exception, by a federal court of appeals in Ohio, led to a Supreme Court review to bring about alignment. In 2015, the debate ended as the Supreme Court declared marriage between same-sex couples a constitutionally protected right.

The Case Discussion

"Marriage" is a cultural artifact – a meme – that the marriage equality debate brought to the fore as a disputed association of meanings. One battleground over meaning was legislative and legal. However, the more important was with citizens and daily life. Marriage equality opponents liked to say that the institution had remained unchanged for millennia. However, change also can be seen as an egalitarian evolution that included redefining women as equals in opposite sex marriage, whereas at one time, they had been treated as their husbands' legal chattel, and had been required to be culturally subservient to them. For example, to get a loan or a credit card required a husband's signature; women were also not allowed to initiate divorce.

In the United States, perhaps the most notable factor in changing the marriage meme to encompass same- sex unions was its self-conscious, disciplined, and stra-tegic campaign nature. Recognition of the battle as being one over "memes" even rose to the fore on the internet with *The 15 Gay Marriage Memes You NEED To See*,[77] *Awesome Gay Memes*,[78] and even the nation's top news magazine ran a story entitled *Here Are Today's Best Marriage Equality Memes*.[79]

The proposition that the marriage meme underwent transformation with marriage equality has strong support. A historically marginalized group gained access to one of the world's most traditional institutions. The pivotal role of procreation as marriage's purpose shifted substantially, with a recognition that many opposite- sex couples marry without such a goal and many same- sex couples marry with having children as a major goal. As well, the issue shifted understand-ings of religion and the sacred, as strong opposition in many religious groups shifted to support for gay marriage. The core definition of "family" was rewritten to include not just same- sex spouses, but also those with children.

---

77   Droesch, Kristen. undated. "The 15 Gay Marriage Memes You NEED To See."
     http://www.yourtango.com/2013188239/top-fifteen-gay-marriage-memes: Your
     Tango: Love Your Best.

78   anonymous. undated. "Awesome Gay Memes." http://likes.com/misc/pro-gay-mar-
     riage-memes: likes.com.

79   Waxman, Olivia B. 2015. "Here Are Today's Best Marriage Equality Memes."
     in *Time*. http://time.com/3938004/us-supreme-court-gay-same-sex-marriage-
     memes/.

"How same-sex marriage ballot initiatives turned around is all about the long game," wrote journalist Nathaniel Frank. "The gay rights movement succeeded using one of the most sophisticated issue campaign operations ever deployed — and by making it stick with old-fashioned commitment, hard work, and face-to-face conversations."[80] This long game was organized as a social movement. Tilly and Wood define such movements by three components: (1) a sustained campaign, (2) a range of political action tactics, and (3) self-presentation as worthy, unified, numerous, and committed. In developing the equal rights marriage movement, there were at least three distinct stages: one was developing the enabling environment by making LGBT rights a legitimate public issue; second was a narrower focus on marriage equality as a grassroots (seen with the FTM) and legal issue; and third was the professionalization of the movement that brought in the more moneyed and connected elites, such as seen with MassEquality. (In the Philippines, the grass-roots/professional NGO distinction is reflected between organizations referred to as "People's Organizations," and those called "NGOs.") After having working for both types of organizations, Friedes comments: "The appropriate grass-roots groups didn't understand how to lobby and raise gobs of money, but they did know how to go into communities to engage people. It was right to start with the social change movement, but then it had to be handed off."

Advancing the marriage equality issue was significantly facilitated by the particular structure and relationships of the LGBT community itself. Once individuals came out of the closet, some families literally disowned them, but a significant majority accepted them with varying degrees of difficulty. Those families included moneyed and well-connected ones with whom most marginalized people would have traditionally had difficulty building personal relationships.

But, the core element in changing memes was personal interactions between people that held different ones. Marriage and family are examples of "successful memes" in Lissack's terms: "Successful memes' meanings transcend situations versus the unsuccessful meme that cannot be understood in contexts different from its original."[81] Waddock, in turn, comments that: "If left unaddressed in change initiatives, the stubborn persistence of old memes can potentially stall or even prevent significant change."[82]

The Natural Environment Change Sphere: The Rise of the Anthropocene

Generic sphere description: The natural environment, in which humans are situated, and humans themselves are continually changing. While "evolution" and "geological ages" dominate much of the discussion, the interaction between these is

---

80   Frank, Nathaniel. 2012. "How Gay Marriage Finally Won at the Polls." http://slate.me/1moCuLZ

81   Lissack, Michael R. 2003. "The Redefinition of Memes: Ascribing Meaning to an Empty Cliché." *Emergence* 5(3):48-65.

82   Waddock, Sandra. 2015. "Reflections: Intellectual Shamans, Sensemaking, and Memes in Large System Change." *Journal of Change Management.*

emphasized with the rise of the concept of the Anthropocene – an era marked by human's impact on the natural environment. Moreover, humans are gaining new abilities to act upon, and direct their own evolution, and indeed even support their displacement by a new species.

Particularly relevant change knowledge traditions: environmental and evolutionary science.

Some key change sphere dynamics: evolution, and geological ages.

Some key change sphere activities: traditional scientific research spanning physical and social sciences, public debate and actions to influence options.

The Case

Within the natural environment sphere, the grandest of scales, transformation is counted in terms of "geological ages" over the Earth's 4.54 billion years. These ages are classified by the International Commission on Stratigraphy based on geological evidence of global events, such as changes in the Earth's orbit around the sun, planetary impact events (e.g., meteors), and mass extinctions. The field of Earth System Science studies these events, which are associated with shifts in the physical composition of land, oceans, the atmosphere, and living organisms. From larger to shorter periods, these times are: supereons, eons (half a billion years), eras, periods, epochs, and ages (millions of years).

Much of this is associated with things, such as the rise and fall of reptiles and dinosaurs as the dominant species, and seems largely irrelevant to change practitioners. However, its relevance is evoked in three ways. Perhaps most obviously, changes in the natural environment have transformative effects. For example, the last glacial period when ice covered much of North America and Europe ended only approximately 11,000 years ago – not so far back, from a historic perspective. Meteors and volcanoes continue to pose real transformative threats, as illustrated by the 1815 eruption of Mount Tambora, on the island of Sumbawa (Indonesia), lowering global temperatures. This led to harvest failures, which in turn, led to mass famine.

A second point about natural environment sphere relevance is that it categorically introduces humans, as we now know them, into an evolutionary trajectory. Our first ancestor recognized as a member of the genus *Homo* (*homo habilis*), emerged roughly 2.8 million years ago. The first *homo sapiens* appeared around 160,000 years ago; they then evolved into what's considered "behavioral modernity" approximately 70,000 years ago. However, as recently as 5,000 years ago, Neanderthals and anatomically modern humans shared Europe. The extinction of the former is hypothesized to be the result of climate change and interactions with the latter.

As highly regarded science writer Michael Tennesen points out in *the Next Species: The Future of Evolution* in the *Aftermath of Man*, this categorically introduces evolution as a factor affecting transformation.[83] There are many reasons

---

83   Isaacs, William. 1999. *Dialogue and the art of thinking together.* New York, NY: Currency Doubleday. Tennesen, Michael. 2015. *The Next Species: The Future of Evolution in the Aftermath of Man*: Simon and Schuster.

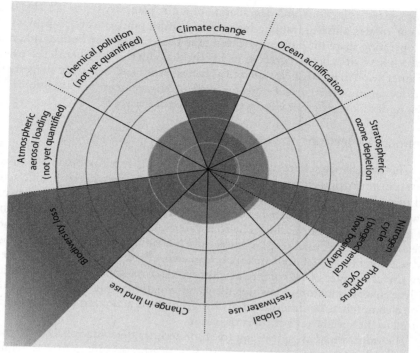

Figure 3E: Planetary Systems: The light shading represents the proposed safe operating space for the nine planetary systems. The dark wedges represent an estimate of the current position for each variable. The boundaries in the three systems (the rate of biodiversity loss, climate change, and human interference with the nitrogen cycle) have already been exceeded. *Source: UNEP Year Book 2010, p. 13.*

to believe that evolution is accelerating. Moreover, technological advances are presenting many possibilities that will become increasingly obvious: modern man may be replaced by anything from cyborgs to robots to genetically created super humans. There is ample reason to believe that these will become the increasing focus of those looking to question transformation.

Even more pointedly for change practitioners, the change sphere of the natural environment's relevance is illustrated with the Anthropocene concept. This is the label that the Stratigraphy Commission has been considering since 2008 for the new epoch in which we are living. Its beginning is proposed as July 16, 1945, the date of the first detonation of an atomic bomb (labeled the Trinity nuclear test). The Anthropocene period is characterized by humans having an enormous impact upon the natural environment.

Discussion

This last point of relevance for natural environment change sphere transformation practitioners brings issues of environmental sustainability front and center. Humans have a huge impact upon the environment, as has been noted with climate change, mass extinctions, and degradation of entire *planetary systems*.[84] This latter concept creates a useful framing for transformation practitioners, as providing a safe operating space for humanity within nine planetary system boundaries, three of which have already been overstepped as the diagram shows (where levels exceed the inner two circles). It helps quantify change issues and implicitly suggests the need for an important framework for systems engagement and attention focus when undertaking relevant large systems change initiatives.[85]

Summary Reflections on Cases

This five change sphere transformation model is distinctive because it aims to place transformation efforts within a comprehensive context, both to guide action and to make sense of many diverse efforts. There are other helpful frameworks as well. For example, one that I'm often asked about, and that I like very much, is the integral framework developed by Ken Wilber. Wilber conducted an enormous investigation into a broad range of knowledge, including consciousness, mysticism, and science. His AQAL four-quadrant framework[86] (that I won't go into here) is very useful because of its comprehensiveness vis-à-vis knowledge. I've used it to analyze change situations. However, the transformational spheres framework aims to be a comprehensive description of change vis-à-vis action. In other words, it is crafted to the specific task of transformation.

The transformation sphere approach underlines the audaciousness of transformational intentions. Acting with such a degree of audaciousness requires humbleness, as well as determination, supported by dynamics that the next chapter explores. Within these chapters, we will return to these cases to apply frameworks, discuss tools, and identify lessons for large systems change

---

84   Rockstrom, Johan, Will Steffen, Kevin Noone, Asa Persson, F. Stuart Chapin, Eric F. Lambin, Timothy M. Lenton, Marten Scheffer, Carl Folke, Hans Joachim Schellnhuber, Bjorn Nykvist, Cynthia A. de Wit, Terry Hughes, Sander van der Leeuw, Henning Rodhe, Sverker Sorlin, Peter K. Snyder, Robert Costanza, Uno Svedin, Malin Falkenmark, Louise Karlberg, Robert W. Corell, Victoria J. Fabry, James Hansen, Brian Walker, Diana Liverman, Katherine Richardson, Paul Crutzen, and Jonathan A. Foley. 2009. "A safe operating space for humanity." *Nature* 461(7263):472-75.

85   Ibid.

86   Wilber, Ken. 1996. *A Brief History of Everything*. Dublin, Ireland: Gill & Macmillan Ltd.

Chapter 4

Large Systems Change Pathways

Chapter Summary

Large systems change is an emergent process, in contrast to a deliberative one. A valuable way to operationalize such a process is through theories of change. Collectively these form pathways to transformation that describe how societal change systems evolve over time to produce transformation. "Pathways" is a useful concept to understand how to move issues from a complex state to one that can be addressed through traditional complicated and simple approaches. It also explains why resilience is so important for transformation. Guidelines for designing resilience are presented.

A hallmark of a successful society is that it addresses transformational challenges, while maintaining the physical and moral well-being of its participants. This is what the Stockholm Resilience Center calls a "resilient society." The Center defines resilience as:

> ...the capacity of a system, be it an individual, a forest, a city or an economy, to deal with change and continue to develop. It is about how humans and nature can use shocks and disturbances like a financial crisis or climate change to spur renewal and innovative thinking.[87]

Yes, climate change is happening and will continue to get worse. Yes, it must be addressed as vigorously as possible. However, climate change also presents an opportunity to actually improve our society in some ways. This is the vision of many in the German energy case who see energy transition as an opportunity to

---

87   Stockholm Resilience Centre. 2016. "What is resilience?". bit.ly/1VvDOIM: Stockholm Resilience Centre.

construct a new decentralized and more resilient energy system. This is the essence of what I meant in Chapter 1 when I wrote that climate change leads to a loss of species and ways of life, but addressing climate change (and other transformation challenges) should be approached with a spirit of joyous recreation.

If resilient societies – ones that can successfully respond to transformation challenges – are a goal, how do we get there? There are two distinct, but very similar, approaches. One is "theories of change" (ToC) and the other is "pathways." The former has generally been associated with project, program, and mid-range goals, whereas the latter has been linked with longer-term directions and addressing much larger concepts, such as evolution and revolution. They are complementary. They bridge traditional outcome-focused planning appropriate for complicated, predictable, and mechanical activities, and emergent approaches to address complex challenges (Chapter 4).

Emergent Approaches Subsuming Deliberative Ones

Large systems change (LSC) strategies reflect an understanding that the core dynamic is emergence, driven by complexity (Chapter 2). This is very different from the production of goods and services, which is most of what governments, businesses, and NGOs do. The production of goods and services requires complicated, deliberate approaches to strategy based in predictability, and primarily concerned with efficiency.

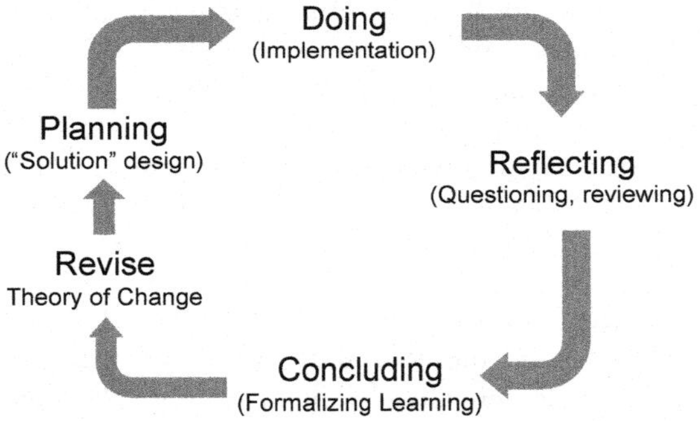

Figure 4A: The Learning Cycle

By "strategy," I mean a process to realize a desired end. A strategy is implemented with tactics (and tactics involve tools/methods (the subject of Chapter 9). A strategy reflects the belief that doing "x" will likely lead to "y." In the corporate world where organizational-level strategy is critical, "deliberate" approaches are associated with Michael Porter[88]. They generally assume a complicated logic: that the operating environment is to a substantial degree predictable, strategy-makers have substantial ability to control organizational direction and goals are clear. "Emergent" approaches, associated with Henry Mintzberg[89], are much more reflective of a complex logic: that major variables are both unpredictable, outside the control of any individual strategist,

---

88   Porter, Michael. 1996. "What is Strategy?" *Harvard Business Review* November-December:61-78.
89   Mintzberg, Henry. 1994. *The Rise and Fall of Strategic Planning*. New York, NY, USA: Free Press, Mintzberg, Henry, and James A. Waters. 1985. "Of Strategies, Deliberate and Emergent." *Strategic Management Journal*, July - Sep.:257-72.

and outcomes are shaped by unanticipated opportunities and impediments. Of course, these are extreme caricatures; most organizations' strategies combine these different approaches.

Deliberate approaches depend on the classic experiential learning process as opposed to an experimental one. This is sometimes referred to as the "Kolb Learning Cycle," referencing the person who defined it although it draws from the work of John Dewey, Kurt Lewin, and others, that David Kolb summarized.[90] The Cycle describes learning as most people think of it: learning from experience and the past. Cycles can be of various lengths, but the period is usually associated with the life of a project, an annual cycle, or even every five years. There are four steps: planning how to address an issue, implementing the plan, assessing results, and finally drawing conclusions to shape development of the next cycle's strategy. This also generates best practices and learning materials.

Emergent approaches are reflected in "learning from the future," a term used by Otto Scharmer. He developed this after deep research, including interviews with over 150 thought leaders about innovation and leadership. The process is sometimes referred to as the "U Process,"[91] because of the shape of the figure that illustrates it (see Figure 4B).

The U Process begins with deep reflection about the current state. In deliberate strategy, this would be associated with situation analysis. However, in this case, it is more than simply assessing intellectually. Scharmer emphasizes the heart and will, as well. This first co-sensing stage involves clarifying your intention. What is the issue you want to address? This analysis identifies hidden assumptions about the way things work and patterns that limit our ability to address an issue. This way this is done is illustrated in Chapter 3 by the individual human revolution case that aims to change debate patterns into generative dialogue. Four key barriers to change are explored: not recognizing what you see, not saying what you think, not doing what you say, and not seeing what you do. In the marriage equality case, there was an assumption that gays and lesbians did not have children and were not families; in

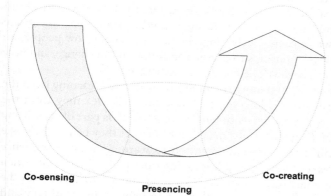

Co-sensing   **Co-creating**

Presencing

Figure 4B: Theory U

---

90   Kolb, David A. 1984. *Experiential learning: Experience as the source of learning and development.* Englewood Cliffs, NJ: Prentice-Hall.
91   Scharmer, C Otto. 2009. *Theory U: Learning from the future as it emerges:* Berrett-Koehler Publishers.

the German energy case, the traditional electric system is based on the assumption that carbon emissions are inconsequential and that alternatives are too costly.

The second stage of the U Process is termed "presencing." This is "...a blend of the words 'presence' and 'sensing,' (that) refers to the ability to sense and bring into the present one's highest future potential — as an individual and as a group."[92] If the assumptions identified with co-sensing are suspended, what new possibilities emerge? What is absolutely essential for us? This often leads to refinement of intention. Often, this stage is associated with solo wilderness retreats, although there are other activities that support presencing too. It is so central to Scharmer that he named his organization, which provides great resources and many sophisticated massive open on-line courses (MOOCs), the Presencing Institute.

By identifying previously unimagined possibilities, the presencing process is very useful for developing transformational change strategies. It supports being open (mind, heart, and will) to emerging possibilities that only become better defined through action to realize them. While conventional analytic knowing of the Kolb cycle is useful, it can also block us from "primary knowing" that connects us to the larger whole. For the case of electricity, that knowing means recognizing that fossil fuels are having a big impact on our planet and that centralized modes with passive consumers are not resilient. How can the electricity system be different, to reflect sustainability imperatives? Although not formally following the U Process, this type of imagining and co-creating is part of what has gone into the German energy transition. Numerous socio-technical experiments are behind it. These experiments are not simply about renewable energy technology, but are also about how people can become prosumers, how relationships to energy consumption can change, and how structures and policies can be developed to support emergence.

Developing transformation requires making emergence and learning from the future the dominant approach. However, this does not make learning from the past unimportant. We still need conventional learning, which is part of co-sensing and co-creating, as well. People identify an action or project they believe will take them in the desired direction, and pay attention to learning as the experience unfolds, adjusting in response. As Zaid Hassan describes in *The Social Innovation Labs Revolution*, these adjustments include both long and very short cycles: he describes the importance of creating a rhythm for revising plans even daily and weekly.[93] The shorter cycles are associated with emergent learning, which should drive longer learning cycles from the past. Chapter 7 has more information on this.

The experiential and emergent activities are the essence of creating a *learning system* consisting of a culture and processes that encourage reflection upon what has been done and the integration of arising knowledge into future actions. Creating a learning system should not be thought of as a great chore or something that requires some huge effort. Rather, it is something that should be integrated into work rhythms. I like the term "action learning" to emphasize that there are not huge gaps between Kolb cycle steps. Instead, the steps come together in daily life (Chapter 9).

---

92   https://www.presencing.com/presencing
93   Hassan, Zaid. 2014. *The Social Labs Revolution: A New Approach to Solving our Most Complex Challenges*. San Francisco, CA, USA: Berrett-Hoehler.

Theories of Change

In 1992, the American National Academy of Science convened what became the Roundtable on Comprehensive Community Initiatives for Children and Families. By 1995, with funding from eight foundations, it had grown to 30 diverse members and the organizing leadership of the Aspen Institute. That year, its questions about how to improve outcomes for families in poor communities led to advancing the ToC concept. It arose out of concern about the inadequacy of traditional evaluation approaches that reflected a linear input-output model that was simply inappropriate for complex systemic change challenges.

Carol Weiss led the development of the idea, contributing a report titled "Nothing as Practical as Good Theory: Exploring Theory-based Evaluation for Comprehensive Community Initiatives for Children and Families" to the Roundtable. Weiss noticed that program designers' and funders' strategies reflected various implicit assumptions, hypotheses and thought processes that very often were not explicit. She referred to these as ToC. This led to an important contribution to rethinking evaluation approaches (Chapter 9), and for clarifying thinking about how to realize desired change.

ToC is simply an explicit description of why change agents do what they do. Weiss gives an example:

> There is a job-training program for disadvantaged youth. Its goal is to get the disadvantaged youth into the work force (thus forestalling crime, welfare dependency, drug use, and so forth). The program's activities are to teach 'job-readiness skills' – such as dressing appropriately, arriving on the job promptly, getting along with supervisors and co-workers, and so on – and to teach job skills. What are the assumptions – what is the theory – underlying the program?[94]

This shows an "A → B" logic: job-training will address the situation of disadvantaged youth. Weiss emphasized two points. One is that multiple theories about how to address an issue have a legitimate basis, such as: youth unemployment is a consequence of youths' lack of motivation, their families' failure to inculcate values of work and orderliness, or health problems. She wrote:

> A program may operate with multiple theories. I do not mean that different actors each have their own theories, but that the program foresees several different routes by which the expected benefits of the program can materialize. ... There is no need to settle on one theory. In fact, until better evidence accumulates, it would probably be counterproductive to limit inquiry to a single set of assumptions.[95]

---

94 Weiss, Carol Hirschon. 1995. "Nothing as practical as good theory: Exploring theory-based evaluation for comprehensive community initiatives for children and families." *New approaches to evaluating community initiatives: Concepts, methods, and contexts*:65-92. P. 67.

95 Ibid. p. 83

To transform the status of disadvantaged youth would likely require addressing more than one ToC.

Weiss' second point is that implicitly there were numerous assumptions behind the job-training program that lead to hypotheses, such as the assumption that youth would sign up for it once they hear about it. These assumptions should be made explicit, to help more clearly "test" them as an explanation of job-training outcomes. In other words, an experimental stance should be adopted, rather than a simple production one associated with repeating well-proven approaches. She wrote that "… (by testing) I simply mean asking questions that bear on the viability of the hypotheses in these particular cases, through whatever methods of inquiry are chosen."[96]

This ToC thinking has had significant and growing influence. However, a web search for ToC maps produces pretty dreary results. They are almost all simply linear activity sets stacked over the top of one another or in columns to produce results, such as: inputs → outputs → outcomes → impacts. They are at the program level, rather than the system level which would emphasize the synergies between the ToCs of different programs. There is little indication of the necessity to develop a series of ToCs and interactions between them for a systemic approach to change; it seems Weiss' message has not been fully understood.

Mapping theories and their associated activities and relationships is one way to map a societal change system. I helped do this to create a map integrating nine CARE programs (change initiatives) to address poverty in Guatemala. We used a methodology called Managing for Clarity (Chapter 9), which maps ToCs. It breaks them down into discrete A → B logics. However, multiple activities may impact B (with multiple arrows pointing to it). As you can imagine, for CARE's poverty programs, this produced a complex diagram that looked like a bowl of spaghetti with arrows to 177 activities. It was though carefully developed with program leads and structured in a easy to understand way. Returning a year later, people were still using it to explain the logic of their vision about how their activity contributes to transforming poverty *and* how they create synergies with others for total societal change system impact.[97] Moreover, the deepened understanding resulted in partnering with new groups to realize an impact on poverty.

Pathways as Revolution and Evolution

This same type of thinking is behind the term "pathways," which has become increasingly popular over the past decade to refer to alternative LSC trajectories.[98]

---

96   Ibid. p. 81
97   Waddell, Steve. 2005. "A Learning History of the CARE-LAC - Institute for Strategic Clarity Guatemala Poverty Project. White Paper on Collaborative Holistic Inquiry Project in Guatemala." bit.ly/1SyZ01u: Institute for Strategic Clarity.
98   The approach is core to the STEPS (Social, Technological and Environmental Pathways to Sustainability) Centre at the University of Sussex in the UK. See: Haasnoot, Marjolijn, Jan H Kwakkel, Warren E Walker, and Judith ter Maat. 2013. "Dynamic adaptive policy pathways: A method for crafting robust decisions for a deeply uncertain world." *Global Environmental Change* 23(2):485-98. Geels, Frank W., and Johan Schot. 2007. "Typology of sociotechnical transition

Rather than looking at the program level, it is usually used to look at the system and a longer-term perspective. Within the pathways discussion, there is debate between what might be termed "evolution" versus "revolution" approaches. This reflects very long historic debates.[99]

The evolutionary perspective holds that small changes build on each other over time to produce a great variation that can be considered transformation. This is associated with Darwin and is based on three principles: (1) traits (genes, cultures) are passed down across generations, (2) modest variations arise amongst the same species/organization type, and (3) competition leads to success of the "fittest." These principles, in a dynamic, changing natural environment, give rise over extremely long periods of time to species as different as man and butterflies. Perhaps, the most recent excitement associated with transformation in this vein came about with Richard Dawkins' 1976 book, *The Selfish Meme*, which claimed memes to be to society what genes are to people (see Chapter 3). A societal example of evolution is the transformation of England from an absolute monarchy into a democracy, reflecting a fundamental shift in values and power structures over 700 years. Some key change events were the 1215 Magna Carta that provided barons' rights, the Glorious Revolution of 1688 that deposed a king, the 1832 Reform Act that gave the vote to one out of five adult males, and the 1928 Reform Act that gave women suffrage.

Table 4A: Conventional Change Pathways Perspective

Change Type	Evolutionary	Revolutionary
Archetypical Actions	Adapting, changing incrementally	Visioning, experimenting, inventing
Time Period	Long	Short
Conflict	Low	Medium-high

The revolutionary perspective holds that transformations occur with a relatively abrupt change over a short period of time, "breaking" equilibrium inertia.

---

pathways." *Research Policy* 36(3):399-417.

Westley, Frances, Per Olsson, Carl Folke, Thomas Homer-Dixon, Harrie Vredenburg, Derk Loorbach, John Thompson, Måns Nilsson, Eric Lambin, and Jan Sendzimir. 2011. "Tipping toward sustainability: emerging pathways of transformation." *AMBIO* 40(7):762-80.

Wise, R. M., I. Fazey, M. Stafford Smith, S. E. Park, H. C. Eakin, E. R. M. Archer Van Garderen, and B. Campbell. 2014. "Reconceptualising adaptation to climate change as part of pathways of change and response." *Global Environmental Change* 28:325-36.

99 They were marvelously summed up in a 1991 article by Connie Gersick, a business school academic. She reviewed others' work with the concept of "revolution" from multiple angles: revolutionary change in individuals, groups, organizations, science as a field (Kuhn, see Chapter 2), biological species, and grand theory (eg: how everything self-organizes). Gersick, Connie. 1991. "Revolutionary Change Theories: A Multilevel Exploration of the Punctuated Equilibrium Paradigm." *Academy of Management Review* 16:10-36.

Think in terms of the impact of a large asteroid hitting earth, an event associated with climate change and species elimination. The French and Russian revolutions are classic examples in the societal sphere. In these examples, the existing power structure, based on near absolute monarchy, was replaced by other logics within a very short period of time. As Chapter 2 described, violent crises are not the only way such changes occur; these changes can occur through inventions, new insights and other factors. The South African case in Chapter 3 describes the importance of the end of the Cold War for ending apartheid. Over a few years, on-line information access has transformed relationships and organizational structures. The centuries-old centralized production of encyclopedias and their industry have been destroyed by the very different dispersed power logic of Wikipedia.

Table 4B: This Book's Change Pathways Perspective

Change Type	Incremental	Reform	Transformation
Archetypical Actions	Copying, duplicating, mimicking	Changing policy, adjusting, adapting	Visioning, experimenting, inventing
Time Period	May be short or long	May be short or long	May be short or long
Conflict	Low	Medium	Medium-high

However, this "evolutionary/incremental versus revolutionary/transformational" view of change is at odds with the view presented in this book. As Chapter 2 described, there are three types of change: incremental, reform, and transformational. These are defined by three different questions, learning, and capacity-development challenges. Without disentangling the qualities of change types presented in Table 4B from the muddle commonly behind the evolutionary versus revolutionary argument of Table 4A, people working on change are limited in their ability to realize transformation and pathway development becomes very confused.

Transformation occurs through many experiments. Transformational experiments try out new ways of seeing, relating, doing, and organizing; they go to the depth dimension of LSC. These experiments tend to be informal, although social change labs (Chapter 7) are creating highly formalized approaches. Experiments may be intentional, as is the case with changes in political structures and revolutions. They may simply be the product of bumbling into something new; this is usually the case with technological innovations that leads to transformation. Transformational change may take place over a long period of time or short periods. Each key change event identified above in England's 700-year march to democracy was, in this view, an "experiment" in the emergence of the democratic paradigm. Each of the events required numerous societal adjustments, and there was always the potential for back-sliding (as occurred with the return of the monarchy after the Glorious Revolution).

Crises and violence may be part of transformation associated with experimental change. In the example of England's democratization, violence was particularly associated with the 1215 and 1688 experiments. The other two were arguably the hallmark of a "resilient" system: the system experimenting with itself. Even if these latter two are popularly referred to as "reform," they represented a transformational change as great examples of "triple-loop learning." Chapter 2 explains that this learning is core to transformation: experimental changes resulted from profound questions about power and core purpose in a march to paradigmatic, democratic change.

Box 4A: Experiments and Scale

A natural tendency is to think of experiments as being of a modest scale. This is a desirable strategy to protect against failure, because this scale requires less effort and investment, and affects fewer people. But, sometimes this is difficult. The German energy transition case of Chapter 3 is a good example of a national-level experiment with new policies and the development of a renewable energy system. One reason for selecting this scale was that the energy production and distribution system is, in important ways, national. Another reason was the perceived urgency of the problem and the value of doing something at scale. There were important benefits of developing the new system at scale, such as lowering per-unit costs for the solar energy generating systems. Germans sometimes say that their renewable energy experiment was a gift to the world.

Trajectories of Change: Keystone Systems

The "keystone species" concept is borrowed from ecology that refers to a plant or animal that plays a unique and crucial role in ecosystem functioning. Without keystone species, an ecosystem would be dramatically different or cease to exist altogether. Bees, as plant pollinators, are an example. Their pollination is critical both for those plants and for other species that depend on those plants. There are some keystone systems whose maintenance is a complex challenge for societies. One set of these is environmental. An approach to defining this set has produced the concept of nine "planetary systems," including bio-diversity and ocean acidity levels (Chapter 2, Natural Environment Change Sphere).[100] Socially, the definition of keystone systems includes: health, education, finance, food production, and governance systems.

Turbulence within keystone systems is caused by activities, such as war, human-caused and natural environmental change, shifts in beliefs and values, and technological innovation. This throws the keystone systems out of equilibrium;

---

100 Rockstrom, Johan, Will Steffen, Kevin Noone, Asa Persson, F. Stuart Chapin, Eric F. Lambin, Timothy M. Lenton, Marten Scheffer, Carl Folke, Hans Joachim Schellnhuber, Bjorn Nykvist, Cynthia A. de Wit, Terry Hughes, Sander van der Leeuw, Henning Rodhe, Sverker Sorlin, Peter K. Snyder, Robert Costanza, Uno Svedin, Malin Falkenmark, Louise Karlberg, Robert W. Corell, Victoria J. Fabry, James Hansen, Brian Walker, Diana Liverman, Katherine Richardson, Paul Crutzen, and Jonathan A. Foley. 2009. "A safe operating space for humanity." *Nature* 461(7263):472-75.

another way to say this is that turbulence forces the keystone systems to find new equilibrium states. That process can be very disruptive, and in extreme cases, leads to the collapse of civilizations. Problems in societal keystone systems led to the collapse of the Roman Empire; problems in environmental keystone systems led to the collapse of the Mayan civilization.

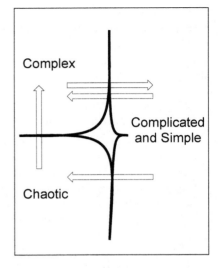

Figure 4C: Cynefin Pathways

Developing transformation pathways is about creating responses to the turbulence. To explore this in more detail, let's return to the cynefin framework of Chapter 2, which is adapted in Figure 4C. Remember that the left-hand side is characterized as "unordered" and the right-hand side is "ordered," where order refers to routinized patterns and activities reflected in organizational structures and the way that work gets done. The complicated and simple in the Figure are combined into one, so we can focus on the movement between them and the chaotic and complex.

Keystone systems are by definition complex: they contain patterns, although these may be harder to see and change more quickly than in complicated and simple states. For prehistoric man, obvious stable patterns were birth and death, the rising and setting of the sun, and seasons. As civilization grew, two things happened with the keystone systems. On the one hand, man began imposing patterns in transformative ways. Governance and other structures were developed to routinize and optimize certain qualities and outcomes. Organizations were developed to handle predictable patterns. On the other hand, science, as an activity that identifies patterns, became a major agent for moving parts of the keystone systems from complex to complicated and simple. Rather than referring to gods and invoking superstitions, people increasingly explained events like weather and metal properties in terms of patterns and qualities arising from scientific analysis. This led to a great variety of technologies and new organizing approaches that shifted issues from the left-hand side of the Figure to the right-hand side.

Let's look more closely at movement between chaos, complex, and complicated. In our daily lives, chaos is associated with disasters, such as earthquakes, wars or tidal waves. All the complicated and simple infrastructure reflected in things, such as power grids, hospitals, schools, transportation, and daily routines, disappear. In the midst of such chaos, the initial response, of course, is usually to rush aid. However, one big initial need is for information to understand how to respond. This information is the basis for identifying patterns in the chaos, such as identifying needs for water and shelter, and the number of people involved.

This data moves a chaotic situation into the complex realm. In this realm, the key distinction from chaos is that patterns start to emerge, although these patterns may be short-lived and ephemeral. Responses to disaster aim to stabilize these patterns, and return the situation over the longer-term to one addressed by complicated and simple infrastructure. For disasters, this usually involves temporary solutions, such as providing tents and trucking in clean drinking water on schedule. These represent simple solutions, pending a return to more complicated ones that require more physical infrastructure, specialized expertise, and stability.

Chaos will always be part of our lives to some degree, due to collapses from various environmental and man-made disasters. Because of turbulence and the very nature of complexity – low predictability, context-dependence, dynamic processes, and changing patterns – the nature of the keystone systems will always be changing. Furthermore, shifting capacities and values, and unintended consequences, will always lead to the obsolescence of complicated and simple responses. **The focus of transformation is on addressing the impact of on-going turbulence that gives rise to new complexity.**

The classic approach to bettering human welfare – even before complexity was understood – was to identify some *part* of a keystone system that can be turned into a complicated or simple response. For example, acute care hospitals are a response to one aspect of the health keystone system, the need to address brief, intense illnesses and support surgical interventions. This particular aspect of the health keystone system has been moved from the complex to the complicated.

From an environmental perspective, consider healthy air as a keystone system. In the United Kingdom, burning coal in London produced perennial fog. Analysis identified patterns, and the reasons for the smog had long been known (mainly homes using coal for heating). Yet, the problems remained in the complex realm. However, the Great Smog (from Friday, December 5 to Tuesday, December 9, 1952) caused an estimated 12,000 deaths. This led to a transformation of attitudes and power balances that produced the 1956 Clean Air Act. The Act was a reform-level change that shifted part of the air quality keystone

Box 4B: Downton Abbey and Evolutionary Transformational Change

The BBC-produced television series Downton Abbey is a great example of a family dealing with a late period of Britain's political transformation from absolute monarchy to democracy; and economic transformation from land-based wealth to industrial. Starting in 1912 and finishing in 1926, the series depicts the response of a wealthy land-owning aristocratic family to changes that result from the First World War, the rise of socialism, the decline of land-based wealth, and the imminent promise of the vote for women.

From the Earl's perspective, he is experiencing destruction of a traditional way of life of lavish lifestyle and status associated with inherited landed wealth, men and aristocracy. It is a good example of how creation – in this case of a more equitable welfare state – is accompanied by destruction.

system into the complicated realm to effectively manage it. A few decades latter attention turned to the threat to our planet's ozone layer that protects us from the sun's harmful ultraviolet radiation. Inertia in the trajectory and power of those associated with increasing chemicals that erode the ozone layer was broken with the 1987 international agreement called the Montreal Protocol. It resulted in reform-level change that prohibited the use of certain chemicals. Carbon emissions associated with climate change are a current challenge, which is an even larger problem since addressing them requires a basic restructuring of energy systems and impacts many status quo interests. These are all examples of moving problems with a keystone system, which have emerged due to turbulence, from the complex to the complicated.

These are transformation pathways, which aim to support movement from the complex to the complicated. However, this almost always also involves destroying aspects of the complicated structures as well. Addressing air quality required destroying production and consumption structures that gave rise to problems. Aspirations for greater wealth equality, to offer another example,

Box 4C: Resilience Design Principles

Over seven years, the Resilience Alliance of Young Scholars network refined seven design principles for resilient societies:

1. Maintain diversity and redundancy: these are key elements in addressing unpredictability;
2. Manage connectivity: ensure healthy interactions between various system components;
3. Manage slow variables and feedback: forces reinforcing and dampening change work at different rates, which may mask important, but not easily noticed, dynamics;
4. Foster complex adaptive systems thinking: this will change behaviors and capacity to address complexity;
5. Encourage learning: resilience is about dealing with change;
6. Broaden participation: this improves legitimacy, expands knowledge, and helps deal with anxieties;
7. Promote poly-centric governance: these are nested institutions connected by values that interact across hierarchies and structures.

These principles are further described in:

- Biggs, Reinette, Maja Schlüter, and Michael L Schoon. 2015. Principles for Building Resilience: Sustaining Ecosystem Services in Social-Ecological Systems: Cambridge University Press.
- Simonsen, Sturle Hauge, Reinette (Oonsie) Biggs, Maja Schlüter, Michael Schoon, Erin Bohensky, Georgina Cundill, Vasilis Dakos, Tim Daw, Karen Kotschy, Anne Leitch, Allyson Quinlan, Garry Peterson, and Fredrik Moberg. Circa 2015. "Applying resilience thinking: Seven principles for building resilience in social-ecological systems." Stockholm Resilience Centre. http://bit.ly/R4A6ul

requires destroying current patterns – attitudes, organizations, and relationships – that sustain inequity. Managing this change on the organizational level – transforming a business organization – is referred to as the need for an ambidextrous organization: one that can successfully grow its new business, while simultaneously destroying its old one. For this type of societal change, Chapter 3 describes how South Africa was able to accomplish this in terms of political racial transition (although it failed at economic-social transformation). The ability to manage this type of movement is the essence of resilience.

Building capacity for resilience is a response to the turbulence caused by activities, such as war, human-caused and natural environmental change, shifts in beliefs and values, and technological innovation. This is a strategy to configure societal-ecological systems to reflect resilience design principles (Box 4C). Resilient societies have a particularly rich array of *mechanisms* to respond effectively to system stress. The "mechanism" concept is core to Generative Causation evaluation approaches (Chapter 9). A match is a mechanism that turns wood into fire. Each of the four strategies in Chapter 4 contain numerous societal mechanisms. They include courts, political processes, public discussion, and multi-stakeholder processes; they also include war, collapse, and mass demonstrations. Resilient societies are ones that have developed effective and peaceful mechanisms to bring about change; brittle societies with low resilience lack these.

Another response to turbulence is to work *within* complicated structures rather than move an issue from the complex to the complicated for transformation. This is reflected by reform efforts to shore up existing systems via adaptation. This is a perfectly satisfactory response to many change challenges, and it is one that we have become quite good at. Business reform is often experienced as a reorganization of some type, such as with internal structures, changing external market focus, and mergers. For governments, it is often associated with new forms of regulation or new agencies. Policy can be a reform change activity, although it is often simply incremental change. Reform strategies are core to the negotiating change approach (Chapter 5).

All this has strategic and tactical implications for change about where to push, what tools to use, and who to engage (Chapters 2, 4, 8). The core implication is that it is important to distinguish between whether transformation or reform will satisfactorily address an issue. With climate change, some people champion reform-as-adaptation through activities, like building dikes and promoting saline-compatible agriculture. On its own, of course, this will not get us to where we have to go. Climate change fundamentally requires a transformative response, outside of currently known solutions. It requires undertaking action that changes the status quo as represented by those currently invested in carbon and its technologies.

This reform-and-transform response to climate change raises the importance of ambidexterity: the need for more than one strategy at the same time. We need to do the reform adapting *and* transformation experimenting. In the United States, this is displayed by some promoting natural gas as a low-carbon technological bridge, while renewables are being developed. The challenge is particularly pressing for electric utilities. They must develop an under-defined and usually under-supported renewable energy business model requiring new skills, while at the same time continuing to provide electricity with a heavy historic investment. This is a resilience issue on the organizational and societal levels.

Complex Pathways

A transformation pathway cannot be defined in advance because of the very nature of complexity. Rather, it has to emerge from experience supported by visioning tools and experimental methodologies (Chapter 9). For example, scenario development can be a particularly useful tool for this process. Typically, it is used collaboratively by stakeholders to identify optional futures, each reflecting different assumptions. The South African case (Chapter 3) described how this was used to identify four possible post-apartheid outcomes. The goal is not to define one future to realize, but to create discussion and awareness about implications of different assumptions, what is possible, and to create a framework for experiments to explored desired futures.

Transformation pathways to an imagined future from complexity to complicated are further described in Figure 4D. Each letter represents an experiment. The Figure reflects basic complexity characteristics described in Chapter 2: low predictability, non-linear interactions, context importance, and emergence. Let's stick with the climate change example to illustrate the diagram's implications:

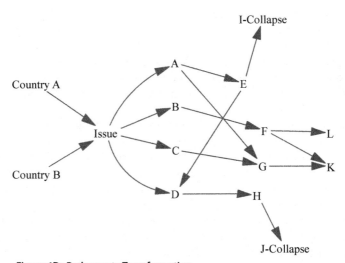

Figure 4D: Pathways to Transformation

- Reflecting the emergent learning quality of complexity, in real life, the actual detailed steps of an experiment will not be known in advance, only the general direction and contours. Detailed steps will emerge out of learning from each previous step. Moreover, in real life, the experiments will only be identified based on the experience of preceding knowledge and experiments. As was said, this is not a traditional planned intervention, but instead one that aims to explore future possibilities (Chapter 4).

- The Figure starts with two countries, reflecting the importance of context. Academics like to talk about "path-dependency," which is short-hand for saying that what happened in the past will influence what will work in the future. Developed countries have significant investments in infrastructure and technological capacity, and are focused on controlling greenhouse gases and energy efficiency. For a developing country, like India, there is much less sunk historic investment, simpler technologies are necessary, and there is a need to increase energy access for the many who do not have it or do not have it in adequate quantities. While this developed-developing country contrast easily illustrates the importance of context, the factors can be much more subtle. It is a key reason why "rolling-out" mass replication strategies are fraught with problems.

- In Figure D, four options are identified (A-D), which is a classic number of scenarios to develop. Reflecting the low ability to predict the impact of interventions in complex systems, experiments can be drawn up around each four, or some sub-set.

- The initial experiments provide data to guide the second pathway experiments (E-H) and ensure against putting all the eggs in one basket that may prove untenable or sub-optimal – without a comparison, it is impossible to know if something is sub-optimal.

- After completing the second round of experiments, those that conducted experiment E concluded there are three viable options: reviewing data from D they decide to try it out; they identify G as an option (as do those who completed C); and they also identify I.

- In the next round, I results in failure (collapse): the outcomes do not provide a possible valid future scenario.

- In the next round, J results in failure, while L and K provide viable options.

For climate change, these different paths may represent different technologies and policies. In a real-life situation, it is highly unlikely that this number of experiments would produce a clear transformative path. Many more could be reasonably expected. As well, it would probably be wise to again increase the number of possible paths, since two (K, L) is very modest.

For illustration's sake, let's pretend that K and L prove viable solutions: they have substantial stakeholder support, reduce emissions, and provide electricity in the desired range. The challenge is then to change the experiment into an innovation where it is widely used. This requires creating an enabling environment through change-as-reform. This shifts markets, policies, and values to support the innovation. Shifting markets and policies might involve market creation, such as the Germans did creating a renewables market through pricing legislation to overcome the inertia power of the traditional energy system and its market. Shifting values might involve influencing consumers' preferences so they switch to renewable energy sources. With this enabling environment established, the attention moves to broadening the approach until it becomes the new normal with incremental change and replication strategies.

The Scale of Transformation Pathways

We must hold ourselves open to options for futures rather than get into a deterministic, traditionally planned mode. However, we still need some guidance and sense of direction. Thinking of the development of resilient societies and flourishing futures for all provides direction; and ToC and pathways guide us in a systemic way to approach complexity. There are indeed multiple paths arising from the diversity of contexts and how flourishing futures and resilience can be imagined.

Together, ToC and pathways present complementary perspectives to support overcoming the intimidation and paralysis that can arise when facing LSC. They provide a way to make sense of individual action steps as part of the larger LSC process. They help bridge the gap between our current state and desired futures, with operational guidance to enhance the impact of our change efforts. In the next Chapter, we will explore how we can better understand relationships between change initiatives at our current point along these pathways.

Chapter 5

Acting with a Full Spectrum of Change Strategies

Chapter Summary

Societal change systems comprise four distinct meta-strategies. Lacking a comprehensive understanding of these while tackling LSC is like working with a hand tied behind your back. Transformational change efforts always involve all four, but change facilitators tend to focus on just one. Understanding how the strategies interact and when to use each one greatly enhances the impact of any action. This is demonstrated by applying these four strategies to the Chapter 3 cases.

Greenpeace grew out of the energy of activists in Vancouver (Canada) in the late 1960s. Today, the organization, based in Amsterdam, is well-known for its high-profile adversarial name and shame change strategy. Greenpeace is made up of a committed and imaginative network of activists who are particularly good at raising awareness and pressing for action on environmental issues. The World Wildlife Fund (WWF) was founded in 1961, in conjunction with the IUCN (the World Conservation Union), a pre-eminent network of governments and conservation organizations. The WWF's strategy is to work closely with governments, foundations, businesses, and individuals, as both funders and project partners. UNEP is a UN agency that is tasked with providing leadership and coherence on environmental issues amongst governments. Its strategy is to leverage its global government legitimacy and networks to develop partnerships with governments and others. To address environmental issues, the Moore Foundation allocates a significant part of its annual $300 million in grants to these issues. Its programs' focus ranges from the Andes-Amazon region to conservation and financial markets. The Sustainable Forestry Initiative (SFI) is an industry response to pressures for more environmentally-sensitive practices; SFI represents an industry strategy to influence these responses.

All these organizations are part of a much larger ecosystem of environmental change initiatives. This chapter describes them from the perspective of their *strategies*, which are necessary to realize transformation. If we think that a range of change strategies is required to realize transformation, how can that be described comprehensively? The answer is important in understanding why some change efforts succeed, and some fail: failure can be associated with the under-development of a particular type of strategy. Individual change initiative strategies are most powerful when they develop with an understanding of the full array of possible strategies and how they interact.

Different people and organizations emphasize, and develop competency in, particular change strategies. Assertions are often made that a particular strategy is right, and another is wrong. In fact, the success of one LSC strategy depends on the presence of other strategies in the change ecosystem. We saw this in the Chapter 3 marriage equality case, in which the success of "professional" change organizations with surveys, focus groups, and media campaigns depended on the work of activist and volunteer organizations talking to individuals about the marriage issue. In the German energy case, developing renewable energy required both small-business people developing renewable energy and activists to keep the government committed to change. The interactions of these strategies are particularly critical. Understanding this calls for a way to map change strategies, just as mapping techniques like social network analysis help us understand the *social relationships* between organizations and individuals (Chapter 9 describes various mapping methodologies). Building on earlier efforts,[101] this Chapter advances the development of the "whole system strategy map."

A Map of Emergent Change System Strategies

Shiva, depicted as Nataraja or Lord of Dance, is a good image for transformation strategists to keep in mind. He dances to destroy a weary universe and prepare for the process of creation. He stands within the universe depicted as a ring of fire. Distinguished by four arms, in one hand is held a drum whose vibrations are an allegory for creation; in another hand is fire, a symbol of destruction; another points to a raised foot to signify being uplifted and liberated; and the fourth hand forms the Abhaya (fearlessness) mudra, bestowing protection from evil and ignorance upon followers.

---

101 These efforts were shared in (1) Waddell, Steven. 2005. *Societal Learning and Change: How Governments, Business and Civil Society are Creating Solutions to Complex Multi-Stakeholder Problems.* Sheffield, UK: Greenleaf Publishing.; and in (2) Waddell, Steve , Sandra Waddock, Sarah Cornell, Domenico Dentoni, Milla McLachlan, and Greta Meszoely. 2015. "Large Systems Change: An Emerging Field of Transformation and Transitions." *Journal of Corporate Citizenship* (58):5-30.

Figure 5A: Shiva as the Lord of Dance

There is a natural tendency for change practitioners to focus on the processes of creation. However, creation is intimately connected with destruction. This observation was made by Joseph Schumpeter in his famous description of capitalism as creative destruction.[102] The transformation of Germany's energy production into renewable energy involves both destroying the traditional system and creating a new renewable energy one. The end of apartheid in South Africa was negatively experienced as destruction by many whites. Change system strategists must be aware of both destruction and creation, which give rise to both resistance and attraction to change.

LSC also has to do with re-creating power relationships (see Box 5A). This is a very tumultuous activity. Unfortunately, it is not just the product of generative dialogue, emergent insights and clear intellectual reasoning. There are also pitched battles, sometimes literally to the death. Change system strategists must also deal with these difficult dynamics.

Figure 5B builds on these insights as a way to map a full range of strategies. The key to understanding this approach is to banish judgment that one strategy is good and another bad. Context, temperament, and the stage of issue development, as well as personal moral perspectives, will all be factors in which strategy is undertaken by any individual or

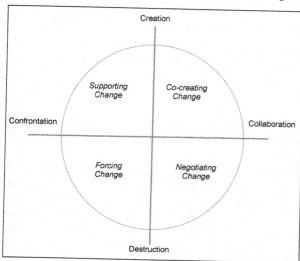

Figure 5B: Change Strategies

102 Schumpeter, Joseph Alois. 1939. *Business cycles*: Cambridge Univ Press.

Box 5A: Power and Change

Adam Kahane in his book *Power and Love*[1] points out that most change practitioners focus on love as a core strategy. This is reflected in multi-stakeholder approaches to get the whole system to work collaboratively to create the future. Power, he points out, is usually under-addressed or even suppressed, as having an important role in change. *The MSP Guide*[2] includes a good description of the six forms of power and ways to address power in multi-stakeholder processes.

- **Coercive power:** the use of physical violence or psychological manipulation to control what others do;
- **Legitimate power:** formal or informal authority given to or taken by a particular individual or group; for example, governments, legal systems, organizational managers, and social group leaders;
- **Reward power:** access to and control over financial and material resources; includes the ability to give rewards, such as money, benefits, time off, gifts, and promotions, to others;
- **Referent power:** the use of ideas, culture, religion, and language to shape the way people see their world and behave (ideologically), and the ability of an individual to use the power of their personality to gain a following and influence (charismatic);
- **Expert power:** the power people derive from their skills, knowledge, and experience; only applies to the expert's specialty area;
- **Informational power:** power resulting from having knowledge that others need or want; the way in which information is used – sharing it, keeping it secret from key people, organizing it, increasing it, or even falsifying it – can shift power within the group.

---

1 Kahane, Adam. 2010. *Power and love: A theory and practice of social change*: Berrett-Koehler Publishers.
2 Brouwer, H., Woodhill, J., with, Hemmati, M., Verhoosel, K., & Vugt, S. v. (2015). *The MSP Guide: How to design and facilitate multi-stakeholder partnerships*. Wageningen, The Netherlands: University of Wageningen. P. 77

collection of individuals. This is why there are so many environmental strategies, as described in the beginning of this Chapter. The goal here is to simply identify a comprehensive map of strategies.

The Figure 5B strategy typology is based on two ideas. One is the creation-destruction idea. The second presents a spectrum from confrontation to collaboration. Some (most change practitioners) focus on collaboration amongst diverse stakeholders to create the new, while others' strategies (usually after the failure of less confrontational approaches) will focus on violence and even terrorism as a way to achieve the new. The South African case in Chapter 3 best brings this dynamic into focus.

First, let's look at the types of strategy from a generic viewpoint:
- *Supporting Change* occurs when power-holders use their resources to realize change, convinced it is for the broader good. They use unilateral action asso-

ciated with "lifting up" and "noblesse oblige." Doing this can be the objective of government legislation, philanthropy, and community organizing, although these actions can be incorporated in other types of change as well, spurring images of a missionary who believes they are bringing out the good in others.

- *Forcing Change* occurs when a stakeholder group acts to grow power in relation to others through confrontational tactics and strategies. Groups do this to educate about, and raise the profile of their issue when they are frustrated with a lack of attention or desired movement. As a strategy, Forcing Change

Table 5A: Change Strategies

Name	Supporting Change	Forcing Change	Co-creating Change	Negotiating Change
Components	Creative power Confrontation	Destructive power Confrontation	Creative power Collaboration	Destructive power Collaboration
Dynamic	Empowering Raising up	Mobilizing Confronting	Collaborating Co-evolving	Fostering minor change Maintaining status quo
Necessary Conditions	Willingness to share power	Willingness to ignore harm	Willingness of everyone to change	Willingness of the disempowered to settle for minor improvement
Popular Terms	Noblesse oblige Upliftment	Forcing	Partnering Collaboration Co-production	Paternalism Being bought off
Danger	Irrelevance	Marginalization	Co-optation	Suppression
Archetypical Role	Missionary	Warrior	Lover	Negotiator
Archetypical Tactics	Rights legislation Legal cases Education Media campaigns	Community organizing State force Strikes (capital, labor) Demonstrations	Multi-stakeholder fora Public engagement Social labs	Reinforcing legal cases Financial pay-offs Consultation
Example 1: SGI	Shakabuku Mentor-disciple	Temple break Komeito Party	District meetings	Hierarchy
Example 2: Energiewende	FITS Cross-subsidies	Demonstrations Referenda	Prosumers	Impact reporting
Example 3: South Africa	Foreign government support	Strikes Boycotts	1990-94 negotiations	Bantustan Black elite creation
Example 4: Same-sex marriage	Sitcoms	Parades Court challenges Lobbying	Religious-LGBT coalitions	Civil unions Separate-but-equal
Example 4: Black American voting rights	Voting Rights Act	King and non-violent action, Malcolm X, Black Panthers	Inter-racial faith coalitions Selma march	Eliminating poll taxes (while maintaining other barriers to voting)
Example 6: Codes of conduct	UN Global Compact principles	Powerful government standards	Forest Stewardship Council (multi-stakeholder)	Sustainable Forestry Initiative (industry controlled)

is often associated with such things as demonstrations, capital and labor strikes, government legal sanctions, and armed insurrections. The archetype is a warrior who sees the change challenge as a battle with a foe who must be vanquished.

- *Negotiating Change* actions are associated with power being used to maintain the status quo. This strategy is often a response to Forcing Change actions, with those opposing meaningful change trying to placate those pushing for it. Consultation by power holders with the marginalized is a common activity: the power holders consult without opening up to sharing power and responding to power dynamic problems. Much government lobbying fits this strategy, as well as top-down government consultative approaches to regulation and multi-stakeholder power cliques. Those taking this approach see themselves as negotiating to retain what they can in the face of inexorable change pressures.

- *Co-creating Change* represents collaborative strategies to develop change. This includes: multi-stakeholder processes to develop principle statements for business and activities to implement them; public-private partnerships; and whole system participation change approaches. A common underlying strategy is to bring together diverse stakeholders with early adopter insiders as a way to transform issues of joint concern.[103] People working to co-create change come from a position of love and mutual respect, believing that problems can be resolved by a deep sense of connection.

Each environmental change initiative highlighted at the beginning of this chapter holds one strategy dominant: the Moore Foundation for Supporting Change; Greenpeace for Forcing Change; the Sustainable Forestry Initiative for Negotiating Change; and UNEP, WWF and IUCN for Co-creating Change.

Table 5A applies these ideas to particular cases by identifying *tactics* that reflect particular strategies. Four of the cases are from Chapter 3. Two others are added to broaden the analysis. Let's look at them individually for some illustrative highlights.

1. SGI: For Soka Gakkai, building a global community to support human revolution is a core activity. This is based on the Supporting Change concept of "shakabuku," which is popularly associated with introducing new people to SGI. SGI describes it as "...the Buddhist method of leading people, particularly its opponents, to the correct Buddhist teaching by refuting their erroneous views and eliminating their attachment to opinions they have formed. The practice of *shakubuku* thus means to correct another's false views and awaken that person to the truth of Buddhism."[104] Supporting Change is also associated with the

---

103 The is an adapted excerpt from: Waddell, Steve , Sandra Waddock, Sarah Cornell, Domenico Dentoni, Milla McLachlan, and Greta Meszoely. 2015. "Large Systems Change: An Emerging Field of Transformation and Transitions." *Journal of Corporate Citizenship* (58):5-30.

104 SGI. 2015. "Shakabuku." http://www.sgilibrary.org/search_dict.php?id=1974: Soka Gakki International.

core "mentor-discipline" relationship, in which individuals relate to people they see as more spiritually advanced as guides.

Forcing Change is less practiced by SGI. However, in the early 1990s, a decision was made to break with what is referred to as the "Temple tradition." Priests asserted themselves as necessary intermediaries on the path to enlightenment, in contrast with the SGI community-centered tradition emphasizing that enlightenment is about discovering and growing the "Buddha within." The Temple tradition "excommunicated" SGI and its members (even though there is no "excommunication" concept in Buddhism). Another example is the formation of the Komeito Party, in Japan, which is closely associated with SGI. The Party engages in traditional political party Forcing Change activities.

Co-creating Change is the dominant change strategy, as experienced in SGI community meetings in which individuals gather to support each other's efforts for human revolution.

There is a side to SGI that I experience as Controlling when people claim permission must be asked to do certain things.

2. **Energiewende:** The two key government interventions in the German energy transition represent Supporting Change strategies: setting attractive rates for those generating renewable energy that must be accepted by traditional utilities (FITS), and distributing the added costs this generates across the electricity system.

In Germany, there was a remarkable sense of unity around energiewende, especially compared with most other countries. Nevertheless, community and environmental groups implemented an important Forcing Change strategy to maintain the transition, particularly after the government tried to weaken the program, as a consequence of the 2009 election.

"Prosumers" is perhaps an archetypical example of a Co-creating Change strategy. The traditional distinction between energy consumer and energy provider is up-ended by those who combine both in generating renewable energy.

An example of Negotiating Change is firms that produce reports describing their social-environmental-economic impacts while staunchly opposing full-cost externality accounting.

3. **South Africa:** Foreign governments implemented Supporting Change for the anti-apartheid movement in various ways, including: increasing the apartheid government's diplomatic isolation, providing training and financial support for anti-apartheid forces, and supporting negotiations to end apartheid.

The critical effort, given the adamancy of the apartheid government, was a Forcing Change one of the community organizing around protest activities, such as strikes, boycotts, and violence.

The rapprochement period of the white government, first undertaken in secrecy and then via public negotiations in 1990-94 with its traditional adversaries, represented a Co-creating Change period. The subsequent unity government is considered a continuation of this strategy by some, although others say that black leaders were by then in power.

The white government's Bantustan policy represented a Negotiating Change strategy. This policy set aside titularly self-governing territories (consisting of very poor quality land) for blacks. It did not work well. However, the more profound strategy of creating a black elite class can be seen as a Negotiating Change strategy that proved very successful at managing political change and preventing profound economic and social change.

4. **Marriage Equality:** Entertainment industry titans – film, television, and music – embarked on a Supporting Change strategy through shows, beginning as early as 1971, that featured positive, anti-stereotypical images of the LGBT community in general and gay or lesbian loving and committed couples later on.

The LGBT community organized itself to undertake significant Forcing Change strategies. With the notable exception of the Stonewall Riots, these were generally not violent, but rather were channeled through change mechanisms associated with a pluralistic society. Parades, marches, and demonstrations were often noted for their color and flamboyance.

The marriage equality movement developed particularly important and successful Co-creating Change tactics to reach out across gay-straight divides to produce gay-straight alliances. This notably included the Religious Freedom to Marry Coalition, and such alliances within schools and universities.

There was a very serious attempt to satisfy marriage equality proponents with separate-but-equal Negotiating Change responses. Those who claimed traditional marriages were devalued by extending the institution to the LGBT community wanted any label but marriage. Although considered a great advance at the time, this was reflected in 1999 Vermont legislation supporting "civil unions."

5. **Black American Voting Rights:** Until the Voting Rights Act of 1965, black Americans' right to vote had been suppressed by a range of measures referred to as Jim Crow laws. The Act was as a Supporting Change strategy, since it resulted from action by predominantly white legislators and led to an on-going set of enforcement mechanisms.

However, this advance only resulted from Martin Luther King Jr.'s Forcing Change strategy to organize the black community into a powerful force to challenge white communities in which the restrictions were the harshest. Most would put King in a different category than Malcolm X and the Black Panthers, because the former emphasized peaceful action, whereas the latter condoned and undertook violent action. However, both employed Forcing Change strategies.

Reaching across the black-white divide as a Co-creating Change strategy was particularly well-illustrated by religious support across racial divides and the famous 1965 Selma to Montgomery march, as well as the Freedom Summer for which large numbers of whites joined blacks.

In 1964, the Federal government made poll taxes[105] illegal, eliminating a significant barrier to blacks' voting rights. This Negotiating Change strategy was quickly superseded by increased pressure for broader change that ultimately led to the Voters Rights Act.

6. **Codes of Conduct:** These codes are a tactic rather than an issue. However, applying strategic change analysis helps distinguish how the same tactic can represent a different strategy. The promotion of the UN Global Compact's principles is really a Supporting Change strategy. The Compact is the government and corporate elites getting together with, in general, a sincere desire for change. Their goal is to influence business standards.

Government regulation is in essence a form of codes that represent a Forcing Change strategy, since they are backed by the coercive power of legal systems.

The Forest Stewardship Council (FSC) and most Action Networks (Chapter 7) represent a Co-creating Change model, in which stakeholders are brought together to define and implement codes.

In contrast to the FSC is the Sustainable Forestry Initiative (SFI), which was mentioned at the beginning of this Chapter. SFI is an industry response to the FSC. SFI is improving forestry practices, but in a less ardent way than the FSC, and in part, it dampens the FSC's change efforts.

Each of these four strategies comes with particular dangers that spell transformation failure. The Supporting Change strategy may be pursued by a small group of traditional power holders, but never get beyond them and remain marginalized. This could be said to be the situation with the business for social responsibility tradition: ardent enthusiasts get pushed out of the market, because the operating environment rules remain old school. Forcing Change strategies face the danger of marginalization. This can be seen with some radical groups, such as Bader Meinhof – the Red Army Faction that operated as a terrorist organization in West Germany, but could never build broad support. The Co-creating Change strategy faces the danger of co-optation, which is arguably what happened in South Africa where Co-creating Change led to the development of a small black elite. The slide into co-optation is easy, given the natural desire of most people to be liked, societal norms of decorum, corruption, and the energy required to continually challenge other stakeholders in a multi-stakeholder forum. For transformation, the danger of the Negotiating Change strategy is that it will be successful and result in suppressing fundamental change. Sometimes radical change may not be necessary, and then this strategy becomes a sort of "negotiating ploy" for the degree of acceptable change.

The four strategies framework allows strategies to be strengthened by asking question, such as:

• Is one of the strategies under-developed, considering current circumstances?
• Is it time to change which strategy is being emphasized?

---

105 Paying a tax was a precondition to being able to vote.

- Is there a need for a better connection between those working on *different* strategies, to address problems of undermining one another or, instead, developing synergies?
- Is there a need for better collaboration between those who are developing the *same* strategy to realize the needed scale or address conflicts?

High-Leverage System Strategies

One of the earliest initiatives to reflect LSC thinking produced *The Limits to Growth* in 1972.[106] Using system dynamics computer modeling to produce future scenarios (Chapter 9) for the world, it extrapolated growth trends based on five variables: world population, industrialization, pollution, food production, and resource depletion. Recognizing the scenarios were predictions "only in the most limited sense," given methodological limitations, two scenarios saw "overshoot and collapse" of civilization as we know it in the mid-21st century, whereas a third resulted in "stability."

Donella Meadows was a lead author of the report. Trained as a biophysicist at Harvard, she worked with Jay Forrester at MIT, who is considered a founder of system dynamics. The report pointed out that growth is a key leverage point for large systems change, that it has both costs and benefits and that most people only consider the benefits. "What is needed is slower growth, and in some cases no growth or negative growth," she wrote.[107] She continued:

> So one day I was sitting in a meeting about the new global trade regime, NAFTA and GATT and the World Trade Organization. The more I listened, the more I began to simmer inside. 'This is a HUGE NEW SYSTEM people are inventing!' I said to myself. 'They haven't the slightest idea how it will behave,' myself said back to me. 'It's cranking the system in the wrong direction — growth, growth at any price!! And the control measures these nice folks are talking about — small parameter adjustments, weak negative feedback loops — are PUNY!'

Her frustration produced a list of interventions to influence a system that is very useful for understanding large systems change strategies and tactics (Box 5B). It arises from system dynamics modeling (Chapter 9). The four strategy archetypes described earlier can be combined to focus on a leverage point for realizing transformation.

The vast majority of attention is focused on leverage point 12, parameters, such as the interest rate set by central banks or who is President or Prime Minister. But, these have very little leverage in terms of LSC goals. They are part of the

---

106 Meadows, D.H., D.L. Meadows, J. Randers, and W.W. Berhens. 1972. *The Limits to Growth.* New York: Universe Books, republished by Productivity Press, Portland, OR.

107 Meadows, Donnella. 1999. "Leverage Points: Places to Intervene in a System." Harland, VT, USA: The Sustainability Institute. P. 1

Box 5B: A Hierarchy of Leverage Points for Change[1]

This list is hierarchical. In other words, intervening by making changes with lever 12 has less impact than using lever 11.

12. Constants, parameters, numbers (e.g., subsidies, taxes, and standards);
11. The size of buffers and other stabilizing stocks, relative to their flows (e.g., in a food system, the number of days supply of stored food is a buffer and daily consumption is the flow);
10. The structure of material stocks and flows (e.g., transport networks, and population age structures);
9. The length of delays, relative to the rate of system change (e.g., the time between planning for a new electric plant and its actual operation);
8. The strength of negative feedback loops, relative to the impacts they are trying to correct (e.g., the cost of switching to renewable energy to address climate change);
7. The gain from driving positive feedback loops (e.g., positive health impacts from cleaner air measures);
6. The structure of information flows (who does and does not have access to information);
5. The rules of the system (e.g., incentives, punishments, and constraints);
4. The power to add, change, evolve, or self-organize the system's structure;
3. The goals of the system (e.g., from energy to clean energy provision);
2. The mindset or paradigm out of which the system — its goals, structure, rules, delays, and parameters — arises;
1. The power to transcend paradigms.

---

1 Meadows, Donnella. 1999. *Leverage Points: Places to Intervene in a System.* Harland, VT, USA: The Sustainability Institute.

existing system and the way it regulates itself to keep away from critical parameters that *would* produce large change. The most powerful interventions concern paradigms referred to in leverage points 1 and 2. These terms refer to patterns, concepts, structures, and power relationships that determine the behavior of a system, such as a pro-growth paradigm and a democratic paradigm.

Changing paradigms, leverage point 2, is what each of the Chapter 3 case studies is about. However, those cases demonstrated that a large number of diverse tactics are necessary to change a paradigm. Moreover, the tactics aimed mainly at leverage points 3-12 on Meadow's hierarchy. This suggests that although there is wisdom in Meadow's hierarchy, to realize transformation is not simply a matter of setting out to shift the paradigm and creating a tool to realize it. To shift a paradigm requires a constellation of actions, and interactions between the levers. For example, a paradigm will not change if the goals of the system are not changed (leverage point 3). One operational insight of the hierarchy is that transformation involves actions throughout the hierarchy.

A second insight of the hierarchy is one that Meadows originally made: when designing a system, do so humbly and pay attention to the relative power of control measures. The negotiators at her meeting were clear about system goals (growth), but they were paying inadequate attention to the impacts of growth. They thought negative impacts could be directed by measures that would be easily overwhelmed by the simplistic pro-growth purpose and underlying paradigm they were working from. Meadows explained that they needed to change the goals of the system (e.g., happiness) and the paradigm (a "happiness" paradigm would make growth a secondary consideration and a function of its ability to produce happiness compared with other functions and growth's impact on them).

The number 1 leverage point might be referred to as the "meta-level" position on change. Meadows describes it as:

> ...keep(ing) oneself unattached in the arena of paradigms, to stay flexible, to realize that *no* paradigm is 'true,' that every one, including the one that shapes your own worldview, is a tremendously limited understanding of an immense and amazing universe that is far beyond human comprehension.[108]

This is a statement that change makers can continually return to during their work.

---

108 Ibid. p. 19

Chapter 6

Creating Societal Change Systems

Chapter Summary

The collective strategies of initiatives addressing any change issue form societal change systems for that issue. These systems are all around us. However, we generally don't see them because our own predilections lead us to focus on particular parts. Without understanding the whole, you can actually undermine your efforts by undertaking poorly-informed action(s) on a part. This chapter presents the idea that these change systems can be developed with three approaches: societal learning and change, the systemic change matrix and social movements. It also summarizes scaling approaches.

In October, 2014, a small group met at Italy's leading business school, Bocconi University (Milan, Italy), to investigate what I now call societal change systems (SCSs). As part of the Global Learning and Organizational Development Network (GOLDEN) under the leadership of Maurizio Zollo, the Energy Ecosystem Lab that I led brought together the GOLDEN and Lab teams, with change initiative leaders in the global electricity issue arena. We built on 18 months of work, and the leaders left enthused with a new approach to their work.

The Energy Ecosystem Lab focused on questions about how to develop an operating environment – markets, policies, and values – that would support the emergence of sustainable enterprise in the electricity arena. The word "ecosystem," which is gaining popularity because of its power to look at complex issues and design actions to address them, in the Lab's name describes this. Originally introduced in the biological sciences and popularized via the Millennium Ecosystems Assessment,[109] the term initially referred to:

---

109 Initiated in 2001 by the UN, the objective of the MA was to assess the consequences of ecosystem change for human well-being and the scientific basis for action needed to enhance the conservation and sustainable use of those systems and their contribution to human well-being. Millennium Ecosystem Assessment. 2005. Millennium Ecosystem Assessment Findings: Millennium Ecosystem Assessment.

... a community of living organisms (plants, animals and microbes) in conjunction with the nonliving components of their environment (things like air, water and mineral soil), interacting as a system.[110]

Applied to social and organizational concerns, "social ecosystem" commonly refers to the relationships among individuals and organizations that interact as a system. The Lab's interest is with societal change (eco) system (SCS) for energy.

Typically, people in one change initiative pay some attention to change initiatives that they come into repeated contact with; sometimes, they intentionally search out partners with specific characteristics. Usually, they pay attention to particularly powerful change initiatives. Most people in a change initiative, however, simply keep their heads down and stay focused on their own work. The number and variety of change initiatives working on their issue is often overwhelming, and frequently seems

> **Box 6A: Societal Change Systems**
>
> A societal change system (SCS) consists of all efforts and initiatives working on an issue to realize transformation with respect to an issue. With respect to social-economic-environmental sustainability, an SCS comprises all those initiatives of governments, business, NGOs and multi-stakeholder organizations that aim to integrate the sustainability imperative into a production system (e.g.: food, electricity, health, peacemaking).
>
> One way to describe an SCS is the Systems Change Matrix, consisting of two components. One is a set of seven functions that are necessary to realize an effective change system. A second is a set of subsystems organized around core tasks with distinct stakeholder groupings.
>
> The SCS concept is particularly important for those aiming for large systems change. It provides an organizing framework for broad and deep impact.

irrelevant. Time spent learning about other initiatives simply seems unproductive compared with "doing the doing."

But, as any systems thinker knows, a shift in one point of a system can have significant consequences on another part of the system. Another core tenet of systems thinking is that a system is not simply the additive output of its components. The whole of a well-aligned system is greater than the sum of its parts. With audacious change goals, *any* change initiative is only one of many addressing any particular issue. There is great value in thinking of a particular change initiative as part of a SCS, and taking action within this context. People working for large systems change (LSC) gain great power by understanding the SCS for their particular issue.

The challenge of developing a powerful SCS can be framed as, "How can coherence be developed amongst change initiatives working on the same issue?" Figure 6A shows the desired shift. Currently, the initiatives are poorly aligned and connected. How can they be bettered aligned, address gaps in needed action, reduce

---

110 Wkipedia. 2014. "Ecosystem." http://en.wikipedia.org/wiki/Ecosystem.

redundancies and conflict, and develop synergies? In short: how can systemic impact be enhanced?

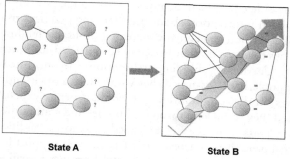

State A   **State B**

Figure 6A: Developing Coherence

The number and variety of change initiatives can easily overwhelm our ability to understand the SCS state for any particular issue. For example, in the electricity issue arena, there are thousands of them. Understanding the state of a SCS involves identifying what people are already thinking, feeling, and doing to transform an issue. Any way of looking at this will be a particular view of "reality." However, it should not be treated *as* reality. Moreover, since SCSs are highly dynamic, any view is simply a snapshot in time. Therefore, understanding is never complete, but is always deepening.

We know that a tenet of complexity is low predictability about the impact of any particular action. However, many change issues have a complicated component where some degree of predictability is possible. For example, we know that increasing the cost of carbon fuels will make the use of renewables more economically attractive. The degree of impact and unintended consequences are the complex quality of the issue. For example, in the German energy case, the development of prosumers (those consuming and producing renewable energy) was novel. How it would emerge in terms of scale, rate, and form was unpredictable. The underpinning question, therefore, is: can we strengthen the underlying change system to enhance the quality of interactions and the impact of change efforts?

There are three particular perspectives that I will share to support understanding the emergence of SCSs. Each of these provides ways to look at a transformation challenge from a comprehensive perspective. The Societal Learning and Change Matrix perspective (Table 6B) integrates levels of change and ways people make sense of reality; the Systemic Change Matrix perspective maps change initiatives to describe the SCS; and developing social movements are presented as an important way to support SCS development, although they are inadequate on their own. The Chapter ends with a description of ways to realize scale.

Societal Learning and Change

In the mid-1990s, I spent time looking at the relationships and fraught history between banks and low-income American communities. Banks simply refused to lend in poorer neighborhoods, particularly in minority communities. Banks claimed lending was high risk, whereas the communities claimed the banks were simply racist and biased against poor people. The federal government passed laws that obliged banks to demonstrate good relationships with local communities and publish information about their lending practices to them. This produced a very different outcome: greatly increased profitable lending, and the ability of communities to invest in their housing, as well as advancement.

Uncovering hidden assumptions accompanied this transformation. For example, banks assumed they would need a brick-and-mortar presence (i.e., buildings) in the communities that would generate expensive overheads. They discovered they could lend through churches and community organizations instead. The banks assumed they would need to enforce lending agreements through costly legal procedures; instead, peer lending and support led to very low default rates.

This is an example of societal learning. Learning is usually associated with individuals, but Peter Senge popularized the concept of the *learning organization*.[111] Learning can also be thought of as a societal activity and that concept permeated my book *Societal Learning and Change*.[112] In all cases, learning is associated with a growth in capacities – something can be done after learning that could not be done prior to it. Learning is also associated with invention and innovation, and is a core activity in all five change spheres described in Chapter 3. Often, the learning process also involves "unlearning," such as with limiting assumptions and understandings that do not align with experience. Examples include believing that: human flight is impossible; the world is flat; democracy will never work; transformation requires violent crisis; and profitable lending cannot be undertaken in low-income communities. With ideas outside our awareness, there is a natural tendency to think they do not and cannot exist. Transformation is often accompanied by the sentiment: "I never thought about it that way before!" Questions about how we unlearn and learn are related to imagining how something can be different, and creating the necessary transformation.

Learning involves exploring and experiencing the unknown. As described in the individual change sphere case in Chapter 3, it includes opening oneself up and becoming vulnerable. This is a core activity of successful multi-stakeholder processes, as people work across stereotypes and assumptions. In the 1990s, the concept of multi-stakeholder processes was still young. We still didn't know how to make them work well. But, important pioneering work had been decades before. A particularly robust strain is associated with the merger of two aircraft engine companies in England headed by Eric Trist, an Englishman, and Fred Emery, an Australian. They built on effective dialogue knowledge to treat "my facts" and "your facts" as "our facts." This opened the door to much more effective planning,[113]

---

111 Senge, P.M. 1990. *The Fifth Discipline: The Art and Practice of the Learning Organization*. New York: Doubleday, Senge, Peter, Richard Ross, Bryan Smith, Charlotte Roberts, and Art Kleiner. 1994. *The Fifth Discipline Fieldbook*. New York, NY: Currency Doubleday.

112 Waddell, Steven. 2005. *Societal Learning and Change: How Governments, Business and Civil Society are Creating Solutions to Complex Multi-Stakeholder Problems*. Sheffield, UK: Greenleaf Publishing.

113 Future Search Network. 2015. "Historical Roots and Theoretical Basis." https://www.futuresearch.net/method/whatis/history.cfm: Future Search Network.

which led to development in the 1980s-90s of the Search Conference as a methodology. It was further refined by Marvin Weisbord as Future Search.[114] With this, the concept of "getting the whole system in the room" developed.

Developing societal learning is facilitated by understanding that *differences in how people learn are embedded in our organizational structures*. Working at the Institute for Development Research in the 1990s with Dave Brown, I had an unusual opportunity to take a broad and deep look at whole system dynamics with business-government-civil society collaboration. Brown was also a professor at Harvard's Hauser Institute for Civil Society, and IDR was known as a global "support organization" for civil society development. Civil society is associated with NGOs, but it is broader than that. It includes forms of voluntary participation that are also associated with religious organizations, trade unions, and credit unions. Sometimes, civil society is referred to as the "third sector" or the "independent sector." This contrasts with the government and for-profit business; I prefer to refer to it as "community-based organizations" (CBOs), because their organizing logic is focused on communities of interest (geographic and/or issue).

Table 6A: Primary Resources and Weaknesses Across Sectors[115]

	State	Market	Civil Society
RESOURCES	Regulatory and taxation powers	Capital and financial assets	Inspirational and volunteer assets
	Enforcement networks	Production networks	Community networks
	Policy impact knowledge	Specialized industry knowledge	Specialized community/issue knowledge
	Government reputation	Business reputation	Community reputation
	Administrators	Entrepreneurs	Community developers
WEAKNESSES	Inflexibility in rule application	Tendency to monopoly	Restricted/fragmented interest focus
	Slow decision-making	Disregard for externalities	Amateurism (from the volunteer base)
	Complexity of jurisdictions/levels	Poor integration of long-term concerns	Material scarcity
	Difficulty with internal coordination	Inequality of outcomes	Difficulty in achieving large scale
	Desire to control other sectors	Ideological ignorance/transactional parochialism	Ideological parochialism (political correctness)
	Partisan-driven posturing	Shareholder fixation	Weak economic understanding

---

114 Weisbord, Marvin, and Sandra Janoff. 2010. *Future Search: Getting the Whole System in the Room for Vision, Commitment, and Action*. San Francisco, CA: Berrett-Koehler.

115 Waddell, Steven. 2005. *Societal Learning and Change: How Governments, Business and Civil Society are Creating Solutions to Complex Multi-Stakeholder Problems*. Sheffield, UK: Greenleaf Publishing.

Questions about the distinctions and relationships between these organizational "sectors" of civil society, business, and government led to funding from USAID, and the Ford and MacArthur Foundations, as well as my title as "Director of Intersectoral Services." I received an unusual opportunity to travel the world looking at, and working with, examples where the sectors interacted. This included housing for the poor in the Philippines, economic development in India, road building in Madagascar, water and sanitation in South Africa, and banking in Brazil. Other relevant experiences included forestry on the Canadian Pacific Coast, addressing poverty in Guatemala, and banking in the US.

I asked questions, such as "What is the difference between the sectors? Why are these multi-stakeholder relationships emerging? Are organizational sectors merely a Western phenomenon, or is there a real foundation for them globally? How can inter-sectoral relationships be effectively developed?" One product of these questions is Table 6A. It came out of the proposition that multi-stakeholder activities arise from distinctive resources and weaknesses of the sectors. Simply put, they aim to integrate their competencies and address their weaknesses.[116] Note, this is another version of "none of them can address some issues on their own." Here are a few important notes on this business-government-civil society world view that help with understanding Table 6A:

- Legal identity is only one quality that indicates which sector an organization will fall into. There are plenty of examples of government agencies that act in many ways like NGOs/non-profits, as well as NGOs that act like businesses, and businesses that act like NGOs.
- Most organizations have some characteristics of another sector, and some aim to categorically integrate them. Social enterprises, for example, are explicit attempts to integrate market and civil society qualities. Most initiatives that aim to integrate all three sectors are thought of as relatively "temporary" and that they will no longer be needed after their task is complete. However, there are many long-term cases (this is discussed in greater detail in Chapter 7).
- Different countries tend to place different emphases on these sectors. For example, the US emphasizes the market first, the government second, and civil society third in terms of power. Europe tends to be relatively balanced, with slightly more emphasis on government. China is clearly government sector-dominant, with business second, and civil society a very weak third. On the other hand, Bangladesh can be seen as dominated by civil society.
- Table 6A suggests another way to think about assessing the success of cross-sector initiatives: identifying particular resources needed and weaknesses that should be off-set, and then seeing whether this is actually being accomplished.
- Academic organizations do not fit neatly into any of the three categories. They are more like civil society as a community; private universities have a clear market orientation; their organizing dynamic is more like a government (administration).

---

116 Waddell, Steve. 2002. "Core Competencies: A Key Force in Business-Government-Civil Society Collaborations." *Journal of Corporate Citizenship* (7):43-56.

Box 6B: The Importance of Relationships in Transformation

Multi-stakeholder relationships are promoted as vehicles for Co-creating Change with relative harmony, compared with other strategies. One reason for this is the importance of learning others' views to create individually and collectively effective transformation strategies – integrating and transcending different perspectives representing the whole system.

But, stakeholders invariably come to the process with different power, financially and socially. Transformation by definition involves changing these comparative relationships. Once rich people get to know poor people on a personal level, the belief goes, the former will be more willing to give up something to support greater equity for the latter. This line of reasoning has a scientific basis. After reviewing experiments in a range of diverse cultures about how people respond to disadvantage, Maria Konnikova concludes that people are "…especially willing to give up…unfair advantages when there's the possibility of strengthening a future relationship."

Applying Table 6A to the banking and communities case helps illustrate the value of intersectoral collaboration. In terms of resources, the government used its regulatory powers to require banks to do something they did not want to; the banks brought in their capital assets; the community brought in their networks and community knowledge to support new lending programs. In terms of weaknesses, the government did not set quotas or targets (reflecting awareness of inflexibility problems). Instead, it simply created reasons for banks and communities to talk to each other and explore possibilities. This addressed banks' tendency to simply disregard the externality of community disinvestment that reinforces poverty. Civil society's material scarcity weakness was addressed through bank lending. Breaking down the barriers to support intersectoral collaboration is an example of how societal learning emerges. Furthermore, it helps build an understanding of the dynamics in developing SCSs.

My most succinct response to questions about the sectors and change is Table 6B. Societal learning arises as change on four levels: societal, sectoral, organizational, and individual. Each of these levels has divisions associated with the three core societal systems: political, economic, and social. Societal learning (at the societal level) involves changing the relationships between these systems, at the organizational sector level between the state, market, and social/civil society level. In terms of organizations, these take the form of government agencies, businesses, and CBOs. In turn, these tend to be aggregates of people with three distinct learning styles: mentally-centered, physically-centered, and emotionally-centered.

Table 6B: The Societal Learning and Change Matrix

Societal	Political systems	Economic systems	Social systems
Sectoral	The state sector	The market sector	The social sector
Organizational	Government agencies	Businesses	Community-based orgs.
Individual	Mentally-centered	Physically-centered	Emotionally-centered

It is this last claim, with respect to the individual level, that has provided me with the most insight. Interestingly, it is also somewhat controversial with many. For me, the critical way to assess such controversies is to ask whether the assertion leads to more insightful and impactful action, or whether it undermines action. In this case, I really find the assertion that individual learning styles generally align with sectors helps action when it is held moderately, rather than deterministically (for example, saying that everyone working within a sector is of this learning style, or that the learning style tells everything about an individual's learning approach). Table 6B proposes that (1) most people have one dominant "learning style," (2) there is a natural tendency to congregate with people with shared learning styles and form distinctive types of organizations, and (3) this leads to distinctions between the three sectors. This claim arose from my reading work on human dynamics by Sandra Seagal and David Home.[117] While I was looking at the distinctions between these sectors to produce things, such as Table 6A, they were looking at individual learning styles: what does an individual focus on and what guides them in making sense and interpreting meaning? Seagal and Home produced tables of characteristics for individual learning styles that mapped almost perfectly with the tables I have developed for the three sectors.

In other words, the mentally-centered tend to analyze and categorize with frameworks. This is reflected in the core work of governments, when they write laws and regulations and create systems to decide what is legal or illegal. The physically-centered focus on concrete manifestations, such as products and services. This relates to the businesses demand to "show me the money." The emotionally-centered know something is real when they feel it in their heart, such as when fairness and justice resonate, which is a matter of particular concern to CBOs. These dynamics were all at play in the banks-community societal learning example, as participants looked at different things to assess whether the relationship made sense.

From an LSC strategy perspective, this table emphasizes the importance of being attentive to these four levels and three systems. Change activity must somehow align (or at least not strongly clash with) any of them. This is particularly useful for creating processes with a "whole systems" perspective, indicating the importance of "making sense" to all interests. The Swedish education system has integrated human dynamics work into its early schooling, realizing that conflict arises from competing assertions of what is important based on learning style. Children are taught how to work with those who have different learning styles, reflecting the belief that such styles are relatively "hard wired" and cannot simply be changed.

When working in diverse groups, an introduction to this perspective usually helps participants work together more effectively. They understand that a significant portion of conflict associated with one claiming to be right and others being

---

117 Seagal, Sandra, and David Horne. 2000. *Human Dynamics: A new framework for understanding people and realizing the potential in our organizations.* Waltham, MA USA: Pegasus Communications.

wrong, simply arises from making sense of reality from different perspectives (such as economic impact versus justice). Valuing differences, such as emphasizing wealth generation versus equity, includes valuing these different ways of making sense of the world. Of course, other differences arise from varied life experiences, values, and other sources. All this provides a valuable foundation for creating societal change systems.

Societal Change Systems

Figure 6B is a map that was produced by the Energy Ecosystem Lab, as one response to these two questions:

- How can the operating/enabling environment (ecosystem) for the electricity sector be enhanced to support the integration of the sustainability imperative?
- How can the change system for electricity be greatly strengthened?

Figure 6B: The Global Societal Change System for Electricity

The map is of websites of change initiatives working at the global level to integrate sustainability into the electricity system. The map includes only *some* of the most important global initiatives and doesn't include change initiatives working at the local, national and regional levels. How can you even grasp all these initiatives and their relationships, let alone identify effective actions for any particular change initiative given this context? These are the questions about the SCS for electricity.

To answer these questions, we looked at organizations at the global action level for electricity, which produced the web crawl map (Figure 6B) of hyperlinks between websites (see Chapter 9 for more information about web crawls). Each node is a website, and the arrows indicate a hyperlink. Larger nodes have more links. Although this global focus level produces initial skepticism amongst many as being too big and complex, it was selected for two reasons. One is that the energy sustainability issue is increasingly recognized as a requiring a global approach. While the national level is the critical regulatory level, markets, technology, companies, and other important change organizations are global issues (see Box 6C). Moreover, energy-related issues, like climate change, are clearly global.

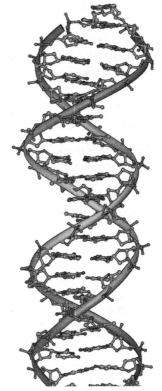

Figure 6C: The DNA double helix as a model for change and production systems

Although there is a complex interaction between global entities and sub-global ones, the global ones can be expected to aggregate major issues. The second reason for the global approach is that starting at a sub-global level always reflects that level's idiosyncratic characteristics, making model expansion problematic. On the other hand, a global approach must be applicable to other geographic levels and must not over-generalize to the point of operational irrelevance.

The project led to the concept of an SCS for electricity, as distinct from the electricity production system. The change and production systems are distinct in terms of their concerns (the integration of sustainability concerns versus electricity provision) and their stakeholders (government, business, civil society, and cross-sector entities, versus utilities and increasingly with renewable energy, other forms of service providers).[118] Visually, one way to think of this as mirroring the DNA double-helix (Figure 6C), as symbiotically intertwined with lots of connections.

---

118 Of course there are many change initiatives of utilities and other service providers.

The production system was defined as the electricity generation-transmission-distribution-consumption linear set of relationships. This is an excellent example of a complicated system. It contrasts with the complex nature of the change system, which was defined as all initiatives aimed at integrating sustainability concerns into the electricity production system. We decided to focus only on multi-organizational change initiatives, reasoning that no one organization would have much global impact and wanting to restrict initiatives to a reasonable number. This includes the initiatives of the utilities themselves, and projects of civil society, business, government, and collaborations between them (Box 6C). Because the United Nations and Bretton Woods organizations, like the World Bank, are government networks, they were included.

We wanted to develop a way to describe the SCS to help those leading change initiatives take more strategic action, and to strengthen the SCS's coherence. We identified 65 particularly important initiatives, and analyzed them in response to the question "What are they doing?" This led to the concept of SCS *change sub-systems*. We identified five of these based on analyzing change initiatives' work and key sub-system stakeholders:

Box 6C: Global Energy Change Initiatives

Some examples of global change initiatives in the electricity change ecosystem are:

- **Sustainable Energy for All (SEFA):** launched by the United Nations to bring all key actors to the table to make sustainable energy a reality for all by 2030.
- **Electricity Governance Initiative:** a network of civil society organizations dedicated to promoting transparent, inclusive, and accountable decision-making within the electricity sector.
- **MIT Energy Initiative (MITEI):** pairs MIT's world-class research teams with the best in the industry, responsible for moving the products of this collaboration into the energy marketplace.
- **ICLEI Local Governments for Sustainability Low Carbon City Program:** the world's leading association of more than 1,000 metropolises, cities, and urban regions dedicated to promoting global sustainability through local actions.
- **Global Reporting Initiative (GRI):** a multi-stakeholder network whose reporting framework promotes energy sector sustainability.
- **IRENA:** an intergovernmental organization that promotes renewable energy adoption and sustainable use.
- **Global Sustainable Energy Partnership:** comprising the world's leading electricity companies and promoting sustainable energy development.

1. **Policy Change Sub-system:** This is the policy-making system of governmental bodies, including regulators and legislators at the local, national, regional, and global levels. Other stakeholders engage in the co-production of rules and policies. This system includes efforts to change the fundamental public policy governance structures.

2. **Technological Change Sub-system:** This sub-system produces new technologies. Its initiating leadership consists of researchers and research organizations, and involves prototyping government agencies, NGOs, and companies that are developing new technologies and innovations. Scaling innovations is part of the service provider change sub-system (below) – the distinction being that different stakeholders and competencies are then engaged.

3. **Finance Change Sub-system:** This sub-system is about innovating financial approaches, influencing financial markets and creating tools to enhance capital flow to sustainable electricity production. This includes both public and private sector capital, with a particular focus on private at the moment.

4. **Service Provider Change Sub-system:** This refers to the changing infrastructure that generates, transmits, and distributes electricity. Historically, it is referred to as "electric utilities," both public and private. Some technological innovations imply significant disruptions in this subsystem, such as decentralized generation. This raises substantial business model issues.

5. **Consumer Change Sub-System:** This change sub-system is about electricity demand and how it is used, how to influence it, and consumers' changing role in the emerging service provider system. Strategically, it is useful to divide the sub-system into commercial and retail consumers.

The research team then asked the key question: "What makes a change (sub) system successful?" and "What must it do well, to realize its change goal?" Academically, these questions lead to questions about *"functions"* or "activities" that are necessary for system and network effectiveness. A review of the answers led to identifying seven activities:

1. **Visioning:** Sustainable Energy for All (SE4ALL) (see Box 6C) plays a pre-eminent system-wide role in this. It creates a much broader vision than the climate change one associated with the Kyoto Process by including the issue of electricity access, which is a big issue for developing countries. It creates coherence amongst intergovernmental organizations. The World Bank, for example, has categorically adopted SE4All goals as its own. However, every change initiative has its own particular focus that is the basis for its work and is critical for mobilizing action. The Electricity Governance Initiative, for example, holds a vision of an electricity sector that is transparent, inclusive, and has accountable decision-making. Issues of change system effectiveness raise the question of

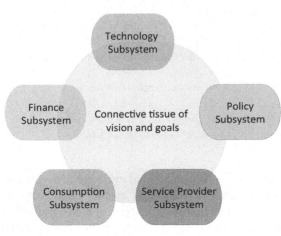

Figure 6D: SCS Electricity Change Sub-systems

whether the visions of individual change initiatives are sufficiently aligned with those of the individual sub-systems that they're part of.

2. **Organizing:** An effective SCS and LSC requires organizing effort and stakeholders in ways that provide coherent aggregation in an appropriate scale. This is most obvious at the global level where no one organization or individual can hope to have substantial impact. For a sub-system to perform effectively, numerous organizations must come together. In the public policy change sub-system, the trade associations for renewables, such as the Global Solar Alliance, play a key role in organizing the voice and effort of their emerging industry. The Carbon Disclosure Project and the Climate Action Network are organizing businesses as consumers to obtain commitments for 100 percent renewable energy use. The World Business Council for Sustainable Development is organizing electric utilities to more effectively work on the service provider sub-system.

3. **Resourcing:** Providing financial and personnel resources is foundational for the change initiatives. To study the population of global networks, organizations participating in change initiatives typically provide resources; in some cases, particularly for NGOs and research work, government and foundation funding supplements this. Development banks, like the African Development Bank, are big funders in the policy and service provider sub-systems. Climateworks, a collaboration of foundations, funds change globally.

4. **Learning:** This critical function to address complex change challenges spreads new ways of thinking about issues and taking action. Learning includes changing mindsets and building capacities at the individual, organizational, and system levels. The International Panel on Climate Change is a pre-eminent example of aggregating scientific data to propel change. REN21 offers a renowned multi-stakeholder network for collective knowledge products concerning renewable energy. The World Energy Council is a multi-stakeholder network focused on creating events, exchanges, and publications to realize an affordable, stable, and environmentally sensitive energy system for the greatest benefit to all. UNEP with developing country governments, and ICLEI Local Governments for Sustainability, also provide critical capacity development for their respective stakeholders.

5. **Measuring:** Each sub-system requires many different measures. Global inter-governmental agreements require a specific array of measures, such as those developed by the UNFCCC on national-level carbon emissions. Both the policy and consumption sub-systems depend on standard-setting measures, such as those produced by the Collaborative Labeling & Appliance Standards Program (CLASP). The Carbon Disclosure Project (CDP) develops measures for companies' and cities' carbon emissions in an attempt to influence investors in the finance and consumption sub-systems.

6. **Advocating:** To be a change sub-system, each sub-system needs the requisite pressure and energy for change. The Principles for Responsible Investment and the Global Investor Coalition on Climate Change, and its members, such as CERES' Investors Network, are good examples of advocating from within

the finance community. Climate Action Network, a global NGO network, lobbies governments at their global meetings.

7. **Prototyping:** This could be considered as part of the learning function. However, because it is critically important for change and has distinct competencies, it warrants listing as a distinct function. Usually, prototyping is associated with new technologies, such as those produced by the MIT Energy Initiative. However, actually testing new ways of organizing, new policies, new financial products, and ideas to influence consumption is also vitally important. The Renewable Energy Energy Efficiency Partnership (REEEP) focuses on prototyping both new technologies and financing approaches.

Table 6C: The Systemic Change Matrix

	Policy	Technology	Finance	Service Provision	Consumption
Visioning					
Organizing					
Learning					
Measuring					
Financing					
Advocating					
Prototyping					

Breaking down SCSs into change sub-systems and functions allows us to describe the SCS, laid out in Table 6C, as the Systemic Change Matrix. This is a map of the SCS (Figure 6B is also an SCS map). For change makers, this table lays the foundation for doing a few important things. One is analyzing the activities of any individual change organization by applying this framework to its work to produce a "change profile." We did this with all World Bank energy change initiatives, classifying them into cells of the Table. Of course, some fit into more than one cell. This exercise then provides a *map* of the Bank's change initiatives and facilitates raising strategic questions with greater clarity:

- Do they reflect the Bank's distinctive and core competencies – is the Bank the one that should be doing it?
- Is there somewhere the Bank *should* be active that it isn't, given its competencies and mandate?
- Is there an unproductive duplication of effort amongst activities?
- Are there synergies to be realized that could enhance impact?

These are questions about the Bank's *roles* in the energy SCS. Verna Allee taught me the importance of roles. She developed a way to map roles in a system, called value network analysis (Chapter 9).[119] Most people think in terms of people, organizations, programs, and projects. Any one of these may have more than one

---

119 Allee, Verna. 2015. *Value Networks and the True Nature of Collaboration:* Meghan-Kiffer Press

role, and any one role may be played by more than one of them. "Role" refers to what they are doing in terms of what a *system* needs done to realize its goals. Roles are nouns, and what they exchange are nouns as well. For example, the electricity SCS needs a "consumer organizer" role to influence consumption. Doing this, requires financial resources, which implies the roles of "financier;" money flows from the latter to the former. The value of this perspective is that it shifts attention to the *system's* needs, rather than those of the individual, project, or organization. This is, of course, a critical step in building coherence and accountability to SCS needs.

But, even more usefully, the Matrix provides a tool for building a collective understanding amongst all change initiatives of the change system. Of course, the Matrix can be filled in by traditional researchers. However, it is better to fill it in through a meeting of change initiatives, and to discuss the questions proposed for the Bank above. This was what we did at the Bocconi meeting, with some leaders of change initiatives in the global electricity SCS. They were excited – relieved? – to finally have a way to wrap their heads around, and think strategically about, their own initiative in relation to others. They discovered, for example, that two initiatives were developing global campaigns around consumption (the Advocating-Consumption cell), which led to discussions about beneficial collaboration.

Box 6D: Creating Coherence in the Financing Function: The RE-AMP Example[1]

By the beginning of this millennium, a plethora of organizations were working to advance clean energy across the six-state Upper Midwest region of the United States. In 2003, the Garfield Foundation committed $2.5 million over five years to determine if systems thinking and a networked approach could lead to greater effort alignment amongst funders and grantees. From an initial gathering of seven funders and 12 nonprofits, today more than 160 organizations are participating in the RE-AMP network with a powerful regional SCS approach. A key activity of their development was use of Managing for Clarity mapping (Chapter 9) to create a shared understanding of their change system; this new knowledge helped identify synergies, respond to gaps in effort, and address unproductive redundancies.

Through their collaborative mapping the NGOs and foundations participating in the Garfield project identified six core strategies to support clean energy. This resulted in six working groups: coal, clean energy, energy efficiency, carbon regulation, transportation, and funders. Funders agreed to align their programs around the five issue working groups; some provide funding for one, some for several. This has led to better collaboration and alignment of activity. There are on-going interactions as a network to learn collectively and adjust the programs in response to the changing context. This has vastly increased effectiveness in such things as closing of coal-fueled plants and legislation supporting a clean energy future.

---

1 McLeod Grant, Heather. 2010. "Transformer: How to build a network to change a system A Case Study of the RE-AMP Energy Network." San Francisco, CA, USA: Monitor Institute.

Some categories for action emerged for which the matrix and parts of it could be used to support coherence and convergence:

- **By geography:** Regional, national, and sub-national jurisdictions can be the basis for applying the analysis to improve change efforts. Different change issues will have different geographic imperatives. For electricity, the national level is particularly important.
- **By sub-systems:** Each matrix column can be the focus of assessing the workings of sub-system functions. For example, in the financing sub-system, organizing financial institutions or prototyping new financial products might be problematic.
- **By change initiative:** Participants saw value in applying the Matrix to their own activities to sharpen their own strategy and priorities, as suggested earlier for the World Bank.
- **By change project or technology:** Issues surrounding a particular activity, such as cross-boundary transmission lines or the adoption of a decentralized energy grid, could benefit from applying the Matrix analysis.
- **By cell(s) or function:** There could be value in taking on a particular function within or across one or more sub-systems. For example, who is doing the measuring in the public policy and finance sub-systems? Are measuring activities comprehensive? Are there integration and comparability issues?

Efforts to create coherence already exist in many SCSs. Some of these have limited geography and stakeholders, such as RE-AMP (Box 6D). In energy, this is essentially the task of SE4All, a multi-stakeholder global initiative that arose from the ashes of the Kyoto Accord. This SCS and matrix perspectives suggest that it should:

- Frame its work as stewarding SCS development, rather than getting involved in any way in technology and the production system development. SE4All should focus entirely on supporting healthy relationships and flows within the SCS, reflecting complex adaptive system (These systems are discussed in Chapter 2) activities of self-organizing, emergence, directional nudges, learning and experimentation.
- Organize activities around sub-systems. This could mean creating five core activities around five sub-systems.
- Create an on-going analysis of the SCS health and sticking points. Participatory analyses can help identify high leverage points to support coherence to guide action. For example, they may identify a specific Matrix cell (e.g., consumption-resourcing) or function (e.g., advocating) that needs attention and then action can be undertaken, reflecting CAS logics.
- Access and develop LSC competencies. A high-functioning change system will have good knowledge about change processes and the capacity to implement them. This includes things such as high competency in scenario development, generative, participatory, and other meeting processes, conflict resolution, mapping, and big data management (Chapter 9).

Box 6E: Healthy Cities: Creating, Scaling Cross-silo Coherence

Integration and crossing silo issues (e.g., water, education, and health), knowledge disciplines, and stakeholders have become particularly popular in the last five years. It is at the heart of the work of Healthy Cities (HC). That network came about as a result of a 1984 conference, and started in earnest in Europe in 1988. HC emphasizes a place-based and holistic view of "health." Within Europe, there are more than 90 Healthy Cities and 30 National Healthy Cities Networks with a designated status from the World Health Organization (WHO) Europe. There are participating HCs around the world. However, their number and degree of engagement have ebbed and flowed. A healthy city is one:

...that is continually creating and improving those physical and social environments and expanding those community resources which enable people to mutually support each other in performing all the functions of life and in developing to their maximum potential.[1]

A city is seen as a networked ecology of organizations, people, and the environment. The HC definition focuses on a continual process of becoming, rather than outcomes. Participation and empowerment are central. HC describes itself as a "movement." However, its multi-stakeholder quality is critical and it can be seen as a form of Action Network and SCS stewarding (Chapter 7) that transcends the movement concept. HC depends heavily on city government. It represents a series of five-year phases of a WHO project. Each participating city makes commitments, financially and in terms of actions. They must demonstrate that they have in place:

- multi-sectoral support for principles and goals;
- an identified co-ordinator;
- a high level steering group;
- a city health profile; and
- integrated strategic planning mechanisms.

A common theme of all the phases is learning and innovation; the WHO umbrella provides legitimacy and space for this. The HC phases are not about applying known "solutions", but developing new approaches, sharing and adapting. In contrast to traditional health strategies, the first five years focused on creating new structures to act as change agents and introducing new ways of working for health in cities. There were three new types of approaches identified:

- partnerships to raise awareness and develop activities;
- networks to exchange information and models of good practice; and
- intermediate support organizations to promote participation and self-help.[2]

Although today this may seem mundane, remember the year was 1994. HC reported:

"Healthy Cities ideas lead to innovation in policies, programs and actions. City projects experiment with new organizational forms such as networks and "one stop" support agencies for citizens. They also promote activities that develop structures and skills for collaboration and exchange. Practical know-how is exchanged at both the local and international levels. Confronting major urban issues – pollution, social deprivation, urban decay – city councils and governments need far-reaching strategies to produce sustainable solutions. An awareness of health impact adds value to strategies for urban renewal and the environment, and the process of public involvement mobilizes greater resources to create effective solutions."[3]

Themes are an important part of the coherence strategy. Themes of the subsequent years were:

- Phase II (1993-97): It was more action-oriented, with a strong emphasis on healthy public policy and comprehensive city health planning.
- Phase III (1997-2002): The core themes were equity, sustainable development and social development, with a focus on integrated planning for health development.
- Phase IV (2003-08): This Phase emphasized equity, tackling the determinants of health, sustainable development, and participatory and democratic governance.
- Phase V (2009-14): This Phase prioritized health and health equity in all local policies.
- Phase VI (2015-20): This Phase supports cities in strengthening their efforts to bring key stakeholders together to work for health and well-being, to harness leadership, innovation and change, and to enhance the potential to resolve local public health challenges.

These themes are supported by annual meetings organized with the support of WHO-Europe. Global meetings are self-organized on an ad hoc basis.

The impact of the WHO European Healthy Cities Network Phase V (focused on health equity) was described in a 2015 report as:

- Translating policy into action - a 'living laboratory' to test countries' strategic health policy commitments (for countries that have member cities);
- Addressing health inequities - health equity has not only remained a critical concern, but has also become an important focus of policy and institutional development in member cities;
- Integrating new governance - the formal recognition of, and commitment to, taking concrete action on governance as a critical driver for health development at every level of society and government has been successfully adapted; and
- Taking innovative action - health equity and governance thinking have been used to develop innovative approaches to broad intersectoral policy development, health equity, health impact assessment, determinants of health and lifestyle interventions, healthy ageing, urban planning and more broadly supportive environments for health.[4]

1   Duhl, Len, and Trevor Hancock. 1988. "Promoting Health in the Urban Context." in *Healthy Cities Paper* No. 1, edited by FADL. Copenhagen, Denmark: WHO Healthy Cities Project Office.

2   WHO. 1994. "Action for Health in Cities." Copenhagen, Denmark: World Health Organisation - Regional Office for Europe. p. 41

3   Ibid. p. 6

4   WHO Europe. (2015). Special report on Healthy Cities in Europe launched.   Retrieved Nov. 1, 2015, from http://www.euro.who.int/en/health-topics/health-determinants/social-determinants/news/news/2015/06/special-report-on-healthy-cities-in-europe-launched

This thinking about the SCS needs much greater development. This is only one way to think about it. Developing a robust SCS in this way could be the task of a group of diverse change initiatives – a sort of multi-stakeholder activity described in Chapter 7 as SCS Stewarding. At different times of any issue's development, different sub-systems/functions/cells will be particularly important. Moreover, the matrix should not be employed dogmatically – different issues will have different sub-systems. The sub-systems will also change as transformation advances. This is seen with the distinction between consumer and service provider sub-systems producing prosumers. However, the functions are generic and will remain constant across all issues.

With this approach, it is very easy to feel overwhelmed with the scale and complexity of tasks. To overcome this, combining audaciousness with humbleness is critical. It is not about "doing it all" or feeling responsible for "it all." That is impossible. Rather, one should use these frameworks as ways to identify some leverage points and/or to understand the leverage point you are working on. The goal is to broaden your understanding of your change ecosystem and your ability to act strategically as opportunities emerge. After all, the added ingredient is the dynamism of change fields: emerging and declining opportunities require reflection about the hard questions of whether to persist in a direction or shift in response to a new one.

Societal Change Systems and Social Movements

Social movements (as we know them) are a large impact, 19th century phenomenon. Many working on transformation promote them as "the answer." They certainly play an important role in developing a powerful SCS. Social movements are the subject of much valuable and relevant analysis.[120] They are associated with three elements:

1. Campaigns: A sustained, organized public effort making collective claims on target authorities;
2. Tools: The employment of combinations from among the following political actions: the creation of special-purpose associations and coalitions, public meetings, solemn processions, vigils, rallies, demonstrations, petition drives, statements to and in the public media, and pamphleteering; and
3. Profile: Participants' concerted public representations of: worthiness, unity, numbers, and commitment on the part of themselves and/or their constituencies.[121]

---

120 Some classics are: McAdam, Doug, John D. McCarthy, and Mayer N. Zald. 1996. *Comparative Perspectives on Social Movements: Political Opportunities, Mobilizing Structures, and Cultural Framings.* Cambridge, UK: Cambridge University Press. Tarrow, Sidney, and J Tollefson. 1994. *Power in movement: Social movements, collective action and politics:* Cambridge Univ Press. and Tilly, Charles, and Lesley J. Wood. 2013. *Social Movements, 1768 - 2012 (3rd edition).* Boulder, CO, USA: Paradigm Publishers.
121 Tilly, Charles, and Lesley J. Wood. 2013. *Social Movements, 1768 - 2012 (3rd edition).* Boulder, CO, USA: Paradigm Publishers.

Mahatma Gandhi noted that attitudes towards great social movements pass through five stages: indifference, ridicule, abuse, repression, and respect.[122]

Generally speaking, social movements are usually necessary, but insufficient, to realize transformation. Movements are particularly powerful when the issue is in the meme sphere; that is, when the issue revolves around a belief or cultural quality, such as with the marriage equality case. Table 6A on sectoral strengths and weaknesses and the systemic change matrix illustrates social movements' strengths and weaknesses related to their civil society qualities. In Table 6B's matrix function, social movements' advocacy role is particularly critical to building and maintaining stakeholders' attention on the need for change, such as in the South Africa apartheid case. Movements also serve important visioning and organizing functions; learning, measuring, and prototyping are often less focal parts of their work or at least ones in which Movements have less pronounced competency. They usually play a negligible financing role, and their resource advantage is people power. In the organizing sphere, their activity is generally restricted to communities and NGO participation, with representatives sometimes participating in multi-stakeholder efforts. Looking at change sub-systems for energy, social movements' role is particularly important in the policy and consumer sub-systems, where members can act as citizens and consumers. In the technology, finance, and service provider sub-systems, they play a more modest role, even in terms of advocacy and organizing.

Social movements are particularly good at advocating an identified "solution," such as with marriage equality. That issue had clearly targeted laws and regulations around which a campaign could be developed to shift memes. Social movements on their own are insufficient for today's challenges, such as climate change, and upgrading the welfare-nation-state-based "solutions" to global responses to perennial issues, such as security, health, education, and the provision of basic physical necessities. One inadequacy of social movements in addressing these issues is that the "answers" to complex issues are not "known" and inquiry is required. For example, we have only a rough outline of what a sustainable enterprise and economy look like – we have no great examples at scale. This means we need to find structures and processes that support an on-going, determined, and focused drive to invent their emergence.

A second inadequacy of social movements for today's complex challenges is that answers cannot be developed by social movements alone. They require a complex inter-weaving of social *and* physical technological experimentation. The answer to universal health care globally is connected to new ways of organizing, new information, and medical technologies and life sciences. Enormous advances have been made in renewable energy to address climate change concerns. However, substantial technological issues remain, such as storing energy, as well as substantial social and power issues, including transforming (dismantling?) utilities and carbon industries into sustainable energy enterprises.

---

122 Gandhi, Mahatma. 1980. All men are brothers: Autobiographical reflections: A&C Black. McAdam, Doug, John D. McCarthy, and Mayer N. Zald. 1996. Comparative Perspectives on Social Movements: Political Opportunities, Mobilizing Structures, and Cultural Framings. Cambridge, UK: Cambridge University Press.

And a third weakness of social movements is that addressing today's complex challenges requires massive financial resources. Ensuring sufficient food for billions of people while sustaining bio-diversity requires massive investment, and mobilizing financial resources are not social movements' strong point.

These are only weaknesses of social movements if unreasonable expectations are placed upon them to "produce transformation." The sectoral and SCS analysis support defining reasonable expectations.

Emerging and Scaling

Realizing a true transformation and tipping point requires lots of people and organizations to change their ways of thinking, connecting, and producing. People often talk about scaling as though it is not happening. It is, but one problem is that the changes, as Chapter 3 cases illustrated, take time. I see lots of scaling change efforts, which makes me wonder if it is invisible to many because they look for it with a traditional hierarchical mindset. Instead, it really requires an emergence mindset.

The Systemic Change Matrix suggest one approach to scaling revolves around connecting existing change initiatives and developing their collective power as a societal change system. The core of any scaling approach requires refocusing effort from experiments and innovation, to broadening engagement. It requires the competencies and resources of all sectors working together.

Michele-Lee Moore and colleagues looked at the scaling challenge through the Applied Dissemination (AD) initiative of the J.W. McConnell Family Foundation in Canada.[123] Over a period of seven years, leaders of more than a dozen diverse national-level initiatives met to investigate scaling efforts. Three types of scaling surfaced:

- **Scaling Out:** One strategy involves replicating programs in new geographies. Sometimes, this is "true" replication; other times, there is a heavy adaptation of principles to new contexts. The latter is undoubtedly more relevant to transformation. People who embrace this strategy often talk about franchising, seeding, developing new branches or nodes, and creating networks. An example is the SGI case in Chapter 3, with a global Buddhist network of Chapters and Districts for human revolution.

- **Scaling Up:** This emphasizes "reform" in terms of changing law and policy. This can support transformation if changes in law and policy reflect the findings of transformational experiments. Federal German law is a very large-scale experiment that is key to the country's energy transformation.

- **Scaling Deep:** This scaling type focuses on the memes sphere as the core transformational focus that will shift other systems. The particular power of this sphere for transformation is reflected in its position in Chapter 2,

123 Moore, Michele-Lee, Darcy Riddell, and Dana Vocisano. 2015. "Scaling Out, Scaling Up, Scaling Deep: Strategies of Non-profits in Advancing Systemic Social Innovation." *Journal of Corporate Citizenship* 2015(58):67-84. See also: Westley, Frances, Nino Antadze, Darcy J. Riddell, Kirsten Robinson, and Sean Geobey. 2014. "Five configurations for scaling up social innovation: case examples of nonprofit organizations from Canada." *The Journal of Applied Behavioral Science* 50(3):234-60.

encompassing three other change spheres (individual, technological, and institutional). The scaling deep work is about spreading new big ideas; this emphasizes the importance of learning systems that reflect the learning imperative associated with "emergence." The marriage equality case focused on broadening the marriage meme. The South Africa case is an example of forcing a change in memes on a resistant group that holds power.

Moore and colleagues also identify "cross-cutting" as a scaling type that integrates all these strategies. This also reflects the analysis of Chapter 3 cases. The marriage meme scaling deep transformation, for example, spread through institutional reform as a scaling up strategy. In addition to scaling up, the German energy transition has involved spreading prosumer entrepreneurs as a scaling out strategy.

Chapter 7

Organizing Change Initiatives

Chapter Summary

Historic organizing approaches cannot adequately address today's transformation change challenges, nor develop powerful societal change systems. In response to this gap, we are seeing the emergence of organizational innovations. Three are presented here: social (innovation) labs, communities of practice, and action networks. Collectively, these approaches power the emergence of societal change systems. There is a need for societal change system stewarding as a new organizing activity.

Transformational change efforts require organizing approaches, power arrangements, and decision-making processes with three critical capacities. These are the abilities: (1) to identify transformational inventions, including adapting and refining diverse contexts; (2) to realize the breadth of the required transformation — in our era, often globally — so inventions do not simply become idiosyncratic islands (such as, cooperatives and intentional communities) in a sea of other logic; and (3) to sustain and promote transformation for the lengthy necessary periods — the examples in Chapter 3 suggest that this period is often decades. In many cases, the organizing structures are not simply supporting a transition, they *are* the transition to a significant degree. That is to say, they should not be thought of as "temporary," because they have long-term roles in ensuring flexibility, resilience, and common good qualities in a flourishing future.

There are three organizing innovations from the past two decades that strike me as reflecting, if not "the answer" to addressing today's complex issues, at least a very good basis for advancing the development of an answer: social (innovation) labs, communities of practice, and action networks. Their work is critical to developing the societal change systems (SCSs) needed to address the huge transformation challenges facing us today. Combining them to realize synergies holds great promise. However, we also need to develop a new organizing effort, SCS Stewarding. Let's look at these approaches individually.

Social Innovation Labs

In June 2004, near the North Sea in Bergen (the Netherlands), an unusual meeting took place. It was unusual because of:
- Its goal of transforming the food system to reflect environmental impact, social equity, and financial concerns;
- The mix of its 33 participants, which included multinational corporations (e.g., Unilever), global NGOs (e.g., Oxfam), foundations (e.g., Kellogg), government officials (e.g., the Secretary of Agrarian Reform from Brazil), a major bank, and a farm workers' leader; and
- The intention to develop and apply leading transformational change knowledge to develop experiments to test and develop responses to the sustainable food goal.

Calling itself the Sustainable Food Lab (SFL), the group identified their main goal as the generation of:

> transformational change of the mainstream food supply by providing key stakeholders in government, industry and civil society with a laboratory where they can create innovations that generate economic value while also meeting social and environmental goals. SFL provides not only this innovation laboratory, but also research, assessment, shared learning, and leadership capacity-building expertise so that transformational change can include leaders themselves, their organizations, and the food sector as a whole.[124]

Over the next two years, the SFL grew to include more than 70 leaders from three continents undertaking six activities. These included:
- A Responsible Commodities team that was developing and testing a benchmarking tool for commodity standards, informed by current commodity roundtable discussions on palm oil, sugar, soy, salmon, and other commodities; and
- A Business Coalition formed by a dozen food-related corporations to drive supply chain and business practice changes, with an initial focus on integrated pest management, animal welfare, packaging, and returning more upstream value to family farmers.

The SFL exemplifies an approach to developing social innovation that is referred to as social (innovation) labs. This approach is associated with a 1960s socio-technical systems perspective that emphasizes the interaction between people and complex

---

124 SFL. Circa 2006. "SFL Phase II (version 4)." Sustainable Food Lab.

work environments. The Tavistock Institute, John Rawlings, Eric Trist, and Fred Emery (all influenced by Kurt Lewin of action research fame) pioneered group and organizational behavior development approaches in the 1950s and 1960s that grew into whole systems processes (e.g., Future Search). Today's labs are the product of three additional roots: design labs (for industrial and architectural design), computer modeling (e.g., system dynamics mapping), and social innovation approaches (e.g., social enterprise).[125] Furthermore, these labs reflect a great deal of learning from many projects by NGOs and others; the distinction is the approach's explicitness and discipline designed around learning, invention, and inquiry.

There are hundreds of social labs globally today. Some are focused on a specific issue, such as the Finance Innovation Lab (United Kingdom), whereas others have broader goals, such as the Social Innovation Lab at Johns Hopkins University (US), the BRAC's Social Innovation Lab (Bangladesh), and UNICEF's Global Innovation Lab. With the Global Organizational Learning and Development Network (GOLDEN), I led an attempt to develop Ecosystems Labs, focused on shifting the operating environment (i.e., the policies, markets, and values) of industries to support sustainable enterprise development. (Its Energy Ecosystem Lab produced the SCS concept and the Systemic Change Matrix described in Chapter 6.)

After reviewing the social lab phenomenon to produce the "Social Innovation Lab Guide," the authors defined a social lab "as a process, one that is intended to support multi-stakeholder groups in addressing a complex social problem."[126] They identified five elements that labs should have:

1. A deliberate intent to transform (as opposed to pushing for incremental change and reform);
2. The ability to take advantage of transitions, thresholds, and crises;
3. The drive to be focused not just on inventing (prototyping), but also on innovating (broadening applications);
4. The focus to pay attention to cross-scale (local to global) dynamics; and
5. The capability to catalyze a range of potential innovations (rather than a few).

Most individuals involved in social innovation labs would agree with these elements. However, they might propose riffs on the very detailed and specific methodology presented in the Guide as a three-step process that includes: (1) initiation, (2) research and preparation, and (3) three workshops: seeing the system, designing, and prototyping. Labs are a process to identify potential inventions that can lead to transformational innovation, rather than the realization of a "tipping point." The latter requires a much larger effort.

Reos Partners has had a particularly important role in developing what they call "Change Labs". Drawing largely on that experience, in *The Social Labs Revolution*, Zaid Hassan writes with scars and smiles from developing numerous labs.

---

125 Westley, Frances, Sam Laban, Cherul Rose, Katharine McGowan, Kirsten Robinson, Ola Tjornbo, and Mark Tovey. Circa 2015. "Social Innovation Lab Guide." Waterloo, Ontario, Canada: Waterloo Institute for Social Innovation and Resilience.
126 Ibid. p. 1

He defines a social innovation lab as a "strategic approach." He goes on to make the following points:

- Strategy is "social" in that it shifts the locus of efforts from already thinly stretched government technocrats to a wider stakeholder base;
- A social lab is a gathering, a coming together of people across the silos that characterize dominant social structures, to attend to a social challenge for as long as necessary to shift the situation;
- Social labs require that participants operate from a place of inner volition and drive;
- A social lab must also work in an experimental and iterative way to address challenges. A program is very different from a lab;
- They must be systemic in orientation, aiming to address social issues at their root cause (My comment: But do systemic challenges have root causes or do they arise from knotty systemic interactions?);
- Labs, whatever their focus, must put inquiry — and not just advocacy — at the heart of their activities.[127]

Labs are clearly about transformation and emergence, in contrast to traditional planning models. They are about advocacy *and* inquiry, with inquiry being dominant, in contrast to social movements. In terms of the four strategies discussed in Chapter 5, labs clearly fit within the Co-creating Change strategy.

Table 7A: Traditional organization – Innovation Lab Structural distinctions[128]

Traditional organization	Lab
Hierarchy	Collective
Static	Dynamic
Singular (expert) focus	Multidisciplinary
Risk-averse	Open to failure
Operations-oriented	Systems approach
Market-driven	User-centric
Production outcomes	Social change outcomes
Linear	Iterative
Prescribed success	Conditional success

Coming from the design root tradition, Lisa Torjman contrasts lab structures with traditional organizations in Table 7A. A social lab's structure shifts throughout its developmental stages. In the early stages, sponsors support lab initiation, and they may continue to provide "Secretariat" organizing support. However, in later stages, labs formed around a specific issue tend to act independently. Developing labs has become the focus of an array of social enterprises, consultancies, and universities,

---

127   Hassan, Zaid. 2014. *The Social Labs Revolution: A New Approach to Solving our Most Complex Challenges.* San Francisco, CA, USA: Berrett-Hoehler.
128   Torjman, Lisa. 2012. "Labs: Designing the Future." MaRS Solutions Lab.

such as MaRS in Toronto, the global network of Reos Partners, the Helsinki Design Lab, IDEO in San Francisco, and the d.Lab at Stanford University.

The SFL itself grew out of an education program called the Global Leadership Institute, the leadership of which included Peter Senge (MIT, *The Fifth Discipline*) and Adam Kahane (now with Reos Partners); program participants included people from Unilever and the Kellogg Foundation. They identified sustainable food as a global issue requiring attention beyond any of their individual capacities. The "U-Process,"[129] articulated by Otto Scharmer (who works closely with Senge), was very important to their subsequent approach.

The SFL developed into three leadership groups. Executive Champions are people in senior leadership positions who stay informed about the lab's activities and provide feedback, credibility, and support to mobilize further resources. Advisors are expert resource individuals who provide advice, research support, and intellectual input. The Secretariat provides organizing support to keep everything moving smoothly.

However, the core organizing component of most labs is *experiments* made up of organizational participants. Participating organizations must commit time, and often money, to a lab. Individuals are not organizational "representatives," but rather must be committed change agents with passion and influence. It is not about "voting" on a matter and then watching others take action — it is about stepping forward to take collaborative action to advance commonly identified opportunities.

"Membership" in a lab, in terms of governance decisions, places second in importance when compared with active participation. The structure focuses on supporting, rather than controlling, participants. An appropriate legal form for international multi-stakeholder collaborations, which labs often are, does not exist. Sometimes, the legal form is found within a university or research institute; sometimes it exists as an NGO. As Hassan comments, overdo the governance structure at your own peril! Keep thinking in terms of "emergence" based on experience rather than theoretical design, which may limit your options.

Within this structure, labs develop a pace of life. There is a general direction, rather than a detailed plan, supported by *agile* processes for timely responses to knowledge as it arises. Labs undertake multiple experiments — reflecting the need when working with complex challenges to try a range of actions to see what might work. Project teams formed around a particular experimental issue and/or action are the core work units. Stakeholders in an issue identify and undertake actions to address the issue through "prototype" projects. "The point of a prototype," Zaid explains, "is to start to deliver results as soon as possible and, in the process of iterating, to improve. That is the difference between a pilot and a prototype."[130]

Experimentation includes important collective reflection and learning processes integrated into action. Hassan describes "scrums" that might be weeklong periods and "sprints" that are daylong periods. There are orga-

---

129 Scharmer, C Otto. 2009. *Theory U: Learning from the future as it emerges*: Berrett-Koehler Publishers.

130 Hassan, Zaid. 2014. *The Social Labs Revolution: A New Approach to Solving our Most Complex Challenges*. San Francisco, CA, USA: Berrett-Hoehler. p. 107

Box 7A: The Sustainable Food Lab Projects[1]

Interview with Hal Hamilton, Founding Executive Director – Sustainable Food Lab

Most projects (experiments) are partnerships between one company and a few NGOs or universities in particular supply chains. Therefore, one company will work on a supply chain for dried vegetables for their soups; we'll work on a specific supply chain for Ethiopian farmers producing beans that go first to an Italian wholesaler, next to a British processor, and finally to a British retailer as baked beans with a social responsibility component. Or, we work with clusters of companies to reduce the climate footprint of their products, which might include tomato, wheat, beef, or dairy production, for example.

We have the largest concentration of supply chain projects in two different areas. One focuses on ways in which supply chains affect the livelihood of small farmers, and the other focuses on ways in which the climate footprint of a supply chain can be quantified with targets set and reduction documented. Climate and livelihood are two main topic areas these days. Some work is also being done on shorter supply chains in the US, where there is an interest in local or regional food.

1 Hamilton, H. (undated) *The Sustainable Food Lab Interview with Hal Hamilton/Interviewer: L. News.* http://www.sustainablefoodlab.org/images/PDF/LIM_interview_with_HH_Issue_112.pdf.

nized daily or less frequent group "check-ins" and progress review cycles to continually and quickly adjust actions and direction based on experience and learning. In other words, there is a disciplined learning process with conscious feedback loops.

Over longer periods, there may be meetings across project teams to share knowledge or investigate new issues; these can include learning journeys, such as site visits (see Chapter 9). Annual reviews by the lead governance group are common.

Communities of Practice

Launched in December 2001, with the support of the Dutch Government, the Collaborative Program on Water and Climate (CPWC) began as a dialogue between diverse stakeholders in the water and climate communities. The Group's concern was climate change impact on water and communities. Their goal was to seek out and assemble scientific knowledge, generate widespread awareness, and identify policy and management options that build coping capacity, making this knowledge available to the most affected communities and decision-makers. Eighteen sites participated, including:

- The Regional Platform of the Small Valley Alert and Flood Vulnerability Reduction Program (SVP) in Central America;
- Bangladesh organizations, including IUCN, that addressed rising sea levels and the salinization of farmland;

- Organizations in the Niger basin of West Africa concerned about increasing drought conditions; and
- Water management organizations dealing with climate change adaptation issues in Russia's Lena basin.

In 2003, I connected with the CPWC, as a result of my work on global networks that address change challenges. Working with Bill Snyder, the community of practice (CoP) guru who coauthored numerous books on the topic with Etienne Wenger,[131] we put together a project to support the CPWC's learning objectives by experimenting with ways to develop its virtual capacity to interact as a CoP. We had painful experiences trying to use first-generation webinar technology, as well as bandwidth challenges and other issues. However, we

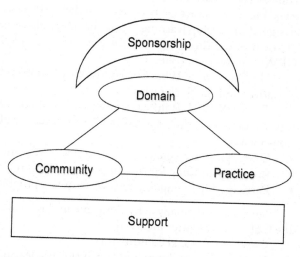

Figure 7A: Structural Elements of Communities of Practice

did advance the understanding of CoP dynamics and structures.

The CPWC aimed to support participating initiatives' activities by forming a network to foster and facilitate communication between parties involved in similar activities between the river basins and other regions. Examples varied from the transfer of technical knowledge (land use, satellite data, seasonal forecasting, and modeling) to capacity building (training and educational tools), as well as the use of awareness-raising materials.

We organized a pilot initiative to explore CoP model application, which included three initiatives: Central America, West Africa, and Bangladesh. We aimed to create interactions within and between them that could represent a microcosm for the CPWC, as a whole.

Figure 7A presents major components in a CoP system, and also demonstrates how we experimented with its application to the CPWC.

---

131 Snyder, William M., and Etienne Wenger. 2004. "Our World as a Learning System: a Communities-of-Practice Approach." Pp. 35-58 in *Creating a learning culture: strategy, technology, and practice*, edited by Marcia L. Conner and James G. Clawson: The Press Syndicate of the University of Cambridge.
Wenger, Etienne C., and William M. Snyder. 2000. "Communities of Practice: The Organizational Frontier." *Harvard Business Review* (January - February):139-45.
Wenger, Etienne, Richard McDermott, and William M. Snyder. 2002. *Cultivating Communities of Practice*. Boston, MA, USA: Harvard Business School Press.

The Domain What: It might be an issue, such as "sustainable water use," or a sub-issue, such as "communications strategies in water." For the CPWC, the over-arching questions concern how climate change impacts connected to water can be mitigated.

The Practice How: These are activities that support capacity development to address the "what." For the CPWC, there was most obviously practice at the 18 sites. However, "practice" here refers to the CoP activity and personal interactions designed to develop learning — via the telephone, email, and webinars —between (1) each of the three sites and Snyder and me, and (2) between all of us and the CPWC Secretariat, collectively.

The Community Who: The community comprised both people involved in the initiatives and the Secretariat.

The CPWC CoP infrastructure was made up of two key components. One was *sponsors,* including the CPWC Secretariat itself and a funder, whose functions included:

- Developing strategic goals with and for the community;
- Providing funding for the support team and regional coordinators; and
- Participating in ongoing reviews to assess progress and foster development.

Support for the daily activities came in the form of Snyder and me developing the CoP. Our activities included:

- Coaching regional coordinators;
- Guiding the development of each site as a learning system case;
- Coordinating the global community;
- Liaising with sponsors;
- Developing the technology platform — including teleconference events and the website (for storing documents, posting messages, and keeping a member directory, etc.); and
- Documenting the methods, results, lessons learned, and proposals for future steps.

Support locally came in the form of *local coordinators* — the lead contacts at each site — who led activities at the regional level to:

- Identify local players to participate in regional learning system initiatives;
- Develop regional case studies — as a baseline for identifying local improvement opportunities and for sharing insights and innovations across regions;
- Coordinate peer-to-peer and cross-level learning at the regional level; and
- Liaise with local institutions: government agencies, NGOs, funders, and others.

We also deepened understanding of the CoP concept by applying it to the Central American site that consisted of river basins experiencing increased flash flooding. To respond to this, it was developing an early warning and other response systems. This is represented in Figure 7B below. It emphasizes the importance of thinking of the CoP as stakeholder groups with common interests. There is the CoP of the CPWC, which is organized around the "water and climate change" domain and consists of 18 initiatives; each of these initiatives is in itself a CoP.

Within the initiatives, there are distinct domains. For example, in the Central American one, there are:

- Policy makers;
- The scientific and technical community;
- Each individual river basin; and
- The river basins collectively.

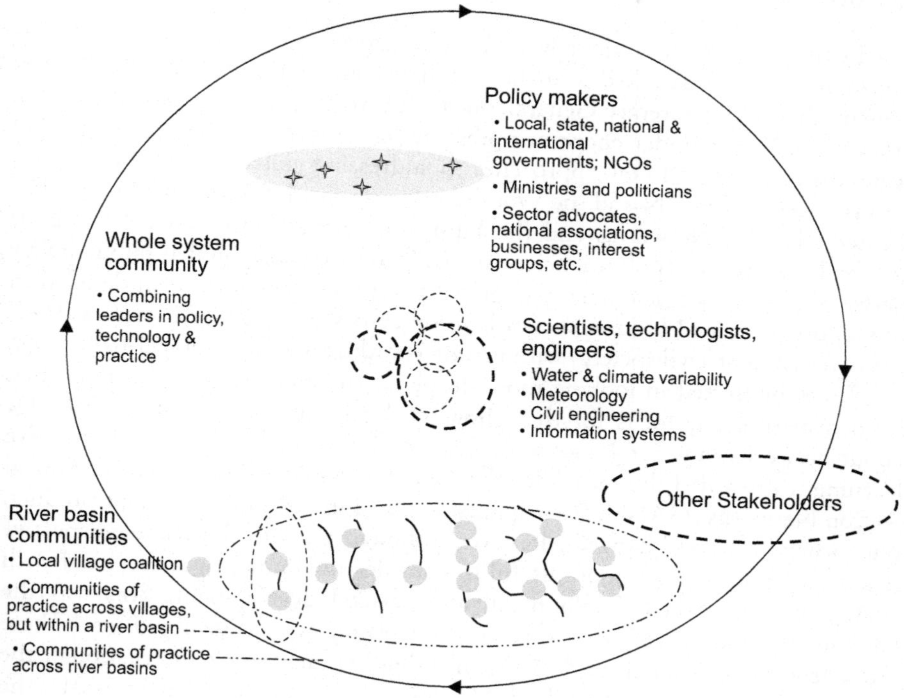

Figure 7B: Central American Small Valleys Project, as a Set of CoPs

Each of these sub-CoPs have their own special issues that require experimentation and learning. Furthermore, there is the issue of how sub-CoPs interact effectively — a consideration that also requires experimentation and learning. If all this seems complex ... well, it is. However, the CoP framework provides a way to organize the complexity and support the emergence of responses. This approach significantly shifts the focus of many people from solely engineering-type technical solutions, helping them understand that their work also involves creating new types of social interpersonal ties, as well as a robust learning system.

While Snyder and I considered the CPWC project a successful learning experience, we did not generate a robust or ongoing CoP infrastructure. There were several reasons behind this. The major one was that there was too much divergence between the sites' issues (the "what") to inspire an ongoing CoP — the local impact of the "water and climate" concept was simply too diverse. A second reason was local coordinators' limited time. Furthermore, we never held face-to-face meetings, which would have built a much stronger foundation. Finally, at the time (2003), the webinar/teleconference/Internet connections we were using were not sufficiently advanced.

Chapter 9 discusses learning methods and tools in greater detail.

Action Networks (ANs)

Because of my work globally on business-government-civil society collaboration, in 1999, I was asked to make a modest contribution to a report for Kofi Annan, then UN Secretary General, on the future of global governance. At that time, the UN was under enormous pressure to "reform." The Secretary General wanted to understand new approaches to addressing global issues. The report, co-produced by the UN and the World Bank, was entitled "Critical Choices: The United Nations, Networks, and the Future of Global Governance."[132] It built on the lead author's (political scientist Wolfgang Reinicke) "global public policy network"[133] concept. The emerging global governance network form detailed in the report combined *horizontal* coordination across organizational sectors (business-government-civil society) with *vertical* coordination (from global-to-local).

I was interested in looking more deeply at these emerging networks. They, in fact, became my focus for the following decade. I deepened my knowledge about networks in general, met with them, and convened them for collaborative learning. I discarded the term "global public policy networks" in favor of Global Action Networks (GANs). Participants do not think of "policy" as their product, but rather focus on "change." Moreover, although a political science perspective is useful, I find it much more useful to consider the knowledge associated with change, organizational development, and societal development. This was the basis for my book *Global Action Networks: Creating our Future Together*.[134] There are a few dozen significant GANs, including Transparency International, the Forest Stewardship Council, the UN Global Compact (founded in 2001), the Global Reporting Initiative, the International Land Coalition, the Alliance for Water Stewardship, and the Global Fund to Fight AIDS, Malaria, and Tuberculosis. Others have referred to a similar group of networks as Global Solutions Networks[135] and Global Issue Networks.[136]

Although I happened to focus on global action networks, many regional and national action networks also exist, and indeed are frequently components of GANs.

---

132 Reinicke, Wolfgang H., and Francis M. Deng. 2000. "Critical Choices: The United Nations, networks, and the future of global governance." Toronto, Canada: International Development Research Council.

133 Reinicke, Wolfgang H. 1999-2000. "The Other World Wide Web: Global Public Policy Networks." *Foreign Policy* (Winter):44-57.

134 Waddell, Steven. 2011. *Global Action Networks: Creating our future together*. Bocconi University on Management. Hampshire, UK: Palgrave-Macmillan.

135 Tapscott, Don. 2014. "Introducing Global Solution Networks: Understanding the New Multi-Stakeholder Models for Global Cooperation, Problem Solving and Governance." *Innovations* 9(1-2):3-46.

136 Rischard, Jean-Francois. 2002. *High Noon: 20 Global Problems, 20 Years to Solve Them*. New York, NY, USA: Basic Books.

I refer to them all simply as ANs. They all share the logic of interorganizational, multi-stakeholder change networks, emphasizing learning and entrepreneurial action. There are many different types of networks that are not action networks, because they lack transformational and action focus. Many multi-stakeholder networks are simply concerned with delivering a service or product, or with talking about policy and shared visions. In contrast, action networks are all of the following:

1. **Systemic change agents:** ANs work to realize transformation in their particular issue;
2. **Diversity-embracing:** Diversity is recognized as both complex and a source of critical value to produce innovative, common good outcomes. This includes collaborating across sectoral (business-government-civil society), linguistic, ethnic, developed-developing countries, and other boundaries;
3. **Interorganizational networks:** Individuals play a role, but organizations are the key participants. This helps realize scale, marshal resources, and engage participating organizations themselves in changing, since change is part of the transformational challenge. As networks, neither hierarchy nor markets provide the principles, values, or capacity. There is an equity principle among participating organizations;
4. **Multi-level bridgers:** An AN may be more locally focused, but its work involves bridging geographic and jurisdictional levels;
5. **Entrepreneurial action learners:** The networks develop new tools, processes, relationships, and actions with a very decentralized decision-making structure that supports responsiveness in diverse contexts;
6. **Common goods producers:** Their activity produces benefits for their diverse stakeholders, both in terms of commonly valued outcomes and those responding to the needs of a particular organization (supporting profitable business, enhancing justice, and realizing public policy goals);
7. **Voluntary leaders:** The networks are driven by the participants' passion and commitment to push the boundaries of enhancing environmental, social, and economic outcomes. Although organizations are the key participating unit, individuals with legitimacy, accessibility, and passion for change are the key to success.

When I started working with people in ANs, they thought of themselves as odd NGOs, weak governmental organizations, or some type of social enterprise. I pointed out that they are clearly none of these. They are an organizing innovation with the goal of addressing a complex change challenge by weaving together business, government, and civil society resources and competencies. Framing them as an organizing innovation is an extremely important point. Previously, they had been considering an inappropriate set of organizations, such as UN agencies and NGOs, as comparison points. Understanding themselves as an innovation allows them to experiment with how to organize themselves and establishes an appropriate set of comparisons. Encouraging this is one reason I created events for people from ANs around specific issues, such as communications, measuring impact, organizing structures, and learning strategies.

Box 7B: Principles for Responsible Investment: A GAN

The "global finance system" hit the wall in 2008 and nearly collapsed. Although many are working on partial solutions from nation-state perspectives, the Principles for Responsible Investment (PRI) Initiative aims for basic global-level change.

In 2005, a group of the world's largest institutional investors, supported by a 70-person multi-stakeholder group of experts from the investment industry, governmental organizations, civil society, and academia, drafted six Principles for Responsible Investment (a seventh tenet has been proposed). These principles aim to change global finance logic to integrate social, environmental, and economic concerns.

The PRI Initiative was launched in April 2006 to give life and meaning to the principles. Key launch partners were the UN, the Global Compact (itself a GAN), and the UN Environmental Program Finance Initiative.

One revolutionary aspect of the PRI is that asset owners, such as pension fund trustees, are in the driver's seat and on the PRI Board instead of the original launch partners, fund managers, and the investment industry. However, all of them are active participants. Another distinguishing quality is that individual investment funds, such as a social responsibility niche fund, cannot become signatories. Rather, the whole investment firm must commit to the principles. By 2015, more than 1,380 institutions representing in excess of US $59 trillion in assets were signatories. Like most GANs, the PRI is a modestly sized organization. Its 2014–15 income was approximately US $8.7 million.

The PRI is developing a new structure to build accountability in the investment system for environmental-social-governance (ESG) concerns. It is an enormous task. After an initial decade of raising awareness, building its network, and establishing foundational resources (such as a Reporting Framework and Clearing House on ESG issues), it is now focusing on implementing its signatories' commitments to the principles. The issues are huge and power-laden. They include changing incentives, building new expertise, realizing transparency, and creating accountability mechanisms for signatories. This is not a top-down strategy. It was defined and will only be realized with deep co-leadership among its diverse stakeholders.

Frustration with the multiple different ways that people use the term "network" led to Table 7B development. This outlines the core structure of ANs and illuminates some sources of organizational confusion. ANs are interorganizational networks — their core participant unit is organizations in the form of government agencies, NGOs, and businesses. "Organization," as used in this table, refers to hierarchies mainly consisting of core participant units that have a key dynamic of "administrating" (e.g., rules and regulations) and "managing" (e.g., attainment of corporate goals).

The key AN *action* unit is organizational groupings around a particular *task*, such as the certification of sustainable forestry in the Amazon (members of the Forest Stewardship Council [FSC]), transparency in the construction of the Berlin airport (Transparency International), or the delivery of a program to address AIDS in Tanzania (the Global Fund to Fight AIDS, Malaria and Tuberculosis). These are interorganizational partnerships; they are organizations participating in the AN and working collaboratively on a particular task. For smaller ANs, partnership task actions may involve all AN participants. When the particular type of task deals with numerous unknowns, it is designated as a complex strategy and experiment (such as with the FSC's first certifications) to produce an organizing "invention" of how to do something. When the type of task closely resembles one that has already been completed, the challenge is one of adaptation, dissemination, and "innovation," organized as a more complicated, deliberatively planned activity. In large ANs, interorganizational partnerships are often organized as sub-units of an AN: sometimes as geographical groupings (watershed-local-national-regional), and sometimes around issues (industry-topic).

Table 7B: Network Types

	Inter-personal	Organization	Interorg. Partnership	Interorg. Network	Societal Change System
Legally Distinct Entities	Many	One	Small to modest	Very large	All stakeholders
Organizing Structures	Informal	Hierarchical	Hub and spoke	Multi-hub	Diffuse
Organizing Logic	Personal	Administering Managing	Coordination	Coherence	Diverse self-direction
Operating Focus	Relation-ships	Organization	Task	System	Definitional
Participation	Open	Closed	Highly controlled	Loosely controlled	External

ANs bridge various levels. If an AN is focused on local action, then it will typically have an important connection to more regional and national organizations and jurisdictions. Because GANs are dealing with global issues, there is also the need to undertake action with global entities, such as intergovernmental organizations (the OECD, the UN, and the World Bank, etc.), global NGOs, and multinational corporations and their associations. This is led by "Secretariats," which are themselves hierarchical organizations with staff who have traditional reporting-line relationships. (I dislike the term Secretariat, because it comes from bureaucratic intergovernmental traditions; a better would be "Transparency International-Global" versus TI-Kenya, emphasizing that they simply operate in different geographic spaces.) The GAN Secretariats are nodes with a multi-stakeholder council. They support network-wide activities (e.g., annual or other meetings; the IUCN meets globally only once every four years) and work with global stakeholders.

Completing tasks requires coordination among participating organizations to access their distinctive competencies. (Recall the sectoral competencies framework in Chapter 6). The AN, as a whole, aims to provide coherence in the change effort between all the tasks of its participants. ANs usually develop one or two dominant functions (out of the seven functions outlined in Chapter 6). The Global Fund to Fight AIDS' key function is resourcing: it is a collaboration of funders who pool their money. The FSC's core function is obviously certification and measurement. Sustainable Energy for All's core function is system organizing: creating effective linkages between organizations for greater coherence around the three energy goals. The goal of ANs is to influence a system comprising all stakeholders in their

Box 7C: A National Action Network for American Health Care

The American health care system is a mess. It is by far the most costly in the world, as a percentage of GDP. The outcomes are among the worst in developed countries, and even with the contentious reforms that went into effect in 2014, about 10 percent of the population remains without insurance.

In 2008, the Robert Wood Johnson Foundation and the Institutes of Medicine launched a two-year initiative to assess and transform the three million member nursing profession. An 18-member committee, comprised almost entirely of health care professionals and academics, produced a 2010 report titled "The Future of Nursing: Leading Change, Advancing Health" to "transform the nursing profession to improve the quality of health care and the way it is delivered." To lead this transformation, a national action network (the Future of Nursing Campaign for Action) was established with the following vision:

Everyone in America can live a healthier life, supported by a system in which nurses are essential partners in providing care and promoting health.

The Campaign's website explains: "We are working to transform health care through nursing by mobilizing coalitions representing nurses, other health providers, consumers, educators and businesses." Today, the Campaign is a network of local- and state-level Action Coalitions (ACs) that are acting as the driving force. The Foundation and the nation's powerful association of people over 50 years old (AARP) provide national support with staffing, offices, and connections to national partners. The Foundation gives up to $150,000 annually to support state ACs if it is matched by at least $75,000 from other sources. Communications, research, and evaluation support are also substantial.

The ACs are composed of diverse stakeholders who are working to transform health care through nursing. Like all ACs, the Texas one has two co-leads, one is from a nursing organization or a nurse, as always, and the other is from a non-nursing entity, in this case a consumer-owned insurer. The Indiana state coalition is co-led by a doctor and a nurse; the executive committee includes two nurses and two doctors, and its 22-member steering committee includes six people who are not nurses, three of whom are physicians.

The work of the Campaign is organized around six themes, referred to as "pillars," that provide network coherence. This includes such things as nursing leadership and education. As part of the leadership pillar, the Texas state AC organizes workshops for nurses to develop their capacity to be on boards and then helps to make those placements.

As part of the education pillar, the Indiana AC is pursuing a shift in the tradition of training health care professionals within their own disciplines—nurses training with nurses, doctors training with doctors—to interprofessional teams. Building partnerships with diverse stakeholders, including leaders in government and education, the AC is leading efforts to support, spread, and implement models of interprofessional collaboration statewide. Interprofessional education has become strongly emphasized between schools of nursing, medicine, and allied health, and state-of-the-art simulation learning experiences are available for nursing, medical, and allied health students in many areas across Indiana.

particular areas of concern (e.g., forestry — all industry, government, and NGOs). Although an AN is large, it does *not* have a mass-organizing goal. Rather, it aims to be a network of organizations that take a leadership role in realizing change (early adopters). If it becomes a mass-member organization, it will absorb all the dynamics of a trade association and work to the lowest common denominator (this has happened with the AN-like Kimberley Process, regarding the certification of conflict diamonds).

There is no available legal structure that reflects the cross-sectoral nature of ANs. Occasionally, GANs are incorporated as intergovernmental organizations (e.g., the IUCN, the International Union for the Conservation of Nature). More often, they are legally NGOs, charities, or nonprofits. GANs face the additional problem of lacking a legal structure that reflects their global nature. Usually, they incorporate separately in the countries in which they operate, and then form a collective association in a particular country for global operations. However, it is critical to success that ANs do not organize their activities as detailed within the legal frameworks. Rather, they must organize themselves based on established experience concerning what gets the job done, while simultaneously providing reports and a formal structure for the government that reflects legal frameworks.

The word "member," like "network," evokes a range of meanings that Table 7C aims to distinguish. The basic common element behind the concept of "membership" is the expression of a formal commitment to an AN's goals. These "participants" are the key to AN success. However, they may or may not formally be "members." Sometimes, membership dues become confused with the funding strategy, which can create innumerable issues with regard to equity.

Table 7C: Aspects of "Members"

Citizen	Participant	Co-owner	Customer
Who is seen as a potential participant/member?	Who is active in realizing goals?	Who makes the decisions/ has formal authority?	Who is paying for the work?

Societal Change System Stewarding

Labs, CoPs, ANs, and social movements (Chapter 6) play particular roles within societal change systems (SCSs). The Marine Fisheries Council, for example, is an AN with a particular role in certifying fish for consumption. There are, of course, many more issues with fish and oceans aside from this one. How do we support the development of coherence, convergence, and action among them? If we are to develop highly effective SCSs, as described in Chapter 6, we need a new type of organizing effort whose role is currently fragmented and poorly defined. Its role is stewarding SCS development.

A well-functioning SCS consists of change initiatives with a high degree of coherence that provides for a convergence of action. We can see many places where the development of coherence is supported. For example, this is a core function of the International Panel on Climate Change (IPCC), with respect to scientific knowledge associated with climate change. It engages all the world's scientists involved in climate change research to collaboratively develop a climate change view based on the preponderance of evidence. Other coherence-generating examples can be found with most issues in meetings around them to exchange information and support the emergence of action. The World Energy Council has such meetings regarding its diverse energy stakeholders; the World Water Forum does the same with water issues. In the climate change arena, there are regular meetings of the UN Framework Convention, which produces the Conferences of the Parties (parties to the Convention, which are governments) that have struggled mightily to achieve coherence and action. However, these are events that focus on particular parts of the systemic change matrix seen in Chapter 6 (often learning) or on particular stakeholder groups. We need to develop more sophisticated approaches to emerging action within the SCS, as described in the last column of Table 7B.

In the energy field, Sustainable Energy for All is at the halfway point between a GAN and an SCS Steward. It does indeed aim to create coherence from the efforts of all system change initiatives. It is still in the programs and projects mode of action, however, which is quite different from the SCS Stewarding mode. Also, it is still quite government-heavy.

What I'm imagining is SCS Stewarding agents that would continually raise awareness of change initiatives about their broader SCS. Initiatives need to develop accountability for not just their individual success, but the effectiveness of the SCS as well. In the Fair Trade movement in the US, for example, although there is a significant awareness of their SCS, they have never been able to realize alignment amongst the organizations; many accuse the largest one of only acting in its own growth and profit interests. SCS Stewarding would absolutely have to be cross-stakeholder in form to gain legitimacy and insight across the change system. It would continually look at a particular SCS, not unlike the way the IPCC looks at climate change with ongoing analysis and review using multiple tools and methods. The SCS Stewarding group would identify opportunities for synergies and problems with duplications, conflicts, and gaps in effort. It would convene stakeholder change initiatives for ad hoc events, or maybe a series of them, around a particular SCS issue. The events would be organized not only for information exchange, but also for collective action planning. The outcome would be change initiatives with a deepened awareness of the SCS, including what is needed to strengthen it, their role in strengthening it, and the commitment of other partners (including financing) to play their respective roles.

Organizationally, an SCS Steward would be very light, much like an AN. It would probably make sense to organize its activities around key sub-systems, such as those identified for the electricity SCS in Chapter 6.

Common Elements of Success

The labs are spaces for experimenting; the CoPs are for building capacity; and the GANs (or regional action networks) are for widespread sharing and adapting. They might be organized separately with only loose ties or more closely share an identity as one network. They are key actors in societal change systems. If there were an SCS Steward, it would organize events to support them in developing SCS coherence and effectiveness. Some shared common organizing principles are listed below: [137]

1. *Organizing is more important than organization.* Practice emergent design around your experience arising from actions on an issue, rather than importing models and valuing permanence and tradition. There are legally mandated reporting requirements and structures, but do not organize around them. Learn what works, and continually integrate that knowledge into the way you organize to address complex challenges.

2. *Consider core competencies.* My work on GANs identified core competencies that suggest functional lines as an organizing basis, and indeed many of them reflect these in the ways they are organized: leadership-as-stewardship, networking/partnership, measuring/evaluation, communications, learning, resource mobilization, and change knowledge/conflict skills.

3. *Organize programs in response to issue characteristics.* There are two particular characteristics to consider. One is geographic often associated with governmental jurisdictions. This association is appropriate if government rules are a key focus of a given change effort. However, jurisdictional boundaries are often part of the problem. There is a need to organize across them to create an innovative geographic space. For example, if a watershed is the focus, organize around it. Often there is a different primary organizing imperative. For example, the Global Reporting Initiative (GRI) is organized around "industries," because it is focused on triple bottom line corporate reporting. This requires industry-specific approaches. Sustainable Energy for All is organized geographically and around certain themes, including: energy efficiency, renewable energy, and capacity development. However, remember that as goals are realized and contexts shift, the focus of the effort and the organizing approach should similarly evolve.

4. *Emphasize participation rather than membership.* Change efforts depend deeply on trust — they are carrots with little in the way of sticks. Both effectiveness and trust that the diverse voices will be responded to, are required. Paying excess attention to membership structures, given complexity, will simply depress change energy. Think in terms of participation infrastructure: support for regular opportunities, activities, and arenas that allow people to connect with each other, solve problems, make decisions, and be part of a community.

5. *Recognize the centrality of learning.* Complex challenges require invention, which requires learning. Pay attention to learning processes and developing capacity; do not treat them as ancillary activities.

6. *Network to connect hierarchies.* A core function of the three organizing approaches is to provide agility to traditional hierarchical organizations by connecting them. Use network spaces to create innovative ways of working, namely those that free participants from restrictive work methods within their own organizations.

---

137 Adapted from Waddell, Steve. 2012. "Design Guidelines to Address Global Challenges: The Case of Global Action Networks." *Journal of Organization Design* 1(3):1-19.

7. *Disperse leadership.* Joe Raelin writes about "leaderful" organizations.[138] People must feel empowered to step into leadership action, rather than having to ask permission;
8. *Embrace diversity.* Transformation requires diverse resources and perspectives. Support interactions between diverse participants. Do not back away from confrontations. Face them directly and turn their energy into change power.
9. *Attend to formal and informal agreements.* Jim Ritchie-Dunham emphasizes the importance of agreements in creating dynamic, strongly-performing organizations. Agreements are formal and informal arrangements or mutual understandings that guide interactions. Often, these are hidden by limiting assumptions that prevent people from performing to their highest potential, thus creating an atmosphere of debilitating scarcity. Fostering enabling agreements is an important factor in high-performance; the agreements can actually be "mapped to identify how to ensure good flows between the diverse parts of complex entities.[139]

Future Directions

The three organizing approaches to transformation are combining in various ways, and new approaches will emerge as new governance forms – processes for making decisions and taking action – because traditional ones cannot address transformation challenges. Derk Loorbach, Director of the Dutch Research Institute for Transitions (DRIFT, a leading center for supporting innovation to address such challenges), wrote:

> In effect, this implies a new balance between state, market, and society and new ways to facilitate and make as effective as possible the informal network processes through which alternative ideas and agendas are generated that are often seen as important in fueling regular policymaking processes with new problem definitions, ambitions, solutions, and agendas.[140]

Loorbach emphasizes distributed, decentralized and self-organizing networks working across scales (eg: municipal-state-national-international) and enabled by new technologies. These appear "anarchic" to traditional eyes. He builds on the word "panarchy", increasingly used by those working in the transitions and resilience traditions, in contrast to hierarchy.[141]

---

138 Raelin, Joseph. 2003. *Creating Leaderful Organizations: How to bring out leadership in everyone.* San Francisco, CA, USA: Berrett-Koehler.
139 Ritchie-Dunham, James L.. 2014. *Ecosynomics: The Science of Abundance.* Amherst, MA, USA: Vibrancy Publishing (ecosynomics.com).
140 Loorbach, Derk. 2010. "Transition management for sustainable development: a prescriptive, complexity-based governance framework." *Governance* 23(1):161-83.
141 —. 2014. "To Transition! Governance Panarchy in the New Transformation." Rotterdam: Faculty of Social Sciences, Erasmus University. Holling, C. S., L. Gunderson, and D. Ludwig. 2002. "In Quest of a Theory of Adaptive Change." in *Panarchy: Understanding Transformations in Human and Natural Systems,* edited by L.H. Gunderson and C.S. Holling. Washington, DC: Island Press.

Chapter 8

Growing Collective Action: Three perspectives

Chapter Summary:

Those working on large systems change have developed ways to describe the process. Three of these approaches are presented here; each focuses on different development challenges. The Collective Leadership Compass emphasizes the dynamics of group formation to develop powerful collective leadership. The Systemic Change Process Map uses system dynamics mapping to describe the way key activities and tools interact as a system. Analysis of the development of Action Networks provides insight into on-going development processes and structures to realize breadth as well as depth. Creating a healthy array of these activities is a key to stewarding development of powerful societal change systems.

All ways of looking at the world are incomplete. Using multiple lenses is one way to enhance comprehensiveness. Three ways to look at transformation development processes are presented in this chapter. These descriptions suggest that the process is much smoother and more predictable than anyone actually experiences it. There is a lot of back-and-forth, and riffs on the approaches are necessary to respond to particular circumstances.

These approaches build on Otto Scharmer's U-Process (see Chapter 4) that identifies learning from the three future stages as co-sensing, co-inspiring, and co-creating. The Collective Leadership Compass looks at transformation as a co-creating change strategy; it focuses on building a powerful set of relationships and competencies necessary for collaboratively co-creating action. The Systems Change Process Map describes the change process in terms of specific activities, using system dynamics modeling to emphasize the relationships between transformation system activities. The Global Action Network development stages framework is particularly valuable for understanding issues related to scaling up co-creation.

These three perspectives support the pathway from transformation to reform to incremental change, as described in Chapter 4. The Compass is particularly useful for initiating transformation processes with a Co-creating Change strategy (see Chapter 5), as well as for development of a powerful Societal Change System (Chapter 6). The Process Map details the movement from the transformation stage to the reform stage, where the enabling environment (markets, policies, and values) shifts and the experiments of the transformation stage become more widespread. A supportive enabling environment is associated with the proverbial tipping point, where experiments become the new norm and incremental change follows. Development of Action Networks is one increasingly common way to support movement through these stages. The development stages of these Networks themselves are associated with the emergence of new, collaboratively-produced norms of a flourishing future.

The Collective Leadership Compass[142]

Introduction

When the Southeast Asian country of Laos decided to pursue a Voluntary Partnership Agreement (VPA) with the European Union to maintain and expand trading rights for its lumber and wood products, it agreed to undertake a national dialogue about the definition of "legal timber" and to develop a socially, economically, and environmentally sustainable supply chain. As part of the EU's Forest Law Enforcement, Governance and Trade (FLEGT) initiative, the country's Ministries of Agriculture and Forestry, Industry and Commerce, and Natural Resources and Environment made significant commitments. Forest degradation and fragmentation in Laos has accelerated since the early part of the millennium with negative repercussions for communities, biodiversity, and the climate. Weak governance permits the forestry sector to be opaque and corrupt. Export of timber from unknown and potential illegal sources is at least five times the sanctioned volume, constituting approximately 80% of total timber exports. The pay-off from the government's commitment could be significant: the agricultural and forestry sectors account for approximately 33% of Laos' GNP, while employing 75% of its workforce. Illegal harvesting means the government is losing out on significant revenues. The agreement would provide access to growing EU markets for sustainably produced timber and related products.

The Lao-EU initiative includes support for creating a licensing system for legally produced wood in a participatory and transparent manner. Due to the country's political history, there is a lack of experience with multi-stakeholder participatory processes. The government is one-party and centralized. Civil

---

142 Case contributors Dominic Stucker, Kristiane Schäfer and Petra Kuenkel of the Collective Leadership Institute, Potsdam, Germany, http://collectiveleadership.com/

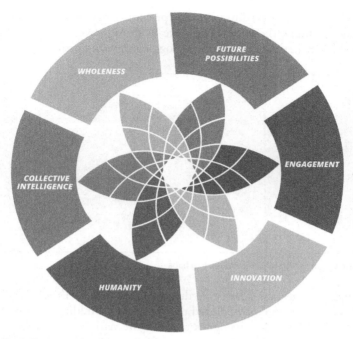

Figure 8A: The Collective Leadership Compass

society is a relatively new concept in Laos, and the "disappearances" of leaders have occurred in the recent past. The forestry sector has several large players that carry considerable influence. Some want to maintain the status quo, whereas others see the benefits in transforming the sector.

Approach

The Collective Leadership Institute (CLI) was engaged by Germany's development agency, *Gesellschaft für Internationalle Zusammenarbeit* (GIZ), to build capacity among key actors for dialogue and collaboration competence needed to transform the forestry sector. In close cooperation with a GIZ program in support of the EU initiative, CLI was charged with bringing a group of key stakeholders into productive and generative dialogue across sectors (see: the Individual Change Sphere case, Chapter 3), catalyzing this team around a shared vision, developing its capacity to design and facilitate multi-stakeholder dialogues in Laos, and building the capacity of a leadership team to realize forestry management transformation. The Ministries of Agriculture and Forestry, Industry and Commerce, and Natural Resources and Environment decided to collectively develop process leadership.

In July 2014, the CLI began with two four-day Art of Stakeholder Collaboration workshops with technical-level officials from the public sector, the wood processing and furniture industries, civil society, and academia. It was the first time these individuals had worked together. To provide a focused environment conducive to team building, the workshops were held outside of Laos in neighboring Cambodia. The beneficiaries from illegal logging were not present.

Figure 8B: The Vision for Sustainable Forestry in Laos

Through round table dialogue designed around CLI's Dialogic Change Model[143], the first workshop explored the context for building a team for change and designing stakeholder dialogues at both the national and pilot provincial levels. Before the second workshop, participants took a two-day break to visit a Cambodian community forest management project, as both a team-building exercise and a learning journey (Chapter 8). The second workshop focused on outlining a dialogic process with resources and agreements for moving ahead. The group articulated and drew a shared vision of sustainable forestry in Laos (Figure 8B) and formed Working Groups related to key parts of the supply chain: log landings in the forest, occupational health and safety in wood processing factories and timber export procedures at the country's borders. Four high-level government officials joined for the last two days. The stakeholders presented their work to them, including their shared vision and an image of the bus with diverse passengers, a metaphor of sharing a common journey. The officials signaled their high-level support by signing their names to individuals at the front of the bus, the drivers of the process. Together, they generated the basis of a shared sustainable forestry vision for Laos.

The next phase consisted of a three-day Art of Leading Collectively workshop in Potsdam, Germany, where CLI is based. The eight participants included high level employees from three Ministries (including those who attended the end of the above-mentioned workshops), in addition to one from the Ministry of Foreign Affairs, one from the National Assembly and two from GIZ ProFLEGT. The workshop was framed around co-creation and collective leadership for shifting a system. Participants built on personal examples of successful collaboration, prac-

---

143 Kuenkel, Petra, Silvine Gerlach and Vera Frieg. 2011. Stakeholder Dialogues: Skills for Better Cooperation. Potsdam, Germany: Collective Leadership Institute.

ticed self-reflection, and developed working groups to support the system shift. This included identifying how to gain the Vice President's support for the VPA negotiation process. This high level leadership team used the six Dimensions of the Collective Leadership Compass to assess and plan their change initiative at the personal, team and system levels. Each participant developed a personal action plan to realize their potential as a collective leader. At the end of the workshop, a special leadership coaching day was organized by CLI facilitators to build further trust and capacity within the group and to identify the key next steps.

Using the Collective Leadership Compass[144]

The Collective Leadership Compass was used implicitly during the planning and facilitation of the above workshops. The Compass is a framework developed by CLI Executive Director Petra Kuenkel that consists of six dimensions. Kuenkel refers to them as a "pattern of human competencies." She emphasizes that the "co-creation" act is at the heart of all human interactions. The dimensions are not treated as "stages" to go through consecutively; rather, they are entry points that represent a comprehensive view of competencies necessary for collective leadership. The Compass is a practice-oriented approach to leading complex change in multi-actor settings. It can be used to strengthen individual leadership skills, to enhance the leadership capacity of a group of actors and to shift systems of collaborating actors towards better co-creation. The Compass can be used as both a planning and assessment tool at the personal, team, organizational and systems levels, identifying strengths and areas that need development for successful collective leadership initiatives. Here are some ways in each dimension in which Compass use achieved tangible results in Laos, building a robust foundation for the ongoing process:

- **Future Possibilities:** Both the process of articulating a shared vision for forestry management in Laos, and literally drawing a picture of the future, created palpable resonance. A select team of participants presented a vision integrating input from all, which was adopted as a guiding document and image for the onward planning process.
- **Wholeness:** The group dove deep into looking at the bigger picture, as they jointly created a network actor map that defined engagement strategies.
- **Collective Intelligence:** Participants learned from one another and facilitators about the delicate balance between administrative procedures, planning processes, and the dialogic quality of the engagement of all relevant stakeholders. Collective Intelligence helped them to work across sectors.

---

144 Kuenkel, Petra. 2016. *The Art of Leading Collectively: Co-Creating a Sustainable, Socially Just Future.* White River Junction, VT, USA: Chelsea Green Publishing.
—. 2015. "Navigating Change in Complex Multi-Actor Settings: A Practice Approach to Better Collaboration." *Journal of Corporate Citizenship* 2015(58):119-36.
—. 2008. *Mind and Heart:* BoD—Books on Demand.

- **Engagement:** This enabled them to move towards engaging relevant stakeholders, planning further processes with attention to process quality, and prioritizing collective action steps.
- **Innovation:** The result was a process map for the coming months. On the final day of the second Laos workshop, the group presented its sustainable forestry vision and plan to high-level actors.
- **Humanity:** In addition to their vision, the group presented a vivid picture of a bus they had drawn as a metaphor representing both stakeholder cohesion and clarity of purpose. The moment had come to see if everyone was "on the bus." And they were! Everyone chose to sign their name to one person on the bus, including high level actors in the drivers' seats.

The next capacity building step in the process was a three-day Art of Leading Collectively workshop focused explicitly on the Compass. Participants included eight high level participants from the three Ministries (including those who attended the end of the above workshops), and one from the Ministry of Foreign Affairs, one from the National Assembly and two from the GIZ program. The workshop was framed around co-creation and collective action to shift a system. Participants shared stories of successful collaboration, practiced self-reflection, and developed informal working groups to support system improvements. This group used the six Dimensions of the Collective Leadership Compass to assess and plan their own contributions in the larger EU VPA process. Each participant developed a personal action plan to realize their potential as a collective leader. At the end of the workshop, a special coaching day was organized by CLI facilitators to build further trust and capacity within the team and to identify next steps for collective action.

At the technical level, a committed cross-sector group, selected from previous participants, took an Art of Dialogue course to build the capacity to design an on-going stakeholder dialogue process in three pilot provinces and to facilitate specific stakeholder dialogue events. With requisite high-level support, the technical-level team took on the responsibility of convening stakeholder dialogues at both the national and provincial levels, as well as applying CLI's Process Quality Monitoring Tool. Through the above-mentioned, multi-sector working groups they also focused on specific issues along the timber supply chain.

GIZ ProFLEGT Project Director, Marc Gross, comments that CLI's approach "... has effectively brought together different interest groups within Laos to start negotiating a Voluntary Partnership Agreement (VPA) for Forest Law Enforcement, Governance and Trade (FLEGT). CLI's methodologies equip stakeholder representatives with tools to engage on the basis of trust, develop solid and fruitful relationships and increasingly value others' viewpoints."

The dialogic change and collective leadership approach has become so well-integrated and applied that CLI support is no longer required. One Laotian participant commented that CLI should work with EU negotiators to have them take more dialogic approach to negotiations, making this a co-creative effort!

The Systemic Change Process Map

Introduction

Leading up to March 1, 2012 in El Golfo de Santa Clara (Santa Clara), where the Colorado River flows into the Gulf of California, Christian Liñán-Rivera from Noroeste Sustentable (NOS: a Mexican NGO) was running after signatures for an agreement on the curvina fishing future. The Curvina Management Agreement reflected long discussions amongst fishers, buyers, government officials, and environmental organizations to find a way to both ensure strong livelihoods and curvina population health. With the final signature, the implementation process began.

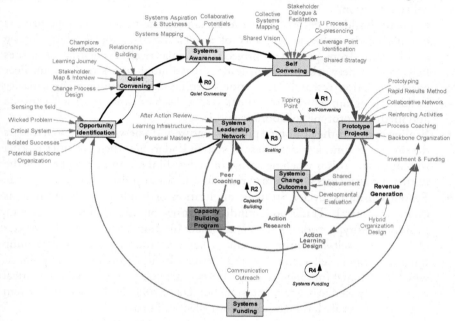

Figure 8C: Systemic Change Process Map (Produced by Joe Hsueh)

This story played a key role in defining the Systemic Change Process Map (SCMP, Figure 8B) by Joe Hsueh, in conjunction with the Academy for Systemic Change. Trained in system dynamics mapping (Chapter 8) at MIT with Peter Senge, John Sterman and others, Hsueh worked with a broad range of issues that follow the transformation pattern that the SCPM describes. Of course, no case follows this exactly. However, the map provides valuable insights into transformational processes and offers guidance for their development. The map identifies key steps as boxes, and describes via arrows how one activity leads to another in causal relationships. A list of possible actions is described for the steps (e.g.: sensing the field as an action in opportunity identification). The small R circular loops describe how activities reinforce one another to create five virtuous cycles:

- **Quiet convening cycle:** This is where the change process begins. Once a systemic change opportunity is identified, a quiet-convening process is initiated by interviewing stakeholders, mapping out the system and building relationships. This raises system awareness and the desire to collaborate across boundaries. The goal is a critical mass of stakeholders who are willing to initiate the self-convening process.

- **Self-convening cycle:** Through the quiet-convening process, stakeholders develop curiosity about the larger system and awareness that no one actor can solve the problem alone. This produces a desire to "self" convene and join other stakeholders in the same room to form a shared understanding of the current reality, co-create a shared vision and identify high-leverage points for collective action.

- **Capacity building cycle:** Critical to sustaining the systemic change process is building the collective capacity of a network of system leaders. Acting and learning from prototype projects and collectively evaluating outcomes help build a network of system leaders distributed across the system. Peer coaching, action research and action learning design reinforce the capacity building program which strengthens system leaders' capacity to self-convene and further prototype collaborative projects.

- **Scaling cycle:** As the prototype projects mature and a network of system leaders develops over time, a critical mass of system leaders and their activities reach a tipping point. This is when new ways of being, thinking and acting become the norms and attractors for others to replicate and scale up elsewhere in the system.

- **Systems funding cycle:** Strategic application of funding to these virtuous cycles is critical. Traditional funding focuses on identifying and scaling proven prototype projects. Systems-based funding focuses on the *process* of catalyzing self-sustaining systemic change by funding and strengthening quiet-convening, self-convening and capacity-building cycles to the point at which traditional funding can support proven prototype projects. It is critical to create a space for funders and stakeholders to collectively sense the system as peers to identify leverage-points for collective impact.

The Story

Christian Liñán-Rivera is a marine biologist and member of NOS, founded under the dedicated leadership of Liliana Gutiérrez-Mariscal, Alejandro Robles-Gozález and Gastón Luken-Aguilar, to develop sustainable coastal communities in northwestern Mexico. They are also community organizers and change leaders. The issues of livelihoods and fisheries had long been identified as a problem in the northern Gulf of California. In 1975, totoaba fishing was outlawed, because the species was endangered. However, there was little capacity to enforce the ban. Growing up to two meters in length and 100 kilos in weight, the totoaba's swim bladder is considered to be a valuable gift by wealthy Chinese who pay as much as $15,000 per bladder. The vaquita – a small porpoise that is an evolutionarily distinct animal endemic to Mexico – is critically endangered, because it is a by-catch in gillnets aimed at other fish and shrimp. The curvina is a beautiful silver migratory salt-to-brackish water fish that is also threatened by over-fishing. All are threatened by dramatic reductions in the Colorado River flow, to the point where it sometimes ceases flowing into the Gulf altogether. A maze of conflicting jurisdictions for government agencies, siloed government ministry traditions and an ineffective top-down style all befuddle efforts to address the entangled issues. Endemic corruption, involving murderous violence and intimidation, are part of the operating environment. The mix is truly a wicked problem to resolve.

These factors led to threats by international environmental NGOs to boycott Mexico at the beginning of the next millennium. In 2005, this forced change strategy produced the Peñasco Agreement under the collective leadership of AGS, a dialogue forum on the Sea of Cortez. However, it depended on government enforcement, and the government was soon overwhelmed. Here, we can see the first Quiet and Self-Convening cycles in the SCPM from Opportunity Identification to Self-Convening and Prototype experience. Government enforcement as a prototype simply failed. The government translated the agreement into a well-funded program, but there was no meaningful stakeholder role in its implementation. There was insufficient stakeholder involvement and commitment, unreasonable expectations of what the government could do on its own, and inadequacy in the quiet convening and systems awareness building steps.

The major outcomes of this first failed prototype were lessons learned and NOS leadership evolution. A re-initiation of the Quiet Convening cycle began with NOS talking to stakeholders and moving from the position of a neutral process facilitator to one of advancing a vision. The profiles of Robles-Gozález and Luken-Aguilar as concerned environmentalists and businessmen, and Robles-Gozález's 30 years of work with Gulf communities, engendered trust. For Quiet Convening, NOS organized meetings with government officials, fishermen, buyers, and the conservation sector. Christian describes this as working with ever-widening, spiraling circles. A reframing of the issue concluded that, "The major weakness was … the lack of capacity of the contributing organizations, not least NOS, to meet the challenges posed by sustaining the necessary behavioral changes within the key parties – the responsible government agencies, the international NGOs and the fishers."[145] In early 2011, Alto Golfo Sustentable (AGS) was re-convened as a multi-sector collaboration network. It represented the first time a community-based approach had been taken. In this second development cycle, AGS represented a prototype platform to carry work forward.

This time there was more focus on building quiet convening and system awareness. "For the first time it was about *creating a collective vision,*" Christian explains. "That phrase we learned made a huge difference. It transformed our way to intervene. We started to focus on the actors, to create a sustainable fishery with well-being for the families and more fish in the water."

145 Olsen, Stephen, and Glenn Page. 2008. "Applying the Orders of Outcomes to NOS Initiatives in Gulf Of California, Mexico." Noroeste Sustentable, Walton Family Foundation.

Traditional meetings were held with officials behind a table at the front of the room and an "audience" in front. The NOS now began meetings sitting in circles, with the leaders as equals. "It generated a very different mood for collaborating and working together," says Christian.

This led to the collective Self-Convenings in November and December 2011, at which Joe Hsueh and Alejandro Flores-Márquez (a NOS systems thinker) worked with participants to develop system dynamics maps (Chapter 8), describing their situation. Particularly powerful was the tragedy of the commons archetype in which short-term individual gain from over-fishing reduces gains for all in the longer term. "Stakeholders realized that they had to collaborate," explains Christian. "They understood inter-dependencies. You heard people say 'Now I've got it. I see why you react like that to me.' It was really dramatic to see adversaries collaborate, because they had systemic understanding of the situation. And it was very easy to go from blaming to action." The shared vision spread.

Prototype action emerged by testing a new approach to a catch-share system (a management framework that had been introduced in Mexico by the NGO Environmental Defense Fund) to organize fisheries. On March 1st, 2012, Curvina Management Agreement was signed. In earlier government prototypes (prior to 2011), an overall quota for the Curvina Fishery had been determined. But, that was all. This time there were quotas for each fishing cooperative and an enforcement mechanism. Local buyers formed a coalition to define a fixed quantity to collectively buy from fishers with a stable price, with the goal of establishing a higher price than fishers had previously received. The fishermen agreed not to fish more than their quota and not to sell to outside buyers at a lower price. This approach aimed to produce higher prices for fishers and buyers, so that they would not lose out financially.

Liñán-Rivera remembers that when the group shared the Agreement with federal authorities, one official said: "What you're proposing has no place under our legal system. There is no way to implement it. But I will find a way, because it really makes sense ... Don't ask me how, but I will."

The first year with the March to May curvina fishing season was very successful. Previously, fishers had fished as much as possible, assuming unlimited curvina. There was substantial spoilage, health issues and prices collapsed from 10 pesos per kilo to 5. Some curving were simply tossed away. For 2012, stakeholders formed working groups to implement the Agreement. Curvina prices were substantially higher and varied between 18 and 20 pesos/kilo.

It was easy to move forward, Liñán-Rivera recalls, because it was the stakeholders' document and they defended it. Moreover, they had developed new capacities for working together and creating solutions. Before, their actions had been limited to such things as manifestos, ineffective complaints and fighting.

Based on the 2012 prototype agreement, a 2013 agreement that integrated lessons learned was signed March 1st of that year. However, the success was not repeated. The federal government was in transition and its role was in disarray. A neighboring community was included in the process, but did not have permits for curvina fishing. They fished anyways, outside the agreement. Also, totoaba fishing escalated despite the outright ban, bringing in the mafia and violence that overflowed into the Curvina Fishery. Corruption and violence overwhelmed all the hard work.

Realizing that pursuing its work required cleaning up organized crime and its ability to act with impunity in the region, NOS shifted its focus for the following year and essentially began a new systemic change process. Meanwhile, international environmental organizations again threatened the Mexican government with a boycott. In response, the government established a 500 million peso program (another prototype action) to keep 2,800 fishers off the water by making payments to them. However, the Curvina Fishery is an exception, since it does not affect the vaquita. The prototype action was more a traditional top-down response to an emergency, rather than the product of a thoughtful, self-convening stakeholder meeting. To receive payments, the fishermen have no obligations for anything, such as community service. This has led to excessive drinking and other social problems. Nevertheless, Liñán-Rivera is energetic and optimistic, commenting "We have to transform the community, the whole system in the Upper Gulf, and this is a great opportunity for AGS."

In this story, the SCPM reveals how cycles operate and repeat themselves. By identifying activities at each step, there is an opportunity for much more disciplined intervention. A simple "decision" can be crafted into an action research and action learning activity, with knowledge and capacity development categorically integrated to support virtuous cycles. As the complex system continues to evolve, the collective capacity of a network of system leaders develops community resilience. They adapt to new circumstances and the systemic change process becomes self-sustaining.

One key audience Hsueh developed the SCPM for, is funders of projects like the NOS one. Most funders are interested in funding specific projects, not processes. Yet, to identify high-leverage projects for systemic change, it is critical to understand the whole system by engaging stakeholders in forming a unified understanding of the complex system and its shared vision. This is the basis for identifying high-leverage points for collective action. He hopes more funders appreciate the importance of supporting the systemic change process by funding quiet and self-convening processes, prototype projects and capacity building, to the point at which traditional funding can come in and scale proven prototype projects. By creating a space in which funders and stakeholders can sense the system in the same room, funders are more likely to collectively fund supporting stakeholder aspirations to achieve collective impact.

Action Networks (ANs)

"In the early 1990s, corruption was a taboo topic. Many companies regularly wrote off bribes as business expenses in their tax filings, the graft of some longstanding heads of state was legendary, and many international agencies were resigned to the fact that corruption would sap funding from many development projects around the world. There was no global convention aimed at curbing corruption, and no way to measure corruption at the global scale."

"Having seen corruption's impact during his work in East Africa, retired World Bank official Peter Eigen, together with nine allies, set up a small organization to take on the taboo: Transparency International was established with a Secretariat in Berlin, the recently restored capital of a reunified Germany."[146] Within a few years, TI was operating globally, as the world recognized corruption as a critical issue.

During TI's beginning, Eigen travelled the world speaking with people to stimulate action. He arrived in Ecuador in the early '90s and met with Valeria Merino, founder of Participacion Ciudadana (PC). PC is a leading citizen sector organization aiming at strengthening democratic participation and civil rights in Ecuador; it monitors country-wide elections.

Their conversation helped clarify numerous things. One was that growing out of his World Bank history, Eigen's strongest network was with governments and associated officials who were concerned about corruption. Second was that the early Transparency International model was based on the idea that individuals concerned about corruption would be the key driver and organizing unit for TI. Third was that PC had been working on corruption issues for some time, and there were also other NGOs around the world that had also been doing so. NGOs, thus, had a clear contribution to make in combatting corruption.

This led to a shift in Eigen's thinking to see *organizations* rather than individuals, as the core members in TI. This was important for scale. Much of TI's work focused on connecting organizations around the world to undertake the local-to-global actions necessary to address corruption. What followed was a development speed globally, in terms of geography and engaged numbers, reflecting how social movements often develop. However, unlike social movements, TI has a leadership role working in a business and participatory manner with a broad array of stakeholders to develop the Societal Change System (SCS) for transparency.

ANs, as Chapter 6 describes, are an organizational innovation of our time. They arise in response to the inadequacy of traditional approaches, such as top-down hierarchies, markets, and social movements. They form locally at the municipal level, globally, like TI, and at all levels in between. TI represents a Global AN – a GAN. Its founding illustrates one of the three ways that ANs are launched: with individual leadership. Another way they often arise is from ad hoc meetings of organizations, such as around a particular crisis or as a committee that looks at an issue. Participants then realize that they need to create a more integrated joint effort. The Global Water Partnership, a GAN, grew out of annual meetings on water issues in the 1990s where funders realized they needed a more sustained collaborative effort. A third common way ANs are initiated is when an organization creates a program with multi-stakeholder ownership that eventually is spun off on its own. For example, the Global Reporting Initiative GAN arose from a program of the American NGO CERES to address the challenge of collecting data on corporations' social-financial-economic impact. Sometimes, there is

---

146　Transparency International. 2015."Our History - In the Beginning." https://www.transparency.org/whoweare/history/: Transparency International.

Box 8A: ANs and Other Organizing Forms

ANs focusing on prototyping will have social innovation lab characteristics; all ANs focus on learning and capacity development and therefore have community of practice qualities. However, a distinctive quality of an AN is that it sees its core role is about organizing, visioning, advocating, and disseminating – actually changing the SCS – by building breadth of engagement and depth of change. It is a key large systems change agent. With a firm foundation developed with processes like the Collective Leadership Compass, an AN develops the system change process identified in the process map (Figure 8B).

a formal consultation process amongst stakeholders that leads to their collective recognition that they need to work together more creatively. This is the story behind RE-AMP, an AN in the north-central US that formed after a foundation conducted consultations and sponsored meetings (see Box 4C). More recently, a new launching process has developed: ANs themselves spin off other ANs. For example, TI has spun off the Extractive Industries Transparency Initiative (EITI) that focuses on a sub-set of transparency issues.

ANs' development can be described in terms of stages. Each stage is characterized by a specific set of questions that must be answered in order to move powerfully into the next stage. These questions are addressed by a set of activities (see Table 8A). This is all presented as a guide and

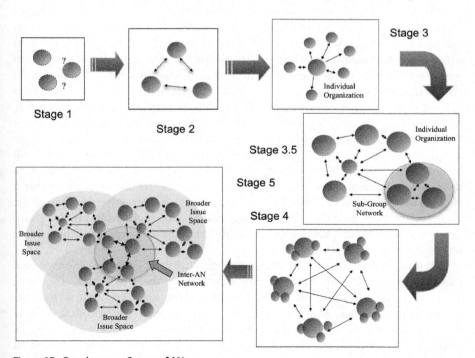

Figure 8D: Development Stages of ANs

different ANs have variations. Moreover, although it is generally true that there is a linear development process, this process is neither predictable nor irreversible. ANs might stop development at an earlier stage and still make important contributions. Moreover, there is more than one case in which an AN became a non-AN. For example, at early stages, the Global Alliance for Improved Nutrition (GAIN) was developing as a dynamic AN, but then, in association with the replacement of its Executive Director, GAIN simply became another bureaucracy with offices in various countries. The Kimberley Process, to stop financing conflicts through diamond sales, was at one point an AN. However, under undue influence from intergovernmental organization models, it expanded to include the governments of countries opposed to basic Process evolution (Zimbabwe, Russia, and Venezuela), and it lost its drive for change and continual advancement.

In the beginning – presented as Stage 1 – an issue is addressed in various ways by different organizations. The organizations start to become aware of each other, such as through Peter's TI investigations. This is a "sensing" stage to understand who is in the change arena, their current relationships, and who to bring together to "steward" AN development. In this stage, participants investigate their larger operating environment and what others are doing around their issue. They broaden their understanding about the collective definition of their shared challenge, diverse perspectives surrounding it and the collaborative effort required to address it. At this sensing stage, the systemic change matrix (Chapter 6) can be of enormous support, along with other mapping approaches (Chapter 8).

At this early stage, one key activity is boundary definition, which is an agreement about who is in and who is out of the emerging network community. This can be contentious, since some see enemies whereas others see opportunities. In Stage 2, this moves into more formal issue definition. The definition of corruption might seem obvious, but there were numerous discussions about the definition that held organizations together to form TI: *Corruption is the abuse of entrusted power for private gain. It can be classified as grand, petty and political, depending on the amounts of money lost and the sector where it occurs.* If an issue definition is too loose, common interests will be vague and there will be insufficient energy amongst participants. On the other hand, if the definition is too tight, there will be no "new" advantage from working together and organizations will drift back to their own individual ways of working. Very often, the definition of the problem changes during a GAN's life, as its participants deepen their understanding of the issue and/or they shift their focus as they realize success. In addition, the group must be able to attract participants of a caliber that make it appear legitimate or it will become irrelevant.

A small group stewards development; this can happen before more formal mapping and system analysis, or may arise out of these activities. The term "steward" emphasizes the collaborative quality of the work and that actions are always being undertaken on behalf of the broader system, which contains many leaders (see Chapter 9). To facilitate expansion, the term supports a dynamic of expanding co-ownership and engagement, in contrast to "permanence" around an individual or a limited number of individuals or organizations.

Table 8A: ANs' Development Stages[147]

	Stage 1	Stage 2	Stage 3	Stage 4
Key Questions	• What is the issue? • What is the vision? • Who should we convene? • How do we convene? Who will finance the exploration?	• What is holding us back from realizing the vision? • What are possible technical responses? • What are the stakeholders' roles in these responses? • What outcomes would individual stakeholders value? • Who/what is a "member?" • Who will finance initiation?	• How do we bring in new participants? • How do we manage global diversity? • How do we create robust sub-global structures? • How do we balance "going deep" and "going wide?" • What is the financial strategy?	• How do we create robust inter-node relationships? • How do we change the culture globally to support our vision? • How can we enhance legitimacy, accountability, and transparency? • How can we provide value on a massive scale? • How do we manage the "tipping point?" • What is the financial strategy?
Activities	• Consultations • Stakeholder identification • Mapping • Convening • Vision creation	• Piloting technical solutions • Creating initial network piloting structures • Defining the problem	• Broadening the application of physical technology solutions • Deepening understanding of social technology challenges • Increasing membership. • Decentralizing the structure	• Spinning off new entities • Mainstreaming issue with other organizations • Increasing the number of network nodes • Broadening to grass-roots

In Stage 2, they start to do something together to address an issue. At this point, they establish a joint identity – sometimes simply named a committee, coalition, alliance – and think of themselves as members or participants. Their actual activity can fall into any of the seven functions identified for Societal Change Systems (SCSs) in Chapter 6. A key activity is developing experiments to illustrate how the diverse organizations can work together to address their issue. This often contributes to issue definition. For example, at this stage, Transparency International developed a way to measure corruption and created the Transparency Index framework. These activities give AN participants the opportunity to learn about each other, including distinct competencies, and get a better sense of their potential. It is important to develop a framework that all key potential participants can identify with and become engaged when applying. Without this shared task, network cohesion will be weak.

---

147 Originally published in: Waddell, Steven. 2011. *Global Action Networks: Creating our future together.* Bocconi University on Management. Hampshire, UK: Palgrave-Macmillan.

Stage 3 is when the attention focuses on further growth in terms of geography and participants. Classically, this is framed as a quandary between "going wide" and "going deep." ANs usually develop highly opportunistic responses to people's energy and resources. More organizations become involved, interactions

---

Box 8B: Great Bear Rainforest: The evolution of complex multi-stakeholder governance[1]

The Central and North Coast of British Columbia (B.C.) (Canada) was branded the Great Bear Rainforest by environmental organizations during their campaign to increase protection of endangered old growth forests. The Rainforest's rich wildlife includes huge grizzly bears and the Spirit Bear, a type of black bear. The remote region traces a narrow strip of Canada's western coastline more than 400 kilometers south to north along the fjords, and 64,000 square kilometers in total size (comparable in size to the German state of Bavaria). Trees average 350 years old, and many individual trees are 1,000 years old or older.

The forests became the center of conflicts in the 1980s as environmentalists waged pitched battles against forest companies and loggers. More than 800 people were arrested in the largest act of civil disobedience in Canadian history when protesters blocked logging roads and climbed trees to protect them from cutting. Forcing Changes strategies also included consumer boycotts that resonated in important Japanese, American and European forest product markets.

Government attempts at land use planning in the 1990s failed. The 2000 announcement of a cease-fire between environmentalists and companies was accompanied by the formation of The Joint Solutions Project (a multi-stakeholder environmentalist-corporation initiative).

Claims to the land by First Nations people (aboriginal Canadians) had standing in Canadian courts, giving them unusual power matched with moral authority. The Turning Point Initiative also was established to ensure that the government and other parties were mindful of the rights and interests of First Nations.

In 2001, all parties and the provincial government agreed to a new land use planning process. With funding from industry, environmental organizations, and the provincial and federal governments, the Coast Information Team (CIT) was created to provide independent scientific guidance. With extensive stakeholder engagement, all parties supported a broadly framed ecosystem based management plan in 2009. Six years later, again with extensive engagement, a detailed plan was approved. In essence, the process marked the evolution of a traditional government-run planning process to a multi-stakeholder one. The role of the government has become more like a secretariat for stakeholders, rather than a hierarchical governing entity. And at the same time, the First Nations evolved into a more powerful and sophisticated governance role.

---

1   *Sources*: Armstrong, Patrick. Undated. "Great Bear Rainforest Lessons Learned 1995-2009 ": Moresby Consulting.
Waddell, Steven. 2005. *Societal Learning and Change: How Governments, Business and Civil Society are Creating Solutions to Complex Multi-Stakeholder Problems*. Sheffield, UK: Greenleaf Publishing.

increase and sub-groups form. The network decentralizes its structure and activities to form subgroups. These might form around some sub-aspect of the issue, strategy and/or task. The application of frameworks, like the Transparency Index, broadens. For geographically expansive ANs, regions emerge, often quite spontaneously: the Global Compact was astonished in an early-stage review to find that participants had developed national chapters around the world. New stewarding groups emerge for these subgroups.

A big trap can be giving too much attention too early to questions about how to organize and make decisions. The answers to these questions should arise naturally from work. Otherwise, it cuts off innovative responses. TI eventually developed around national federations, referred to as Chapters, and the Global Reporting Initiative developed around particular industries and their idiosyncratic reporting needs. Often, at this Stage, there is a need for leadership renewal, since growing the network requires different skills from founding it.

The core organizing imperative is a commitment to a change mission and vision (remember, it is a complex vision about direction, rather than a complicated goal), as well as mutual accountability between the nodes as they undertake action. This is usually associated with statements of values and principles that must be interpreted within local contexts. For example, the Forest Stewardship Council is organized around three core stakeholder groups: business, environmental NGOs and social impact NGOs. But, in Canada, the First Nations people ("Indians") have a particularly important role and this led to organizationally recognizing them as a fourth stakeholder group. The mutual accountability principle requires ways to eject participants not working in accordance with the purpose. For example, the Global Compact "delisted" thousands of companies that were not fulfilling reporting requirements; the TI-Kenya office itself became embroiled in corruption, which resulted in its decertification (and later restarting with a different group).

Figure 8C shows a Stage 4 network without a center. The AN operates as a dispersed set of activities, with modest reference to each other as nodes specializing in different regions or other sub-groups. It is a mistake to think of the nodes operating within a geographic hierarchy (eg: for GANs, thinking that the global node directs other nodes). Unfortunately, people very easily slip into this thought pattern since it is so clearly a part of their organizational experience. For GANs, a global node is not a "head office" in any command and/or control sense. Rather, it has two functions. One, as with other nodes, is to work with organizations within its issue sphere; however, it focuses on global organizations. For example, TI worked with the OECD to establish a convention on corruption. Second, the global node supports network participants at global events, such as through TI's annual assembly. Similarly, it provides communications support and ways for members to identify global issues needing attention. In a highly functioning Stage 4, network nodes do not "go through" the global node to communicate with one another – they communicate directly. No "approval" is needed. Most GANs refer to their global node as "the secretariat" – a term I dislike because it sets up intergovernmental organizations, like the UN that uses the term, as comparable. I prefer simply "TI-Global," just like TI-Bangladesh.

Increasingly, ANs are entering Stage 5, recognizing the need to create connections between issues. At this stage, ANs focused on different issues start working together to overcome issue silos. They share "logics" in the way that they work and their values, which makes this relatively easy. On the global level, this collaboration occurs in conjunction with intergovernmental organizations. We can see the UN Global Compact taking leadership on economic-related issues with GRI, TI, and the Principles for Responsible Investment, in particular. Around the Food and Agriculture Organization in Rome, we can see something potentially emerging, such as connections between it and GANs, like the International Land Coalition, the Sustainable Food Lab, Ecoagriculture Partners and the Blue Number Initiative. With regards to health, the World Health Organization has taken a role in developing numerous GANs, including: the Stop TB Initiative, the Global Alliance for Improved Nutrition (which is no longer really a GAN) and the Global Fund to Fight AIDS, Tuberculosis and Malaria (which is by far the largest GAN financially, distributing billions of dollars).

The true power of GANs is still to be realized. In Guatemala, a colleague and I brought together the Forest Stewardship Council, the Youth Employment Summit, IUCN, TI, the Microcredit Summit Campaign, Social Accountability International, The Access Initiative and others to test our hypothesis that they would, because of similar organizational logic, be able to easily work together. This was supported by a two-day meeting, which resulted in a proposal to focus on the country's Cotan watershed to collaboratively apply over three years GANs' expertise and resources to advance development opportunities. Unfortunately, we could not find the funding resources to support the initiative.

Even with their global reach and scale, GANs do have ability to tip systems into true transformation. They are a part of the larger SCS, even if they are major players. They play within the Co-creating Strategy quadrant described in Chapter 5. Other strategies are needed. Even within the Co-creating Strategy, GANs participants include only some initiatives in their issue arena.

Chapter 9

Applying the Appropriate Tools: Which One, and When

Chapter Summary

There are an overwhelming number of tools to support large systems change analysis and organizing events. Which methods and tools are appropriate for use at what times in the transformation process? How should they be used? This chapter aims to address these questions, with a particular focus on mapping approaches useful for seeing and developing various aspects of change initiatives and SCSs.

Societal change systems (SCSs) and the field of large systems change (LSC) knowledge and practice are still at a relatively early development stage. This is reflected in the fragmentation of knowledge, tools, and methods amongst pioneer innovators and their specialties: collaborative impact is associated with FSG, David Cooperrider is associated with appreciative inquiry, Peter Senge with system dynamics (mapping), Otto Scharmer with Theory U, Dave Snowden with SenseMaker, Juanita Brown with World Café, Steve Borgatti and others with Social Network Analysis, Reos Partners with Change Labs, Petra Kuenkel with Collective Leadership, and Verna Allee with Value Network Analysis, etc. How can the enormous range of approaches be understood so that you know when to use each method and tool?

I want to suggest a distinction between a "tool" and a "method." Scharmer's Theory U, for example, is a methodological approach (see Chapter 4). It describes a way to frame and investigate the LSC process; it is the strategy that gives rise to tactics as the process unfolds. While acting with this approach, numerous tools are available. For example, social presencing theater is a tool promoted for moving from an intellectual and mental understanding to an embodied physical-emotional experience of the Theory U. However, the distinction between methods and tools is hard to maintain. Even in this chapter, I will move back and forth, but will put more focus on tools.

There are different ways to organize tools to help you more easily identify the one that is appropriate for your needs. Tool choice is influenced by where you are in the change process described in Chapter 8. Many are useful at multiple places in that process. The application and use of "process tools" that engage people should be understood as a means of supporting a change process, rather than as the process itself. There is a tendency, for example, for people to become "event- and meeting-centric" – that is, to think of meetings and events as being the change process itself, rather than as important, but modest, milestones that require substantial preparation and follow-up if they are to be effective.

There is still way too much use of panels and people talking *at* others, particularly in academic and government forums (most particularly, in UN-associated organizations). These are erroneously viewed as examples of "tools for change." I remember a meeting of the Youth Employment Summit at the Alexandria Library (Egypt) attended by hundreds of energetic youth from around the world. The activities were organized around speakers and panels of officials in a large theater with fixed seating, such as is historically common in universities. Of course, the youth were not having much of that. They were meeting in hallways and other spaces to share their knowledge and make plans. I had unsuccessfully encouraged the event organizers to think of the event as an action planning event. This would mean organizing activities so that: participants could do at least some work in advance; coherence around a vision would be reinforced; participants could develop clear ideas about the next steps in giving life to their vision; and people could leave with a personal network to support realizing their vision. In the case of the Alexandria meeting, I was told that government pooh-bahs needed star time in front to massage their egos and to create amongst the pooh-bahs event visibility, legitimacy, and funding. LSC and ego-based pooh-bahs do not work well together.

Way too many resources and precious face-to-face time are spent on "cold" interactions, like document and information exchange that can usually be handled via virtual exchanges. Face-to-face interactions should ideally focus on "warm" co-creation and co-development activities. The latter are core dynamic and "tools" of LSC. Warm activities are grounded in the understanding that (1) *everyone* present has some expertise and a critical role to play in the change effort (or else they should not be there); and (2) people playing their roles effectively requires meaningful engagement in strategy development, so they understand well enough to work independently with a coherent dispersed action logic, rather than a top-down approach. The LSC emergence dynamic, with many unknowns, means that people undertake independent actions, rather than "checking back" for approval when new questions inevitably emerge as they experiment.

LSC and SCS development is dominated by collaboration, rather than consultation. The distinction between these two is very often missed. Consultation means you ask for opinions and information in response to some specific pre-s questions and goals. Consultation is an important LSC activity. However, any consultation is subsumed within the over-arching collaboration dynamic, which means collectively defining goals and processes to realize them. Of course, we are not speaking of complicated goals, but rather complex ones (as distinguished in Chapters 2 and 4).

Table 9A organizes some tools for LSC processes by categories described by their purpose. Within the rest of this chapter, I spend significant time distinguishing between Systems Mapping methods, because I have not found a place where this is done well. The Intra-Meeting and Collective Action Processes are so numerous and well-documented elsewhere that I share an overview of the U.S. National Coalition for Dialogue & Deliberation, and I also refer you to other resources. With social media, a burgeoning field, I suggest a way to categorize approaches based on their function in a social change system. With learning processes, I focus on learning system development. To address Assessment Processes, I share some key ideas about how to approach the issue; and with Big Data, I note its importance.

Table 9A: Transformation and Change Tools

Tool Category	Purpose	Examples (illustrative, not comprehensive)
Systems Mapping	Develop an understanding of the change system and its dynamics	Social Network Analysis, System Dynamics Analysis, Value Network Analysis, Strategic Clarity Analysis, Systemic Change Matrix, Web Crawls, and Sense-Maker
Foresight, Scenarios	Create alternative views of timelines and possibilities	Trend Projection, Problem-Focused Scenarios, Actor-Centric Scenarios, Reflexive Interventionist/Multi-Agent-based Scenarios
Intra-Meeting Processes	Generative dialogue, honoring differences/ commonalities	Process Facilitation, World Café, Open Space, Charrettes, Wisdom Circles, and 21st Century Town Meetings
Collective Action Processes	Develop action that transcends differences	Future Search, Consensus Conferences, Sustained Dialogues, Appreciative Inquiry, National Issue Forums, Public Conversations, Theory U, and Rapid Cycle Prototyping
Social Media	Connect large numbers of people and organizations	Avaaz, U-Tube, MadMundo TV, MOOCs, Crowdfunding, Facebook, Kickstarter, and Razoo
Learning Processes	Invent and build capacity	Action Research/Inquiry/Science, Learning Histories, Learning Journeys, and After Action Reviews
Assessment Processes	Understand how to do better	Developmental Evaluation, Outcome Mapping, and Other Mapping
Visual Analytics Big Data Collection	Understand the change field	Analysis of spatial relationships, text and concepts, time/trends, and objects' relationships

Systems Mapping

Large numbers of people and organizations with a wide array of roles and relationships are part and parcel of LSC. LSC's scale and complexity commonly provoke confusion. Describing relationships to support seeing "the whole" is important for strategic action. There are various ways of doing this by visually showing connections between resources, concepts, organizations, systems, data, and individuals. This is what I mean by "mapping."

Some people associate mapping with long-worded descriptions and extensive lists of who is doing what; generally, I do not find that useful because holding this in my head is impossible. Rather, I prefer visual explanations with diagrams and tables that are supported by a modest number of words.

This type of mapping makes an enormous contribution to strategy, enhancing the collective impact in a complex system. Mapping's greatest strength is its ability to create good conversations amongst stakeholders to understand a system; its greatest danger is the ease with which people can think of it as *being* reality, rather than simply one representation of it. Mapping:

- Builds a common understanding of the *system* that is the objective of change, ensuring people are talking about the same thing;
- Develops an understanding of how a particular organization, concept, activity, program or action "fits" in terms of prioritizing and crafting actions;
- Identifies important leverage points to enhance collective action by addressing gaps, potential synergies, blockages, and redundancies.

Mapping can also play an evaluative function. In LSC a common goal is reconfiguring structures and relationships. Repeated mapping at reasonable intervals shows how a system is changing. One time series over five years in the media sphere, starting in 1999, showed Google as a small, peripheral actor with the New York Times a central player. Five years later, Google was much more central, and the Times was dramatically less so. Of course, causal relationships and attributions that explain change are often much more difficult to identify.

Maps can be generated by "experts." But generally, mapping is a great participatory collaborative activity undertaken by people working face-to-face on an issue, supported by experts. It helps build a common understanding of "what is" through discussion from individuals' perspectives about the current state of the change system. All mapping includes the:

- Purpose of the system being mapped, such as food production or ideas relevant to climate change;
- Boundaries, which decide what organizations/people/roles/concepts to include and exclude;
- Relationships between concepts, organizations or people, defined by exchanges or linkages; and
- Nodes, which are the unit of focus, such as an activity, individual, organization, role, or concept.

Sometimes in the mapping process, and always in the LSC process, the definition of a purpose changes as people deepen their understanding of needs and possibilities, potential purposes, and the range of purposes associated with an issue. For example, in the German energy case, the system purpose shifted from simple energy provision to clean energy provision. This also changes maps' boundaries, relationships, and nodes.

Table 9B: Important LSC Mapping Methods

Method	Map Focus	Core Output
Societal Change System Mapping	Change initiatives	Map issue change system in terms of key sub-systems and functions
Concept Mapping	Concepts	Map relationship between ideas
Managing for Analysis Clarity	Theories of Change	Map integrating change theories within the issue arena
SenseMaker	Stories	Map beliefs in terms of relative strength
Social Network Analysis	Relationship Structure	Map individuals'/ organizations' relationships
System Dynamics	System forces	Map stocks and flows with organizations and activities
Value Network Analysis	Value creation	Map relationship between roles and exchanges
Web Crawl	Virtual reality	Map virtual relationships and list websites

Table 9B offers an overview of some mapping methods I've found particularly useful for LSC. These are described in greater detail below. Note the listed outputs are simply the distinctive ones: all methods can include on their maps a lot of information about the characteristics of their focus, such as distinguishing between size, type, and the strength of nodes and connections.

A danger in presenting maps as I do here is that you will simply be overwhelmed or frustrated by them, because they contain so much information. One challenge for change makers is to spend time studying maps – think of them as replacing many pages of text.

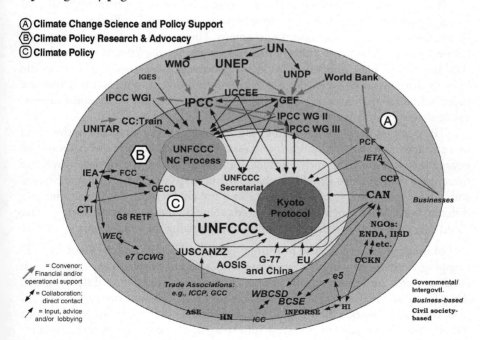

Figure 9A: Concept Map of the Climate Change System

Societal Change System Mapping: This mapping approach was a focus of Chapter 6, so I won't go into more details. But remember it is part of your mapping options! It is particularly useful when there is a need to build coherence with a large set of change activities.

Concept Mapping: Sometimes, it is valuable to show the relationship between different aspects of an issue – such as geography, players, and roles in a development process. Concept mapping can take numerous perspectives to describe a space in ways that provide strategic insight. This approach is associated with mind-mapping, an approach commonly used in planning meetings.

Several years ago, the Figure 9A map was developed by Tariq Banuri and myself to understand climate policy development. This is an extremely complex field, and the multitude of relationships is very difficult to grasp. How can this be described in a way that is sufficiently comprehensive, relatively easily understood, and summarized on a page? The product in Figure 9A integrates a type of Social Network Analysis (SNA: see further on) with networks and their role in three major concept activities of (1) science and policy support, (2) research and advocacy, and (3) climate policy. Policy is the central process, and the United Nations Framework Convention on Climate Change (UNFCCC) and the Kyoto Protocol were central to policy development, so we put them at the center. Then, we analyzed the major roles of *networks* (rather than organizations, to cut down on the number of actors) – there is a wide range of players who provide support, advocacy, research, lobbying, citizen voices, and information.

It was important to distinguish the sector (business, government, and civil society) associated with networks, since they come with such different concerns – hence, the different type faces for the acronyms. There is a slew of alliances between networks that are also important to describe, so connecting lines were introduced. And the players have different roles in the process, so arrows were placed on the lines to distinguish between three particularly important roles. Some actors are more influential than others, so as a very rough estimate of influence, some organizations were given larger acronyms than others.

The completed diagram describes the dynamics and participants in the arena in a succinct way that facilitates discussion. Are the stakeholders who should be engaged, engaged? Sufficiently engaged? Engaged in the appropriate way? Are there ways relationships should be changed…perhaps made more direct? Should some "new space" be created, because some stakeholders need connections in a different way? Maybe the whole arena needs some fundamental rethinking – what could that look like? The diagram facilitates addressing these questions.

Managing from Clarity Mapping (MfC): This is an off-shoot of SD mapping, developed by Jim Ritchie-Dunham. Different people in any issue system (such as water, peacekeeping, global finance, and health care) have different goals. They focus on different parts of the system and have different understandings of how "the system" works: they have different "mental models" and theories of change (Chapter 4). Mapping with the strategic clarity framework developed by Ritchie-Dunham makes these differences explicit so people can more effectively work collaboratively and the "whole system" can see itself.

A MfC map includes a description of how each stakeholder's actions and incentives impact the intended and unintended actions of other stakeholders, and how this set of actions impacts the overall system intention. The framework provides the basis for identifying potential highly strategic leverage points that could "shift" the system's behavior in the desired direction.

This mapping framework based upon mental models is grounded in systems theory and decision sciences. The framework

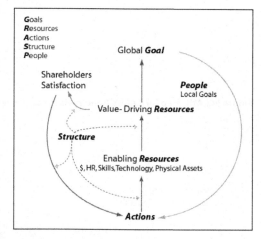

Figure 9B: Generic MfC Map

provides five principles to describe a complex issue system: **Goal**, **Resources**, **Actions**, **Structure**, and **People** (GRASP).

- **Goal:** Why does the network exist?
- **Resources:** Which resources drive stakeholder value and which enable work to be done that creates stakeholder value?
- **Actions:** Which actions most effectively leverage enabling resources?
- **Structure:** What are the linkages among the goals, resources, and actions?
- **People:** What do people care about in this system?

These principles are structured in a map in a specific order, as shown in the generic MfC map in Figure 9B in which actions are at the bottom and the goal is at the top.

In 2004, I worked with Ritchie-Dunham and CARE in Guatemala to use MfC to understand the dynamics of poverty and actions to combat it. This was done very interactively with people in CARE and those working on poverty alleviation. The maps were developed by interviewing people about why they do what they do, defining their own change theory with respect to their specific work. In the Guatemala case, people were carrying out a wide range of activities to address poverty, from supporting education to digging wells. They all have distinct ideas about how their activities impact poverty. Figure 9C is part of the map, developed with the person leading land reform programs. Nine similar maps were made around other activities. These were then integrated with some activities for CARE (as an organization). That produced a spaghetti diagram with 177 variables that appears overwhelmingly complicated. However, because it was developed by system participants, they understood it intimately. On our return a year later, we discovered that they had a large printed version in their office that they referenced when thinking through strategic questions. Even more importantly, they had significantly changed their relationships and the people and organizations that they worked with to better align with their change strategy.

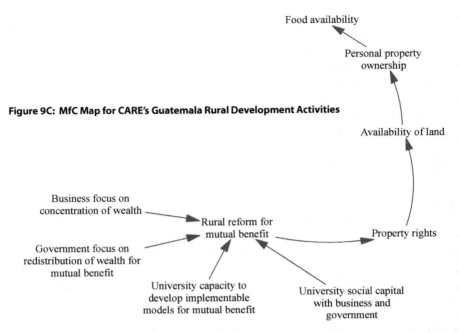

Figure 9C: MfC Map for CARE's Guatemala Rural Development Activities

MfC was the critical framework to transform very poorly connected efforts to address climate change into a powerful change system, called RE-AMP (see Box 6C).

More about this approach can be found in Ritichie-Dunham, J., & Rabbino, H. (2001). *Managing from Clarity: Identifying, Aligning and Leveraging Strategic Resources.* Chichester, UK: John Wiley & Sons, Ltd. Contact Luz Maria Puente: luzma@instituteforstrategicclarity.org

SenseMaker: Developed by Dave Snowden of cynefin complexity fame (see Figure 2A), SenseMaker® has been used with a wide range of issues, such as terrorism, the role of girls in Rwanda, and health care in the United Kingdom. It is a story-telling research methodology that captures and analyzes large numbers of very short stories about individuals' experiences (with respect to an issue). It bridges a gap between case studies and large-sample survey data to identify patterns and trends. The questions are always about how to "shift" attitudes, behaviors, and beliefs from current problematic ones to preferable ones. The data describe an issue in terms of "sets" of attitudes, behaviors, and beliefs; this produces maps that identify sets that are more desirable and have the potential to become dominant via interventions.

In Rwanda, Girl Hub asked caregivers for stories describing a moment or event when they felt encouraged or concerned about girls' situations. The open-ended nature of SenseMaker prompts allows storytellers to share stories of their own choosing and enables researchers to collect narratives on the same topic from various perspectives. Each respondent also gives his or her story a unique title. Following this, respondents convey the meaning of their stories by completing analytical questions called the 'signification framework.' That framework is a set of questions based on predefined topics of interest for investigation, which allows the storyteller to analyze his/her own story. Girl Hub first developed these topics during participatory research with girls and continues to evolve them to address specific research questions. Patterns and linkages later emerge during the analytical process, enabling people to make sense of the diverse and complex stories being shared. The analysis led Girl Hub to revise its advocacy and program strategies, to prioritize addressing violence. Stories also were integrated into radio drama. [148]

In another case, the goal was to encourage behaviors and attitudes that would enhance safety in handling chemicals. The data was transformed into Figure 9D. This is like a topographical map, but rather than representing increasing elevations, the lines represent an increasing concentrations of responses (each circle is a response).

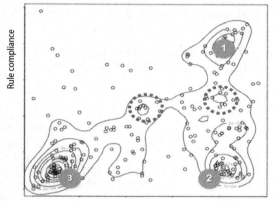

- In the top right, we have a pattern of observations that represent both compliance with organizational rules and chemical handling procedures and task completion.
- Area two, bottom right, represents a pattern of getting the job done regardless of rules.
- Area three, bottom left indicates (depressingly) indifference to rules and a lack of task completion.

Figure 9D: SenseMaker Map

The two dotted circles represent patterns of behavior that are an improvement on the current state, and closer to it than the ideal. In complexity, this is known as the *adjacent possible*. It represents an achievable point to move Area 2 and 3 to 1. So, the facilitator could now sit down with the participants, point to the dotted area, and ask: *What can we do tomorrow to get more like this?* They can also do the same with areas two and three and ask: *And what can we do to create fewer situations like these?*

The visualization shows the disposition of the system (how it tends to behave), and indicates how it can be nudged to move towards a more desirable state.

Social Network Analysis (SNA): This form of mapping describes relationships between individuals; individual-level information can be extrapolated to identify relationships between organizations. This is a labor-intensive form of mapping and demands the most stakeholder time. Survey and interview data iden-

---

148 Cognitive Edge. 2014. "Using Sensemaker to Understand Girls' Lives: Lessons Learnt From GirlHub": Cognitive Edge.

tify relationships that individuals have with others in the studied system – in LSC, it is usually an inter-organizational (rather than intra-organizational) system. Maps can provide various qualitative indicators, such as intensity and strengths of relationships. They describe how information flows in the system and who is connected to whom. Following are key concepts:

- Hubs: these are nodes that are connected to numerous system participants, and they are important both to engage and to investigate as possible bottlenecks.
- Structural holes: these refer to a lack of connections, where connections are required for effective network functioning.
- Cliques: these are "sub-systems" of well-connected system members, often requiring a collective strategy to bringing them into a new initiative.
- Bridging: some participants have unusual relationships that connect to people outside their clique; these are important to know about, particularly in structuring multi-stakeholder networks, since these people have comfort and facility crossing stakeholder lines.

There are many software programs that support SNA. The one most popular with academics is UCINET, which provides detailed data. However, much of the

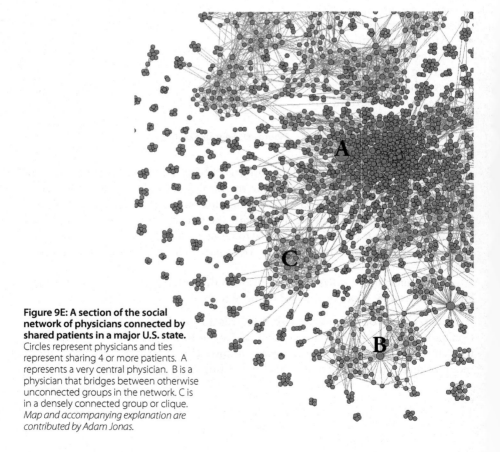

Figure 9E: A section of the social network of physicians connected by shared patients in a major U.S. state.
Circles represent physicians and ties represent sharing 4 or more patients. A represents a very central physician. B is a physician that bridges between otherwise unconnected groups in the network. C is in a densely connected group or clique.
Map and accompanying explanation are contributed by Adam Jonas.

detail is not really helpful for the vagaries of large system change. Other software produces much more powerful visual images.

Figure 9E is from a big data project on the nationwide social networks of U.S. mental health physicians. In the whole visual (this is only a section), 3,386 physicians are represented as circles. Each of the 12,007 ties denote sharing 4 or more patients. Patient sharing has been found (in previous research) to be a reliable proxy for social relations between physicians. The larger circles are doctors (e.g.: A) who have the highest degree of connections to other doctors via shared patients. These doctors are highly central and serve as hubs. They may be influential both through direct social connections to others and indirectly by high network visibility. Once identified, these doctors would be critical to reach if you were trying to spur systemic change, since they are highly connected and likely influential.

Upon further inspection of the social network map, you notice that many dense clusters of socially connected doctors exist within the state. Often, these are associated with geographic closeness. Clusters in which everyone knows everyone else are what network researchers call cliques. Cliques are densely connected social groups that can serve as incubators for certain ideas or behaviors. In this particular study, statistical analysis showed doctors within these groups tended to prescribe similarly priced medicines. If you are seeking a second opinion or if you want a cheaper generic medicine, it may be important to find a doctor who is part of a different clique.

Some doctors form bridges between groups. These doctors, despite maybe not being as immediately central, are especially important to the entire network, since they connect otherwise disconnected groups (this is referred to as spanning structural hole in SNA jargon), allowing resources to flow between groups. These brokers are vitally important to changing large social systems since they can reach different groups and help others understand what resources certain groups have compared with others. However, if certain individuals or organizations in the network bridge a substantial portion of the network, they can become a bottleneck for the system and can act as a gatekeeper, leveraging their position for their gain, often to overall system detriment.

If you want to try this out for your own network, you can do this for your LinkedIn contacts by going to: socilab.com. It is really a great way to start to understand SNA power.

System Dynamics (SD) Mapping: In every system, a range of forces is pressing for diverse ends. Understanding how these forces interact is critical to network development. They often have unpredictable collective impacts, often referred to as "perverse" and "unintended" consequences. System dynamics describe the forces and flows in complex systems to help understand the impact of possible interventions. The following are core SD mapping concepts:

- Causal structure: the most basic illustration of this is that doing "x" produces "y;"
- Feedback loops: when "x" produces "y," there are outcomes that flow back to "x" – either directly or indirectly through other variables;
- Flows: these are system activities that produce stocks;
- Stocks: these are the products of the flows of a system (for example: the number of trees in a forest, and the financial assets of an individual);

- Time delays: often, there are delays in the impact of "x" on "y" that must be accounted for when undertaking interventions.

SD mapping requires background research and interviews with stakeholders representing a microcosm of the system. Once the underlying causal structure is identified, the SD map can be used for a scenario analysis of the dynamic impacts of various interventions. It helps guide both internal strategic planning and external stakeholder engagement vis-à-vis the goal of increasing a specific stock. However, it is important to remember that SD is best for a *complicated* system with engineering-type relationships; in complex systems, relationship patterns, as well as goals, are always changing.

Figure 9F is an example of a SD map prepared by Joe Hsueh to support

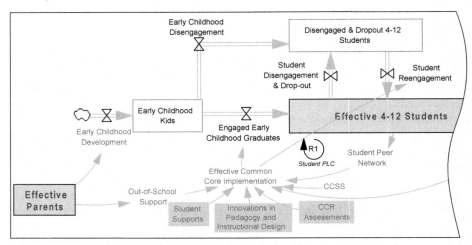

Figure 9F: Education System Dynamics Partial Map (Produced by Joe Hsueh)

addressing concerns about school drop-outs. The purpose of the system is "Effective, Responsible, Happy Citizens." It identified "Effective Common Core Implementation" as a key intervention. In this example:

- **Stocks** are exemplified by rectangles, such as "Effective 4-12 Students;" the intervention aimed at increasing this stock. Effective Common Core Implementation is driven by the stocks of Out-of-School Supports, Student Supports, Innovations in Pedagogy and Instructional Design, College and Career Readiness CCR Assessments, Common Core State Standards CCSS, and the Student Peer Network, among others.
- **Flows** are indicated by the **hollow arrow** with valve signs indicating what is moving. The core flow is newborns growing from *Early Childhood Kids* to *Effective 4-12 Students* to *Higher Education Students* to *Entry-level Job Employees* to *Effective Responsible Happy Citizens* – the vision of the education effort.
- **Solid Arrows** represent the direction from cause to effect: e.g., more *Effective Parents* lead to higher *Early Childhood Development* and *Out-of-School Supports*.

- **The R sign** indicates a positive reinforcing **feedback loop**. The R1 Student Peer Network (PN) Loop: more *Effective 4-12 Students* lead to a more effective *Student Peer Network*, which enhances *Effective Common Core Implementation* through peer learning and creates more *Effective 4-12 Students*.
- **Reinforcing feedback loops** are key to scaling up systemic change as various interventions catalyze circular self-reinforcing processes.

In this case, an identified goal was investment in various high-leverage points to the extent where the system tips into self-sustaining change processes. One example is Effective Common Core Implementation.

An example of an adapted SD map is the Systemic Change Process Map (Chapter 8). Another valuable development of SD mapping is identifying "system

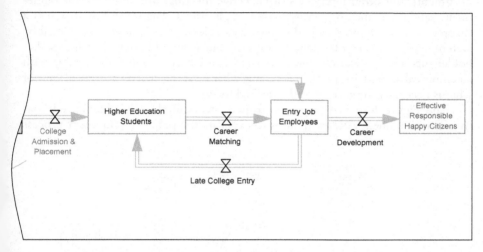

archetypes:" commonly found patterns. For example, one common archetype is the Tragedy of the Commons. This describes the dynamics that give rise to the phenomenon in which people who have common, unfettered access to a common good, such as air, will tend to abuse it (hence, air pollution). There are nine such archetypes, and they can often be found as the basis for LSC issues.[149]

Value Network Analysis (VNA): Designs for potential futures is best done in a way that gets people outside of their organizational boxes and loyalties, and that emphasizes their interest in realizing the over-arching system purpose. To reorient people to the system, rather than specific organizations that may be operating within that system, relationships can be usefully described by two aspects:
- Roles: What kinds of actors are necessary for a system to realize its goal? This is related to the concept of the "function" of an organization in a system. So, while an SNA map has individuals or organizations as network nodes, a

---

149 Kim, Daniel. 1992. *The Toolbox Reprint Series: Systems Archetypes I.* Waltham, MA: Pegasus Communications, Inc.

VNA map will show the role or *type* of actor as nodes within the network. Roles are nouns, like educator and financier.

- Exchanges: What flows between the roles can most helpfully speed the system's success? In a well-defined system, these can be thought of as "deliverables." So, where an SNA map has only one link showing that two nodes are connected, VNA "unpacks" that link into multiple interactions and deliverables that actually define that relationship. Exchanges are nouns, such as money and information.

VNA data can be obtained in two ways. One is an empirical approach that looks at current organizations in the issue arena (or SCS) and analyzes their current roles and exchanges. This data can often be gathered from websites and documents, but often interviews or collective meetings are necessary for refinement, validation, and to identify action implications. The second approach is a theoretical one of imagining the necessary roles and exchanges for a healthy system. Again, this can be done by experts, but is much better done in a stakeholder meeting. Of course, these approaches are best combined – starting with an empirical approach, and then assessing what exists against a theoretical view of what is necessary for success or the desired future.

The Figure 9G VNA map arose from the work on the Global Finance Initiative. The simplified VNA map aims to explicate the policy development process

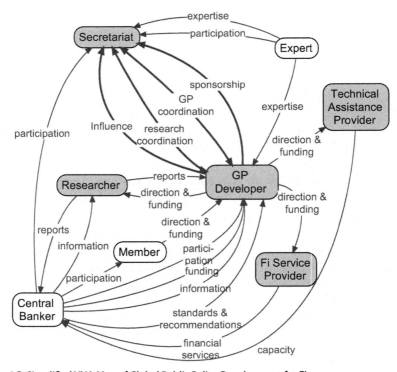

Figure 9G: Simplified VNA Map of Global Public Policy Development for Finance

at the global level for finance. The Bank for International Settlements (BIS), a major international banking organization, plays the roles of global policy (GP) developer, secretariat, technical assistance provider, researcher and financial assistance provider. Those roles are shaded rectangles, with other major roles in clear rectangles. The arrows indicate the exchanges that are critical for the system to work. The diagram helps move people outside of their traditional organizational mindsets to discuss how well particular roles are being played and exchanges being made; THEN, people can get into discussion about organizations and the way roles and exchanges are allocated.

This approach has been pioneered by Verna Allee. See more at vernaallee. com and in Allee, V. (2015). *Value Networks and the True Nature of Collaboration:* Meghan-Kiffer Press.

Web Crawl Analysis: This is a comparatively easy way to analyze an issue in terms of "virtual space *website* relationships." With increasing accuracy, these reflect real life inter-organizational relationships. These maps are developed using software that identifies "hyper-links" embedded in organizations' websites, linking

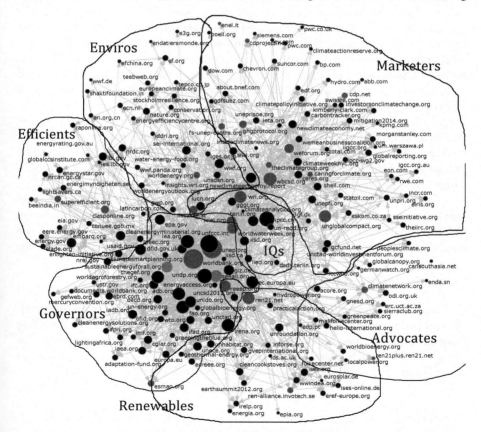

Figure 9H: Web Crawl Map: The Global Electricity Change System

them to another organization's site. This produces two types of useful outputs: one is a diagram that visually represents relationships; a second is a list of websites that are connected and the number of connections. Unlike other mapping, this mapping is simply software-generated, and there is no role for collaborative development. It is very useful to generate conversation collectively, however.

It is important to remember that these maps represent virtual, rather than actual, reality. Their value depends on the quality of websites in your issue arena. To analyze global issue arenas, web crawls are particularly useful: an organization seeking a role in a global issue arena that does not have a relatively good website is probably not much of a player. Web crawls can also be conducted for constrained geographic regions. However, the more local they are, the less informative. The maps should be treated as very generalized data, rather than as surgically accurate data. They are a way to look at patterns, rather than relationship details. For mapping software, I use www.issuecrawler.net (supported by www.govcom.org).

Figure 9H is an example of a web crawl map that I developed for the Energy Ecosystem Lab (Chapter 6). The larger the node, the more links. Software places nodes in "neighborhoods" with the closest connections. This helps understand the "natural" organizing structure. In Figure 9H, there are seven relatively distinct groups that I identified by being familiar with the issue arena and nodes: those focused on influencing the market (Marketers), those primarily concerned with the environment (Enviros) or energy efficiency (Efficients), policy and intergovernmental organizations (Governors), those focused on renewable energy (Renewables), those whose primary activity is advocating for change (Advocates), and research organizations (IQs). This provides valuable insight into natural groupings, but you can see that there is no common denominator. Some congregate by strategy (Advocates), some by role (Governors), some by concern (Efficients, and Enviros), and some by change focus (Marketers). As Chapter 6 explains, mapping the players as a SCS within the systemic change matrix can provide much greater power.

The second web-crawl product is a list of websites identified for the issue arena. It ensures a comprehensive view of who is working on the issue. In Figure 9H, the crawls identified 265 organizations within the issue arena (not all on the map), leading to a list of 65 to focus on in the subsequent more in-depth analysis.

Foresight and Scenarios

The South Africa transition from apartheid involved numerous scenario development processes (as described in Chapter 3). These processes support expanding imagination about possible futures and pathways to them. Again, it is important to engage diverse stakeholders – and as many as possible, if the results are to lead to action. Below, I describe three types of scenario development processes.[150]

---

150 This typology is based on Wilkinson, Angela, and Esther Eidinow. 2008. "Evolving practices in environmental scenarios: A new scenario typology." *Environmental Research Letters* 3(Oct-Dec).

Problem-Focused Scenarios: The goal here is to create accurate maps of the future, enabling others to reach a destination as reliably and efficiently as possible. These are the most common type of scenarios with the longest history. They are associated with war game analysis, and somewhat later, with MIT and the work of leading academics, such as Jay Forrester and John Sterman. They are the product of extrapolating trends, observed or anticipated. They were popularized with the Club of Rome's *Limits to Growth* report, published in 1972, which predicted widespread collapse by 2030 without substantial transformation.[151] It resulted from computer models that extrapolated such things as the amounts of available resources, different levels of agricultural productivity, birth control, and environmental protection. These models are commonly used in economic forecasting. It is the central instrument of the International Panel on Climate Change.

This form of scenario development is especially useful for focusing on issues that need addressing and generating discussion about what to do. It is based on a predictive, complicated approach to issues that requires substantial assumptions about trends and stability.

Actor-Centric Scenarios: "Actor" usually means an organization or group of organizations surrounding an issue. The image here is setting out on a journey and inviting the whole crew to help draw a map of the route that they need to take as an organization or as a system. The questions are about possible futures, and the usual goal is to understand possibilities to more effectively build organizational resilience to respond to various scenarios, undertake interventions to try to support a particular future, or to at least incorporate (potential) implications into strategies and planning. The development of this approach is associated with Shell (the oil company) Intuitive Logics. This is the approach used with South African apartheid (Chapter 3).

This type of scenario is not a forecast about what will or should happen, but rather stories about a few possible futures and how they might come about. Classically, between two and four possible futures are described to emphasize the emergence and range of possibilities with stories that are relevant, challenging, plausible, and clear. In Brazil, Christel Scholten of Reos Partners led this type of investigation into the future of education. The four scenarios arose from discussions with stakeholders from across the education system over three workshops and they varied in the way they combined six dimensions:

1. Diversities and inequalities;
2. Participation and social control;
3. Role of the State (government);
4. Education paradigm;
5. Management model;
6. Public-private balance.

---

151 Meadows, Donella H, Dennis L Meadows, Jørgen Randers, and William W Behrens III. 1972. "The limits to growth. Club of Rome." *New York, Universe.*

The only consensus is on whether the resulting scenarios are plausible – different participants might prefer different scenarios. The scenarios are typically named in a way that will readily bring to mind the scenario in question. In the Brazil case, they were named after birds: the canary scenario had an education system led by the State with pressure and involvement of civil society, maintaining a traditional type of education; the hummingbird scenario emphasized social-technological innovations with different education models in which learning moves beyond school walls through public-private partnerships; the hawk scenario highlighted a reduced role of the State and the transfer of responsibility for delivering education to the private sector, and focused on developing the workforce; the tico-tico bird jumps in the same spot to get its food, and this scenario represented a continuation of the status quo with government incapable of universalizing education, where quality is for only a few and with increasing violence and religious influence.

Reflexive Interventionist/Multi-Agent-based (RIMA) Scenarios: The image associated with this scenario approach is setting out on a journey in which environmental scenarios help to shape not only the route, but also the ship, its crew, and the ocean itself. Rather than being responsive to situations, as in the previous two scenarios, this approach is creative. It represents a way to advance transformation, rather than serve as a one-off series of activities. The route, inquiry, and perceived destination all can change in response to what is learned during the exploration. Continual collaborative thinking and action are emphasized to spur imaginative future thinking. This requires attention to signals about potentially emerging scenarios, and the ability to build on scenarios as they emerge. Stakeholders change as the issue continues to evolve. This approach depends on the ability to articulate, share, and potentially transcend diverse world views.

The RIMA approach was applied in scenario work conducted by Angela Wilkinson that looked at Resource 2050 and the Futures of Low Carbon Mobility.[152] She explains that:

> One way to think of this is as a fusion of sciences - natural and social - a new kind of global systems science - or as design science as some now call collaborative transformational actions. I can confirm that effective intervention results from approaches that use mixed methods (e.g., scenario planning, agent-based modeling, visioning, backcasting and horizon scanning) to avoid the false dichotomy of quantitative versus qualitative. The mix of methods depends on users and their uses/situations and, in particular, the emphasis on reactive (agile, adaptive) and proactive intervention (innovation to create new future possibilities). So, think mid-range theory/ professional practice/critical constructivism rather than empirical research versus subjectivity. The European Community has expressed interest in this method of combining systems sciences with trilateral collaboration to enable transformation policies. It has a grand challenges agenda and there is

---

152 WBCSD. "Vision 2050: The new agenda for business." Geneva, Switzerland: World Business Council for Sustainable Development.

no predictive theory of evolution of living systems and no agreed economic theory for managing the messy multi-dimensional transitions needed in a fast paced, turbulent era of more global and more local, unpredictable uncertainty and unprecedented collaborative potential. So I am glad to be one of many players/niches all striving to find effective alternatives.[153]

Intra-Meeting Events and Collective Action Processes

Intra-meeting processes are associated with meeting "facilitation." During transformation work, this can be enormously helpful in decision-making. A range of tools help support things, such as creativity, synergy, integration of diversity, and transcendence.

I distinguish intra-meeting *events* from collective action *processes* that involve meetings, but also require substantial preparation and follow-up. The meetings are merely a milestone in a more involved process. Classic examples are commissions typically formed by a government to respond to a particular issue. However, they are about reform rather than transformation. The World Commission on Dams (WCD), for example, was formed in the late 1990s in response to a controversy about the impacts of very large dams the World Bank was funding. With multi-stakeholder leadership, the WCD undertook a 2-year process that included extensive hearings and research.

Collective action processes are something between a tool and a theory (based on how I use these terms). Multi-stakeholder approaches grew out of socio-technical traditions of the 1950s and open systems theory with participative design approaches that were most often applied to organizational issues. Fred Emery and Eric Trist were important pioneers (1960s-1980s) for this work, which then expanded to broader issues and produced the Search Conference methodology that was further advanced by Marv Weisbord and Sandra Janoff, as Future Search.[154,155,156] Key concepts are "whole systems" and "stakeholder co-creation," contrasted with the prevailing tendency to approach issues by cutting them into ever smaller parts and having outside experts say what should be done. The collective action processes typically involve a range of activities (for example, mapping) with a focus on collaborative visioning and action planning. This line of work has been more recently popularized by FSG with the term "collective impact".[157] Chapter 8 provided more details about structure.

153 Personal communication, Oct. 25, 2015
154 Bunker, Barbara, and Billie Alban. 1996. *Large Group Interventions : Engaging the Whole System for Rapid Change*. San Francisco, CA, USA: Jossey-Bass.
155 Weisbord, Marvin, and Sandra Janoff. 2010. *Future Search: Getting the Whole System in the Room for Vision, Commitment, and Action*. San Francisco, CA: Berrett-Koehler.
156 Holman, Peggy, and Tom Devane (Eds.). 2007. *The Change Handbook: The Definitive Resource on Today's Best Methods for Engaging Whole Systems*. San Francisco, CA, USA: Berrett-Koehler.
157 Kania, John, and Mark Kramer. 2011. "Collective Impact." *Stanford Social Innovation Review* Winter:36-41, Kania, John, and Mark Krarner. 2013. "Embracing Emergence: How Collective Impact Addresses Complexity." Blog Entry: Stanford Social Innovation Review.

These collective action processes are Co-creating Strategy (as discussed in Chapter 4). They require that participants are committed to addressing the issue, or at least are sincerely interested in exploring ways to address the issue. Some collective action processes purposefully do not engage all stakeholders. WHO, when it started its tobacco-free initiative, specifically did not include tobacco companies that had core purposes opposed to the initiative's goals. The companies could reasonably be expected to slow down and undermine the initiative. Of course, the role of the companies in the change system was a critical concern, nevertheless. Collective action processes require participants to be potential earlier adopters. If a stakeholder cannot commit to change aspirations, it is usually better to approach them with a forcing change strategy.

A great resource for both Intra-Meeting and Collective Action Processes methods is the *Engagement Streams Framework*. This was developed by Sandy Hierbacher and the U.S. National Center for Dialogue & Deliberation (NCDD) to encourage relevant methods to support productive exchanges amongst stakeholders. Table 9C categorizes dialogue and deliberation approaches into four streams (based on one's primary intention or purpose): issue exploration, conflict transformation, decision-making, and collaborative action. A second Table drawn from the NCDD's work describes each process/tool/method in terms of which engagement stream it supports. You can find more information about the NCDD's approach, with good information about 200 methodologies, at http://ncdd.org/rc/item/2142. Another good resource is: Holman, Peggy, and Tom Devane (Eds.). 2007. *The Change Handbook: The Definitive Resource on Today's Best Methods for Engaging Whole Systems*. San Francisco, CA, USA: Berrett-Koehler.

Media/Social Media

Print media has a long history of supporting transformations. Books, newspapers, and pamphlets play key roles in sharing ideas, creating visions, and connecting people. Television has had a similar role. Towards the end of the Cold War in the 1980s, there was an amazing series of broadcast television town hall meetings that brought together small groups of citizens from the Soviet Union and the United States. For the first time, many Americans saw that Russians did not all dress alike, that they had opinions, and could articulately share them. The series humanized what had previously been the 'enemy.'

While traditional media continues to be important, social media is the new power house for transformation. It supports other change methods by connecting very large numbers of individuals. It has developed particular capacities and sites that have made their own distinct additions to transformational change. These can be categorized by how social media contributes to the key functions or activities necessary to realize transformation (as described in Chapter 6 with the Societal Change System matrix).

Visioning: Creating visions of how the world can be different is a core function of many social media discussion groups. These support understanding issues from diverse perspectives, to help create common visions. One particularly sophis-

Table 9C: Engagement Streams Framework

Engagement Stream/ Primary Intention	Key Features	Important When…	Examples of Issues	Organizer's Strategy	Appropriate D&D Processes
Exploration **To encourage people and groups to learn more about themselves, their community, or an issue, and possibly discover innovative solutions**	Suspending assumptions, creating a space that encourages a different kind of conversation, using rituals and symbolism to encourage openness, emphasizing listening	A group or community seems stuck or muddled and needs to reflect on their circumstances in depth and gain collective insight.	Strengthening democracy, understanding a community of practice	To encourage new insights and connections to emerge by creating a space for people to share both their thoughts and their feelings.	Conversation Café, Intergroup Dialogue in the classroom, Wisdom Council, Wisdom Circles, Socrates Cafe, World Café, Open Space, Appreciative Inquiry, and Bohm Dialogue
Conflict Transformation **To resolve conflicts, to foster personal healing and growth, and to improve relations among groups**	Creating a safe space, hearing from everyone, building trust, and sharing personal stories and views	Relationships among participants are poor or not yet established and need to be. Issue can only be resolved when people change their behavior or attitude, expand their perspective, or take time to reflect and heal.	Political polarization, Jewish-Muslim relations, race relations, value-based conflicts, and healing after crises or trauma	To create a safe space for people with different views to talk about their personal experiences and feel heard. Often, to set the groundwork for deliberation and action.	Sustained Dialogue, Intergroup Dialogue in communities, Victim-Offender Mediation, PCP dialogue, and Compassionate Listening
Decision-Making **To influence public decisions and public policy and improve public knowledge**	Naming and framing, weighing all options, considering different positions (deliberation), revealing public values, and brainstorming solutions	The issue is within government's (or any single entity's) sphere of influence.	Budgeting, land use, health care, and social security	To involve a representative group of citizens in thorough conversations about complicated policy issues. Ideally, the group is empowered by governance.	National Issues Forums, Citizens Jury, Deliberative Polling, 21st Century Town Meeting, Charrettes, Citizen Choicework, and Consensus Conference
Collaborative Action **To empower people and groups to solve complicated problems and take responsibility for the solution**	Using dialogue and deliberation to generate ideas for community action, collaboratively developing and implementing plans	The issue/dispute requires intervention across multiple public and private entities, and any time community action is important.	Regional sprawl, institutional racism, youth violence, and responding to crises	To encourage integrated efforts among diverse stakeholders, sectors, and organizations, etc., involved in the problem.	Study Circles, Future Search, and Appreciative Inquiry

ticated application was *Madmundo TV,* developed by Patrice Barrat of The Bridge Initiative. Barrat integrates social media, mobile phones, video, television, email, web-conferencing, and other technologies to create conversations about critical issues. With Madmundo, he started with a citizen with a compelling question and brings these questions to Presidents, Prime Ministers, CEOs, Executive Directors, and other leaders.

For example, Barrat did a production with the Global Fund to Fight AIDS and a South African AIDS-infected child. The child asked, 'Why must I die?' Busi – a South African activist – brought her question to G8 participants, including the UK Finance Minister, the World Bank President, and the UN Secretary General. Their video responses to Busi stimulated video and written exchanges on the web; after several months of conversation, a film was produced integrating the contributions.

Organizing: This is perhaps the pre-eminent contribution of social media, since its distinctive capacity is the number of people it can connect with relative ease. One of the best examples of social media being used for organizing is the Arab Spring. New York Times' columnist Thomas Friedman described this from the perspective of Wael Ghonim:

> Ghomin (is) the Egyptian Google employee whose anonymous Facebook page helped to launch the Tahrir Square revolution in early 2011 that toppled President Hosni Mubarak — but then failed to give birth to a true democratic alternative. In the early 2000s, Arabs were flocking to the web, Ghonim explained: "Thirsty for knowledge, for opportunities, for connecting with the rest of the people around the globe, we escaped our frustrating political realities and lived a virtual, alternative life."

> And then in June 2010, he noted, the "internet changed my life forever. While browsing Facebook, I saw a photo ... of a tortured, dead body of a young Egyptian guy. His name was Khaled Said. Khaled was a 29-year-old Alexandrian who was killed by police. I saw myself in his picture. ... I anonymously created a Facebook page and called it 'We Are All Khaled Said.' In just three days, the page had over 100,000 people, fellow Egyptians who shared the same concern."

> Soon Ghonim and his friends used Facebook to crowd-source ideas, and "the page became the most followed page in the Arab world...Social media was crucial for this campaign. It helped a decentralized movement arise. It made people realize that they were not alone. And it made it impossible for the regime to stop it."

> Ghonim was eventually tracked down in Cairo by Egyptian security services, beaten and then held incommunicado for 11 days. But three days after he was freed, the millions of protesters his Facebook posts helped to galvanize brought down Mubarak's regime.[158]

---

158 Friedman, Thomas L. 2016. "Social Media: Destroyer or Creator?" Pp. A23 in *New York Times.* New York, NY, USA: New York Times Company.

Learning: Learning naturally occurs in most social media exchanges. However, Mass Open On-line Courses (MOOCs) have taken social media learning to new levels of sophistication. In Q1 2015, Germany's development agency, GIZ, offered a 7-week open online course "Leadership for Global Responsibility," focusing on transformational leadership. It explained that participants:

> ...will embark on this journey with international experts...as well as experienced practitioners and regional facilitators from around the world. You will engage with global issues, reflect upon values, develop your own competencies and meaningful solutions for urgent leadership challenges. The course will provide the space for you to connect with others to take innovative action. Using live webinars, individual exploration, co-creative assignments and online conversation, we will enquire into the principles of cooperation, international diversity, innovative collective action and transformation.

> The MOOC will support participants on their personal and collective journeys, providing you with supportive tools to enhance your reflection, collaborative action and transformative change initiatives.[159]

The course attracted 30,000 participants.

Measuring: Social media and the internet more broadly present a new array of tools and ways to measure change activities and impact. This includes:

- Website Analytics: Understanding the traffic on your website, such as the number of visits and their length.
- Social Media Analysis: Data about your reach and engagement on platforms, like Facebook and Twitter.
- Online Polls: On-line surveys provide extensive feedback (and overwhelm recipients with the number of requests!).

Financing: Crowdfunding is the big new financial innovation of social media. It focuses on social media's ability to connect people to initiatives that they want to support. It is still at an early development stage. However, in 2015, it raised an estimated $835 million for more than 153.4K crowdfund projects started during the period; of the campaigns which ended and reached their goal, each raised $25.4K (on average).[160] In addition to raising money, other benefits include: creating buzz, building a network, engaging historic supporters, and gauging public interest. There are a few different approaches:

- Rewards-based: Raising money for a project before it starts with the prospect of gaining a percentage of profits. This may include everything from films to inventions.

---

159 GIZ. 2015. "Leadership for Global Responsibility (GC21)." http://bit. ly/1o6MpqX: MOOC List.
160 Centre, Crowdfunding. 2016. "2016: The State of the Crowdfunding Nation Global Report." http://thecrowdfundingcentre.com/index.php?page=login#report|page/ report/?: Crowdfundingcentre.com.

- Equity: This raises money for going concerns and translates it into partial ownership.
- Debt-based: Borrowers apply on-line, and investors make loans.
- Litigation: This allows plaintiffs or defendants to raise money and provide a reward based on the outcome of a legal case.
- Charity: Investors bank-roll a project without an expectation of a return on their capital. Increasingly, this is connected to specific advocacy messages.[161]

There are many on-line platforms that support crowdsourcing. They are specialized by approaches and many other qualities.

Advocating: Some platforms have specialized in advocacy campaigns, such as Avaaz, which describes itself as "…a global web movement to bring people-powered politics to decision-making everywhere." The platforms develop processes for receiving and reviewing requests for help to advance a cause. They then proceed to obtain signatures and financial support (a form of crowdfunding). The signatures are communicated to influence decision-makers; the sites utilize a range of other advocacy strategies.

Change organizations, like Greenpeace and Amnesty International, have integrated the social media advocacy strategy into a range of more traditional approaches.

Prototyping: This function – experimenting with new ways to approach change challenges – is perhaps the most difficult one to integrate into social media strategy. However, Otto Scharmer's Presencing Institute has launched a MOOC to support developing the U-Process capacity (Chapter 4). It integrates the initiation of prototypes into the end of its U.Lab course. In Q4 2015, the MOOC brought together 43 Impact Hubs in global cities; it was open for the Hubs' 11,000 members. Participants developed both individual and group prototypes.

Social Media Summary: There is enormous excitement with social media and its role as a transformation tool. It has much to offer, and there is still additional potential to develop. However, there is also perhaps a little naivety, as Friedman suggests at the end of his Arab Spring column, about the organizing power of social media:

> Alas, the euphoria soon faded, said Ghonim, because "we failed to build consensus, and the political struggle led to intense polarization." Social media, he noted, "only amplified" the polarization "by facilitating the spread of misinformation, rumors, echo chambers and hate speech. The environment was purely toxic. My online world became a battleground filled with trolls, lies, hate speech."

> Supporters of the army and the Islamists used social media to smear each other, while the democratic center, which Ghonim and so many others occupied, was marginalized. Their revolution was stolen by the Muslim

---

161   Wkipedia. 2016. "Crowdfunding." https://en.wikipedia.org/wiki/Crowdfunding#-Types: Wikipedia.

Brotherhood and, when it failed, by the army, which then arrested many of the secular youths who first powered the revolution. The army has its own Facebook page to defend itself.

Here is what he concluded about social media today: "First, we don't know how to deal with rumors. Rumors that confirm people's biases are now believed and spread among millions of people." Second, "We tend to only communicate with people that we agree with, and thanks to social media, we can mute, un-follow and block everybody else. Third, online discussions quickly descend into angry mobs. ... It's as if we forget that the people behind screens are actually real people and not just avatars.

And fourth, it became really hard to change our opinions. Because of the speed and brevity of social media, we are forced to jump to conclusions and write sharp opinions in 140 characters about complex world affairs. And once we do that, it lives forever on the Internet."

Fifth, and most crucial, he said, "Today, our social media experiences are designed in a way that favors broadcasting over engagements, posts over discussions, shallow comments over deep conversations…It's as if we agreed that we are here to talk at each other instead of talking with each other."

Ghonim has not given up. He and a few friends recently started a website, Parlio.com, to host intelligent, civil conversations about controversial and often heated issues, with the aim of narrowing gaps, not widening them… "Five years ago," concluded Ghonim, "I said, 'If you want to liberate society, all you need is the Internet.' Today I believe if we want to liberate society, we first need to liberate the internet.[162]

Learning Processes

Learning is a core element of transformation, since transformation intimately involves discovery and learning how to do, think about, and organize things differently. This is both learning from historic experience, and learning from the future (Chapter 4). Here, however, I will focus on the former. As the societal learning and change matrix (Chapter 6) points out, this is learning for individuals, organizations, networks, sectors, and societies. It cannot be treated like a nice ancillary activity for LSC and SCS development – it is the core since LSC is about learning how to do things in new ways.

But, learning usually does not have much to do with classrooms and capacity development, as traditionally construed. Most learning happens via informal activities. The 70-20-10 rule estimates that 70% of learning comes through experience and practice at doing a job, 20% through other people and conversations, and 10%

---

162 Friedman, Thomas L. 2016. "Social Media: Destroyer or Creator?" Pp. A23 in *New York Times*. New York, NY, USA: New York Times Company.

formal learning processes.[163] Organizing work-lives and routines to categorically integrate learning is valuable. Most organizations and initiatives involved with transformation already spend considerable time and resources on learning: just think about all the time and money (direct and indirect) spent in collective meetings, knowledge sharing, report writing, and knowledge development. However, there is rarely much organizing behind this learning system activity.

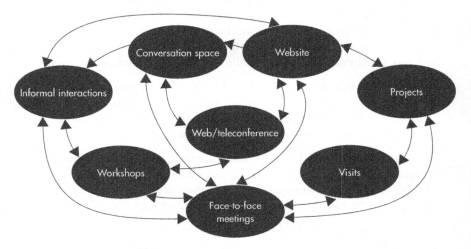

Figure 9I: Ecology of Learning[164]

Coherent learning approaches are needed. A helpful core concept is the "ecologies of learning," which was introduced by community of practice gurus William Snyder and Etienne Wenger (Figure 9I). Their concept supports vastly enhanced opportunities for learning and raises particular questions about the pace and sequencing of these types of interactions. The ecology of learning does not focus on a top-down process or expert knowledge or knowledge management. Rather, it emphasizes horizontal exchanges.[165]

The basic concept behind the ecology of learning is to list all the ways that learning takes place, and then draw out relationships between them to develop a strategy that can integrate various activities. Some of these learning vehicles are identified in Figure 9I. However, these can be further refined into activities, such as learning journeys (where people travel together to see how each other is working) or learning histories (documenting processes to reveal hidden and explicit learning).

163 Jennings, Charles. 2011. "Social & Workplace Learning through the 70:20:10 Lens." http://charles-jennings.blogspot.nl/2011/08/social-workplace-learning-through.html: Charles Jennings.
164 Snyder, William M., and Etienne Wenger. 2004. "Our World as a Learning System: a Communities-of-Practice Approach." Pp. 35-58 in *Creating a learning culture: strategy, technology, and practice,* edited by Marcia L. Conner and James G. Clawson: The Press Syndicate of the University of Cambridge.
165 Waddell, Steve, Heinz Greijn, Koen Faber, Jonas Haertle, and Annalisa Mauro. 2013. "Inter-organizational Learning: A new frontier." *Capacity.org* January(46):3-6.

In LSC activities, learning involves the personal and introspective, as well as the external and learning about others. Learning supports reflection and individual change with processes that produce generative dialogue (Chapter 2, the individual change sphere) about new ways of acting and seeing. Good for this are many processes associated with intra- and inter-meeting tools, like World Café and Appreciative Inquiry. The following are some learning-specific approaches that are also good for this.

Action Research/Learning/Inquiry: In complex situations with many unknowns, disciplined investigation processes to accompany action are enormously helpful. These action methodologies provide immense help in creating learning systems that address complexity and guide disciplined action. Action research is defined as:

> ...a democratic and participative orientation to knowledge creation. It brings together action and reflection, theory and practice, in the pursuit of practical solutions to issues of pressing concern. Action research is a pragmatic co-creation of knowing *with*, not *on or about* people.[166]

This describes an overarching learning stance that is valuable for transformation. Action research emphasizes experiential and emergent evidence, in contrast with conventional research that emphasizes historic experience. Action research can be thought of as research *with* people, applied research is *for* an organization or people, and conventional research is done *on* and *about* people and situations. All three research approaches are of value to change processes, but action research is the most important.

Action research works with stakeholders to emerge action. In this activity, the boundary between the researcher and other stakeholders becomes blurred. For example, while I worked in Guatemala on poverty, those working in poverty programs were actively part of the research team and did interviews; analysis was a collaborative process. The researcher had a distinctive role and responsibility for supporting the research aspect of the activity and developing the capacity to do the interviews and co-develop interview questions. But, the overall aspect is one of a team. This stance greatly enhances and embeds learning with those doing the doing.

There is a range of "action" methodologies, such as action learning, action inquiry, and systemic action research. But, they all share the same stance. In traditional academia, action researchers are not held in high regard because others think their work lacks objectivity. Applied and conventional research are much better with simple and complicated situations, but action research is better for complex ones (see Chapter 2 for the distinctions). This means that while other research approaches can be useful, in transformation processes they should be subsumed within overarching action research understanding, rather than dominating the processes.

---

166 Bradbury, Hilary. 2015. "Introduction: How to Situate and Define Action Research." Pp. 1-12 in *The Sage Handbook of Action Research*, edited by Hilary Bradbury. Boston: Sage. P. 2

Box 9A: The Systematic Knowledge and Learning Approach: An example of a learning system approach

The International Land Coalition (ILC) is a global multi-stakeholder network with a transformative vision for land governance, as a strategy to address hunger, poverty, and equity. They took a big step forward in developing these ideas with the Systematic Knowledge and Learning Approach (SKLA). It is an approach and not a strategy, because it is meant to change mindsets, not to provide a rigid framework. The SKLA is designed around five axes, each with unique tools.

- **1st axis: make effective knowledge connections across levels.** Knowledge and skills should not be shared only between members (horizontally), but also between global, regional, and local levels (vertically). *Related tools: cross-cluster/cross-level reviewing; database of good practices; online monitoring of knowledge demand; forums; and publication series.*

- **2nd axis: take advantage of network capacities.** This requires first systematic mapping of knowledge resources and the needs of members; second, understanding the information and knowledge they are willing to share; and third, the skills that can be put at the disposal of the coalition. *Related tools: network book 'Connecting the Dots;' horizontal mentoring through the 'Talent Map.'*

- **3rd axis: orient knowledge and learning activities towards change.** The ILC needs to ensure that members actually adopt and embody knowledge so that they can apply it to generate actual change within the policy arena. *Related tools: learning journeys; trainings on knowledge for advocacy/action.*

- **4th axis: learn from monitoring.** Moving towards the change ILC wants to achieve is complex. As a result, ILC needs to continuously learn from its own experiences, such as projects and partnerships, in order to fine-tune its day-to-day activities, and in order to find new ways towards the envisaged change. This internal learning needs to build on the monitoring and evaluation (M&E) system. *Related tools: internal learning notes; thematic reports.*

- **5th axis: make the roles of ILC entities complementary.** ILC is a knowledge broker and this brokering requires complementarity of roles for the different entities that compose the Coalition: single member organizations, subgroups of members such as thematic working groups, regional platforms, national platforms, and the global secretariat.

These axes provide a valuable distinction between systemic strategic elements of a learning system, and the content/issues or learning events/platforms that usually are the most sophisticated approach achieved. The former are critical to develop coherence amongst the latter – otherwise there are simply many poorly connected activities with undeveloped synergies, gaps, and duplications.

Learning Journeys: These are actual site visits to deepen knowledge about the experiments and how people address challenges. They comprise diverse stakeholders, supporting a range of views and discussion from various perspectives. The goal is to get people outside of their comfort zones to stimulate more creative thinking. Learning journeys are distinguished from "field trips" by rigorous design.

Learning Histories: This is a way to record and share experiences by including multiple narratives. Classically, one column focuses on factual events as they have occurred, and the second column contains quotes from participants to illustrate events from their diverse perspectives. It can be an on-going diary to support a change process, if it is regularly reviewed and discussed by participants. Sometimes, the record is multi-media. This is a good tool for collectively making sense of various experiences.

Assessment Processes

There is perhaps no greater impediment to transformation initiatives than traditional measurement and evaluation approaches. Input output models appropriate for simple and complicated processes (Chapter 2) are inappropriate for the complexity of emergence and transformation – although they can be useful guides for modest work *within* these activities. In complex situations with many actors, attribution to the creator of an outcome, a cornerstone of traditional impact measurement, proves highly problematic. Yet, funders commonly cling to such approaches (e.g., USAID's notorious log-frame), even when they actually undermine their objectives (Of course some of USAID's work *is* industrial product and service production, for which log-frames are appropriate.).

One major reason for the dominance of the input - output model, with its core $x -> y$ framework, is accountability. Funders want to know whether a grantee has done what they said they would, and flexibility then becomes problematic. This evaluative approach requires defining a goal and steps to realize it in advance. This has two problems for addressing large systems change. One is that it eliminates the possibility of *learning* as an activity is underway: learning that the original goal was inappropriately defined (maybe something better has come up!) and/or that the steps to reach it were inappropriate. The second big problem is that all the focus is on project performance, rather than considering the real system change goal, which takes significant time and multiple actors.

Moreover, given the traditional approaches' focus on whether a project has hit its target, it does not say anything about how it worked, with whom, and why. In transformation and emergence processes, "assessment" is much more about *understanding context* and *learning*, which are critical ingredients in complex environments. The assessment approach must consider:

- The complexity of relationship interactions in a change arena, including porous and changing boundaries to define the "problem/opportunity" and stakeholders.
- How change involves destruction, as well as creation (a systemic understanding of this is required).
- There is not one, but an emergent number of possible pathways that require exploration and development to address issues.
- Change networks' visions require a long time to realize while there is significant change in their operating environments.

- Change networks usually do not aim to "take credit" for actual valued outcomes (such as healthy, happy people). They aim to take a back seat in favor of their participants' being recognized for their work.

Box 9B: Systemic Action Research and the Myanmar Conflict Transformation[1]

As its name implies, the systemic action research (SAR) brand emphasizes systems thinking. Moreover, it underscores complexity and change, and presents a particularly valuable approach for large systems change and the development of societal change systems.

Like other action research processes, SAR creates the iterative learning processes of Kolb's four stages, as presented in Chapter 4 (planning-doing-reflecting-concluding). SARer Danny Burns introduces an important addition to the cycle with the step of revisiting the theory of change that is the basis for action. Moreover, in comparison with conventional research, SAR makes these cycles much more frequent to assess the next steps, and it engages the whole system in them rather than just researchers. SAR emphasizes the importance as well of identifying questions from the perspective of various stakeholders within the issue system, and of recognizing the distinct roles of different stakeholders to undertake action. It, therefore, does not emphasize consensus. Rather than change *within* the system dynamic, SAR focuses on *changing* the dynamic of the system. These multiple perspectives support identifying novel and creative actions in response to intractable problems.

"Intractable" is a description of how people experienced conflict in significant portions of Myanmar. Religious and ethnic differences, drugs, and the military government have provided a potent stew of tensions for many decades. The SAR intervention assumed that underlying economic and social issues must be addressed. In numerous townships, the SAR process engaged the stakeholder system. They were organized into trained SAR groups, which collected and analyzed stories, and developed a map of the conflicts' system dynamics. This led to identifying convergence points between internally displaced people (IDP) and a host of issues, such as cutting timber. Economic issues were also forcing the IDP and host communities to cut trees, resulting in wood scarcity and tensions. This analysis identified three sub-issues and then a new round of story collecting and analysis.

A series of meetings with diverse stakeholders identified some actions they wanted to undertake. Among other things, actions led to the formation of youth groups and activities to stop bored youth from drifting into town and causing trouble. "In the context of north Myanmar," commented Burns, "where there's been almost no organization allowed for 50 years, the development of these youth groups is a major story in its own right."

1 Burns, Danny. 2007. Systemic action research: A strategy for whole system change: Policy Press. Burns, Danny, and Stuart Worsley. 2014. Navigating Complexity in International Development: Facilitating sustainable change at scale. Warwickshire, UK: Practical Action Publishing.

Much greater development of assessment tools is required. However, here is an introduction to four approaches that gives a sense of how assessments for complexity are different from traditional approaches. The first two – Development Evaluation and Generative Causation – are strategies and approaches, whereas the third – Outcome Mapping (OM) – is a method with particular steps. The fourth, Systemic Evaluation, emphasizes relationships between all the sub-systems. Each of these is different from data collection tools (e.g., surveys, and participant observations) which would be used in each of them. These all emphasize the importance of theory development as a core part of the process. In the case of large systems change, this means Theories of Change (ToC: see Chapter 4). While the word "theory" can cause anxiety amongst non-academics, it simply refers to an explanation about why something happens. For management-oriented folks, it is really very similar to strategy. The ToC describes what you are doing and why, as well as the relationship between various action steps.

Developmental Evaluation (DE): This is the framework developed by Michael Quinn Patton, former President of the American Evaluation Association. DE is a **stance:** as with action research, the evaluator is a co-participant in developing the initiative, actively working with others to draw out learnings and integrating them into actions with the action-reflection-planning-action cycles being built into daily worklife. DE is a practice that aims to pragmatically guide workday actions and promote a dispersed leadership culture that is so important for change networks.

In *Developmental Evaluation,*[167] Patton presents cases that illustrate when and why to use particular methodologies. For example, two cases are:

- Many different agencies and project teams working collaboratively on the same problem with complicated interactions, impossible-to-attribute outcomes, and diverse responses to unexpected events…the challenge is ongoing development of the collaborative effort and providing feedback about its effectiveness.
- (A) major systems change initiative in which the intervention initiative aims to "tip" a system in a major new direction…

Patton brings up learning as loops, as described in Chapter 2: **single-loop** learning for incremental change (asking questions within the established policies, structures, and goals – e.g., are we doing well providing people fish to eat?) and **double-loop** learning for reform change (asking questions about the policies, structures, and goals – e.g., should we instead be teaching people how to fish to feed themselves?). Oddly, he does not broach **triple-loop** learning for transformation (asking questions about how we think about an issue – e.g., how do we understand the eco-systems-fish-consumption relationships?). Patton places DE's focus more at the double-loop level; I would say that it moves into the triple-loop as well. (In subsequent correspondence, Patton commented: "I agree that the omission of triple-loop learning is an oversight on my part…the actual processes of, and interactions around, developmental evaluation more often than not involve and include triple-loop learning.").

---

167 Patton, Michael Quinn. 2010. *Developmental Evaluation: Applying Complexity Concepts to Enhance Innovation and Use.* New York, NY, USA: Guilford Press.

Box 9C: The Emerging Assessment Field

By: Fred Carden, *co-developer of Outcome Mapping (OM), and evaluation and research consultant*

Complex problems have generated a strong interest in mixed methods, because in complex settings you need multiple different methods for different aspects of the problem. This is more or less accepted now in most funding agencies. What has not changed in development evaluation is the level at which evaluation takes place in most bilateral and multilateral agencies, and foundations. Evaluation takes place at the project and program levels, when it should actually take place at the theory level. Outcome Mapping (OM) starts to move in that direction by identifying boundary partners (those you are most likely to influence), and the use of progress markers with the proposition: "we think that if you apply these interventions, you will progressively change behaviors in these ways, leading to the sustainable change you seek." What we learn from that is whether or not, and where, the theory of change we have constructed using OM works and where it does not; we learn how to tweak it. We learn not so much if the intervention works, but where it works, for whom, and in what contexts, giving us a much richer basis on which to consider using the theory of change for other interventions.

The two main analysis units in learning-oriented evaluation (accountability evaluation is a different matter), should be the theory of change and the context within which the intervention hopes to have a positive effect. By collecting and codifying evaluations around theories of change at play, we learn about how, where, and with whom interventions are effective. We can use the outcomes we collect through evaluating theories to assess future interventions, modify them, and in turn modify the theory of change itself based on new information and experience from new interventions. Context, as a unit of analysis, implies looking at interventions in the settings to identify how the intervention has made a difference in the setting, or how a set of interventions has made a difference in a setting.

For theory assessment, we are concerned with the way of working, the 'how' (what we control); in context assessment, on the other hand, we are more focused on how the setting is changing and how that affects our intervention. These are the things we do not control, but that we need to understand if we are going to be successful. It is about broadening our horizons. For example, take a maternal and neonatal mortality program that interacts with other economic development programs in a region leading to improved economic conditions, and improved educational opportunities, etc. The point is that it is not only about reducing neonatal mortality, but whether and how this interacts in the system: if we are only saving more babies so they can be stunted by malnutrition, receive poor or no education, and be functionally unemployable, then we have not helped by reducing neonatal mortality. Instead, we have increased the burden on the community and the State in caring for additional members of the community.

Realist Evaluation (RE): This approach has been promoted by Ray Pawson.[168] The term "generative" is similar in meaning to "emergent;" it emphasizes that the

---

168 Pawson, Ray. 2013. *The science of evaluation: a realist manifesto*: Sage.

ToC is continually being reassessed and revised to integrate feedback arising from actions. In traditional complicated (e.g., building a dam) projects, a theory (engineering strategy) is identified in advance to realize a pre-determined goal with the assumption that the theory is "correct." In traditional research projects, the tentative theory is identified in advance, actions are taken, and then the theory is reassessed based on data arising from the actions.

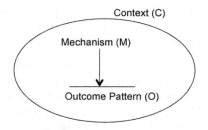

Figure 9J: Generative Causation Model

The RE approach is much more like action research (see above). Rather than thinking in terms of one (or several) factors in a traditional causal approach, interactions between the elements are considered in a manner reflecting system dynamics (see Mapping above). The three *elements* of this approach are identified in Figure 9J:

- Outcomes (O): These are described as a *pattern* rather than as a point (as in traditional evaluation). For LSC, it might refer to a range of possible transformations in the organization of governance or agricultural-food systems. RE's goal is to explain why a particular outcome is produced. Rather than focusing on just one outcome, RE assumes that there will be a range of outcomes given the two other elements.

- Mechanisms (M): These are the trigger that explains why outcomes turn out as they do, as well as the overall shape of the outcome pattern. The mechanism is part of the wider system, and the questions concern what it is about that system that causes certain outcomes. What are the constraints and avenues that lead to specific choices? Are there mechanisms to effectively express dissatisfaction, for example, and realize change? Is decision-making decentralized? Do attitudes support centralized decisions?

- Context (C): A rich set of qualities surround any action. Contexts are pre-existing institutional, organizational, and social conditions that sometimes enable and sometimes constrain choices. For example, consider a country's economic development, the level of income inequality, and violent crime rates – these can be factors that come together in different ways in different countries.

As a simple illustration, consider a forest fire. The context may be years of drought, good fire response preparation, wind, thick underbrush, or mountainous terrain. The mechanism might be things, such as a burning cigarette, lightning, or a spark from equipment. A range of outcomes is possible, from only a few trees destroyed because the fire was caught early, to thousands of trees destroyed followed by desertification because of continued drought, or soil erosion from downpours, or regrowth through carefully managed efforts. These three elements are well-aligned with complexity qualities: they provide for multiple outcomes (O), a range of mechanisms (M) that are the product of specific cultural and historic qualities (path-dependence), and a great diversity in contexts (C).

Outcome Mapping (OM): This approach was developed by the (Canadian) International Development Research Center (IDRC) with Sarah Earl, Fred Carden and Terry Smutylo. It focuses on creating feedback systems both to respondents and to those who want to know how the work is going. The sub-title to OM is "Building Learning and Reflection into Development Programs." The developers explain that:

> The originality of the methodology is its shift away from assessing the products of a program (e.g., policy relevance, poverty alleviation, reduced conflict) to focus on changes in behaviors, relationships, actions, and/ or activities of the people and organizations with whom a development program works directly.[169]

The focus on learning and behavioral changes arises from the observation that the aspired to changes usually occur a significant time after an action or program, and that the outcomes might be *different* than originally expected (rather than worse/better), because previously unperceived ways of thinking about the change process and outcomes have developed. One core concept is "boundary partners," which recognizes that any initiative is only a single actor in realizing change, and that there are complicated interactions with participants in realizing change. Therefore, the approach does not aim to attribute an outcome to an action, but instead looks to understand the contributions the initiative makes to an outcome, as well as its boundary partners.

OM assesses strategies, issues, or relationships. There is a three-stage cycle to designing an OM plan, usually conducted in a workshop with participants:

- Intentional Design: This aims to ensure a consensus about the definition of macro-level changes, by answering Why? Who? What? How?
- Outcome and Performance Monitoring: Its learning emphasis means OM is based on principles of participation. The OM process itself is designed to support outcome development. A disciplined process of participant record-keeping and observation is key.
- Evaluation Planning: An evaluation plan identifies the main actions to be undertaken to apply the OM framework.

Process and outcome evaluations are integrated by collecting observations about process implementation and results achieved by participants.

There are substantial on-line OM resources and an active community of practice.

Systemic Evaluation[170]: There are three key principles to systemic evaluation:

1. It is vital to take multiple values and perspectives, processes of marginalization and power relations into account when deciding on the boundaries of what to evaluate. Boundaries define who and what to include in the evaluation. Up-front boundary critique (thinking about the consequences of employing

---

169 IDRC. 2010. "Outcome Mapping." Ottawa, Ontario, Canada: International Development and Research Centre. P. 1.

170 This description was contributed by Gerald Midgley. See also: Midgley, Gerald, Robert Y Cavana, John Brocklesby, Jeff L Foote, David RR Wood, and Annabel Ahuriri-Driscoll. 2013. "Towards a new framework for evaluating systemic problem structuring methods." *European Journal of Operational Research* 229(1):143-54. Reynolds, M. (2015). (Breaking) The iron triangle of evaluation. *IDS Bulletin*, 46(1) pp. 71–86.

different values and boundaries for the evaluation) is therefore vital, and this needs to be revisited periodically.
2. There are very different types of evaluation available, and we should design an appropriate approach for the context (drawing on parts of other approaches as needed), as defined through a boundary critique.
3. There should be a seamless movement from evaluation to design, so an evaluation doesn't stop once comments are made on what is being evaluated – the design of changes should be just as systemic as the evaluation.

In terms of drawing on other approaches, there are three major types of evaluation:
1. Stakeholder –qualitatively exploring the experiences of those involved or affected by what is being evaluated, with no pre-set agenda.
2. Goal-based – setting goals, targets and measuring performance with a view to instigating improvements.
3. Organizational – assessing an organization's ability to deliver on its goals and remain resilient in a turbulent environment.

There is a logical relationship between the above, as stakeholder evaluations can be used to define the right goals, the achievement of which can be evaluated through goal-based evaluations, and the ability of organizations to deliver can be enhanced through organizational evaluations.

Note that the seamless flow from evaluation into design is a significant and almost unique feature of Systemic Evaluation, and there are a whole host of systemic and participative design methodologies to draw upon. Examples are Soft Systems Methodology, Interactive Planning, Systemic Dialogic Design, Viable System Modeling, etc., and these can be integrated into an evaluation approach along with Stakeholder, Goal-Based and Organizational Evaluation.

Big Data Collection and Visual Analytics

Jerri Husch (jerrihusch@gmail.com) is the lead author of this section.
Both big data[171] and visual analytics are burgeoning fields, arising out of the ability to use the Internet to collect data at an unprecedented scale *and* pace. This requires more creative ways to represent information through "visual analytics:" a representation of systems, data, and relationships in terms of summary visuals of figures and diagrams.

The field's growth is propelled by increasing computing power and the proliferation of databases, ranging from scientific ones and those of government agencies to the internet and social media. The ability to collect current data, particularly with respect to the internet and social media, greatly decreases the traditional time gap between data collection and analysis.

---

171 For an overview see: Technology, Parliamentary Office of Science &. 2014. "Big Data: An Overview." in Postnote. London, UK: Houses of Parliament.

The modern use of the term "big data" gained momentum in the early 2000s, when IT analyst Doug Laney provided a clear set of criteria and articulated a definition of big data that had three key attributes: "volume, velocity and variety."[172]

- **Volume** refers to how data is collected from various sources, including business transactions, social media, and information from sensor or machine-to-machine data. New technologies (such as Hadoop)[173] have eased the burden of working with enormous data sets and the quantity of data available has multiplied exponentially over the last decade.
- **Velocity** requires that new programs can deal with data streams that operate at an unprecedented speed and must be dealt with in a timely manner. Very high velocity allows real time data collection.
- **Variety** recognizes that data comes in all formats – from structured, numeric data in traditional databases to unstructured text documents, email, video, audio, stock ticker data, and financial transactions.

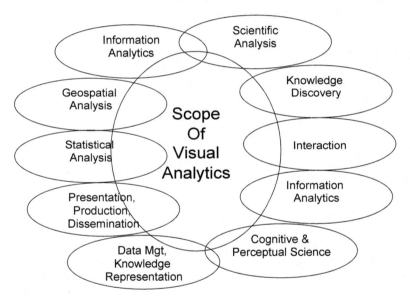

Figure 9K: Scope of Visual Analytics[174]

---

172 Laney, D. (2001), '3D Data Management: Controlling Data Volume, Velocity, and Variety', Technical report, META Group.

173 In 2008, Yahoo released Hadoop as an open-source project comprising distributed computing and processing. Today, Hadoop's framework and ecosystem of technologies are managed and maintained by the non-profit Apache Software Foundation (ASF), a global community of software developers and contributors. For additional background see, Ashlee Vance, NYTimes, "Hadoop, a Free Software Program, Finds Uses Beyond Search", March 16, 2009. Retrieved, 1 Nov 2015, http://www.nytimes.com/2009/03/17/technology/business-computing/17cloud.html?_r=

174 Keim, Daniel A, Florian Mansmann, Jörn Schneidewind, Jim Thomas, and Hartmut Ziegler. 2008. Visual analytics: *Scope and challenges*: Springer.

To this preliminary definition, other attributes, such as **"complexity,"** have been added as data is collected from multiple sources. Multiple and diverse data create the need to link, match, clean, and transform data so that they can be integrated and compared across systems. This requires creating relationships, hierarchies, and multiple data linkages. Big data is "complex data" that can quickly be overwhelming.[175] Given these evolving definitions, in recent years, Laney's view has been expanded so that "big data" is now viewed as:

> …high-volume, high velocity and high variety information assets that demand cost-effective, innovative forms of information processing for enhanced insight and decision making[176]

Box 9D: Paris COP-21 Big Data Commitment[176]

At the climate change summit, Schneider Electric, the global specialist in energy management and automation, announced it will provide access to data generated from its WeatherSentry weather intelligence platform as part of the UN's Data for Climate Action campaign. In December 2015, Schneider Electric announced it had networked more than 4,000 disparate rural area weather stations to provide a more holistic view of rural weather patterns across the US; now it is making this data available globally.

The data will be used to provide developing countries with the critical resources needed to assess weather impacts on agriculture and improve crop yield and soil conditions, specifically in rural communities. Ron Sznaider, senior vice president, cloud services, Schneider Electric, commented: "As part of our recent climate commitment pledge…we also commit to work with the global research community to cooperate on big data analytics as it relates to agriculture and weather."

Many tools now being developed can be used across disciplines to link data as disparate as agricultural production measures, weather patterns and disease surveillance, census records, and airline passenger lists (see Box 9C)[177].

Visualization of Big Data: Generating data volume and velocity are now less of a concern than the challenges of making sense of all of it. Innovative visual analytic tools offer ways, beyond pie charts and graphs, to deal with visual complexity and have affected analytic methods in various fields. The lists of websites produced through web crawls described under mapping tools are an example of big data; the maps visualize that data. Other mapping techniques do not, however, involve big data, since they are based on original data generation, rather than secondary existing sources.

---

175 SAS Institute, (2015) website. Retrieved 11/2015.
http://www.sas.com/en_us/company-information.html#history
176 Gartner (2015) http://www.gartner.com/it-glossary/big-data. Retrieved 5 November 2015.
177 Schneider Electric. 2015. "Schneider Electric pledges open access to proprietary weather data to aid research on global food production". http://www.pandct.com/media/shownews.asp?ID=45070. Dec. 10

Figure 9L: Visual Analytic Examples: Top right clockwise: spatial analysis, network analysis, complex data analysis, and semantic analysis

Visual analytics is a multi-disciplinary field that has transformed how we visualize complex and dynamic phenomena in the new Information Age; it has also transformed how we optimize analytical reasoning and make sound decisions with incomplete and uncertain information (Figure 9K[178]). Visual analytics is especially concerned with sense-making and reasoning. It is strongly motivated by the desire to solve problems and make sound decisions. The science of analytical reasoning is central to the analyst's task of applying human judgments to reach conclusions from a combination of evidence and assumptions. Under the influence of Jeff Thomas, at the National Visualization and Analytics Center (NVAC),[179] visual analytics centers exist throughout the world. Universities have integrated visual analytics into their core information sciences curricula. This has made the new field a recognized and promising offshoot of information and scientific visualization.

Examples of new visual analytic tools, all now easily available, include the use of Geographic Information Systems (GIS) for spatial analysis, text and linguistic

178 Keim, Daniel, Florian Mansmann, Jorn Schneidewind, and Hartmut Ziegler. 2006. "Challenges in visual data analysis." Pp. 9-16 in *Information Visualization, 2006. IV 2006. Tenth International Conference on*: IEEE.

179 Gartner (2015) http://www.gartner.com/it-glossary/big-data. Retrieved 5 November 2015.

tools for content analysis, object relation tools for social network analysis, and dynamic timelines for temporal analysis.[180] GIS, for example, can capture, store, manage, and analyze spatial data from various sectors. Visual tools can quickly place data on geographic and topographic maps, allowing information to be seen simultaneously from a "macro" planetary level to a "micro" local street level. Examples now abound of satellite monitoring providing geo-spatial positioning to follow human movement anywhere in the world – allowing millions of people to access and immediately share information through interactive mapping applications on smart phones. The digital convergence of people, GIS information, and data resources helped provide assistance during crises, such as Hurricane Sandy, and it is increasingly well-documented in crisis informatics.[181]

Box 9E: Regulator Warns Tech Companies of Big Data Bias

In a report on the use of big data by businesses, the US Federal Trade Commission asked companies to consider whether their data sets represented the user population, whether algorithms were insulated against social bias, and whether the predictions they generated were accurate.

Bias can be difficult to weed out of big data programs, as a string of public incidents has revealed. For example, a company that advertises services to customers who apply through social media may neglect less tech-savvy populations, the report said. Alternatively, software that tries to identify promising job applications by factoring in graduation from top schools may inherit college admission biases.

The FTC urged companies to remember the golden rule of logic: Correlation does not equal causation. "Companies should remember that while big data is very good at detecting correlations, it does not explain which correlations are meaningful," the report said.

Exhibit A: *Google Flu Trends, the Alphabet Inc. GOOGL-1.38% division's technology for predicting flu outbreaks. Google's algorithm attempted to use search queries on flu-related topics to detect the flu incidence ahead of government estimates. It proved accurate initially, but overshot the prevalence of the illness in subsequent years, leading to an ongoing debate about whether data mining techniques and new data sources should be used to make big public health predictions.*

Source: Dowskin, E. (2016) *Regulator Warns Tech Companies of Big Data Bias.* Wall Street Journal, Jan. 7. *on.wsj.com/1JxlBsf*

---

180 Husch, J. (2013) Action Intelligence and Climate Change Adaptation, AAP Internal Report, NYHQ, NY.
181 Liu et al. (2014) Crisis Crowdsourcing Framework: Designing Strategic Configurations of Crowdsourcing for the Emergency Management Domain. Computer-Supported Cooperative Work (CSCW) special issue on Crisis Informatics and Collaboration

New digital mapping tools (DMTs), such as Gephi,[182] and CorTexT Manager,[183] can add additional dimensions of visualizing data to help social scientists trace and make sense of textual and "big" linguistic data.

Large Systems Change uses: The use of big data and visual analytics is evident across practically every social sector. For example:

- **Governance:** Harnessing and applying analytics to big data, governments gain insight into challenges, such as economic development, infrastructure use, managing utilities, managing ministries and agencies, dealing with traffic congestion, or preventing crime. Governments increasingly, however, have to address accountability, transparency, and privacy issues.

- **Health Care:** Big data is being used to predict epidemics, cure disease, improve the quality of life, and avoid preventable deaths. With the world's population increasing and most living longer, treatment delivery models are rapidly changing, and many decisions behind those changes are being driven by data. The drive now is to understand as much about a patient as possible, as early in their life as possible, cutting across traditional data silos.

The LSC use of big data is still not well explored. However, their use can be expected to fall into two categories:

1. Situation analysis: Entering change processes requires understanding "what is" in terms of interactions across related fields that have traditionally been treated as unique silos. For example, showing relationships between agriculture and water and nutrition issues could be valuable.

2. Rapid responses and assessment: Rather than waiting to gather data to understand impacts, big data collected in real time can greatly diminish the delays associated with traditional data collection. This allows more rapid assessments and the adjustment of actions in response.

To take full advantage of these new methodologies requires rethinking approaches to project action and design. Data collection strategies and how to represent data must be thought about up front.

---

182 http://gephi.github.io Retrieved, November 1, 2015.
183 http://www.cortext.net/projects/pulseweb.html Retrieved, November 1, 2015.

Chapter 10

Stewarding Change: Our Role as Large Systems Change Makers

Chapter Summary

The real-life experiences of change agents can provide invaluable guidance to support you in your large systems change and societal change system development work. Five key qualities of successful change agents and four roles are discussed in this chapter.

I often ask myself questions such as: "how should I *be*, as an LSC change agent? What should I *do* to play this role? How can my distinctive abilities contribute to the transformation I perceive is emerging, to realize a direction that supports increasing people's ability to realize happiness and their highest aspirations and potential?" As I have pondered these questions personally and with others, and as I have seen others do the same, some key points have emerged for me.

Change Maker Qualities

Attentive to your own life balance, well-being, and happiness. Deep concern for others and our planet can easily lead to manic behavior (with elation and depression), a lack of perspective in which everything becomes a crisis, and inattention to physical and mental health. Being valued and in demand can easily lead to an overwhelming focus on work-associated activities with resulting crazy work and travel schedules. This can dull your ability to successfully interact with others and respond to important emerging opportunities that demand shifts in focus and relationships. Focus on payments rather than the compensation needed to live well (or well enough) can easily lead to a focus on narrow elites who pay generously and reform, rather than transformation. Comparing with others, rather than centering on making one's own distinctive contribution, can breed unproductive competition and unhappiness. Pay attention to behaviors that are part of the source of out-of-balance life ecosystems.

Being attentive requires setting boundaries and protecting routines. I remember Peter Senge explaining that he was not going to travel in June. Many integrate a meditative or spiritual practice into their daily routines and some attend annual retreats. It's also important to get adequate exercise; guard your physical health; treasure family and make time for close colleagues; spend time in nature; and, when possible, build in an extra travel day or two to simply enjoy being in a different place.

Humble. The challenges are indeed huge. I often feel the need to laugh at the scale of ambition, to help put it into perspective and understand there is a "craziness" about what is being attempted. Claiming the mantle of a great expert is not appropriate when there are so many unknowns and variables, and when so many lives can be affected. Each of us contributes what is possible, along with many others who are doing the same, and who are simultaneously balancing many life demands. Any one of us can contribute to addressing an issue. However, as time passes and actions unfold, individual contributions will pale next to collaborative work.

When approaching any change challenge, honoring the work of others is of paramount importance. Many have been toiling in the field to address these challenges and associated issues, and none of us comes with "the answer" or the proverbial silver bullet. We contribute within the context of enormous efforts by others.

Audacious. Being humble and being audacious may seem contradictory. However, being humble while working towards an audacious goal is a critical combination. People in change efforts constantly say they would never have started a project if they had understood the depth of the challenge. Ignorance can be bliss, but audacity to continue in the face of recognizing the scale of a challenge is crucial.

Understanding what I am working on in the big picture is important. Audaciousness can be at a very local level, such as with those at the Southern African Food Lab who are working to change the opportunities for small farmers and the nutritional impact of their work. By doing so, they are challenging the very power structure of the food-agriculture system. This is the deep audaciousness of transformation, in contrast with reform.

The societal change system challenge is also about the breadth of impact. It is about reaching the proverbial tipping point, which requires massive audacious organizing and ways of handling the complexity that large numbers of people and organizations involve. Audaciousness requires engaging with scales of challenges that have never before been addressed, arising both from unprecedented opportunities and threats, and globalization.

Empathetic. LSC involves destruction, as well as creation, as described in Chapter 5. Usually change agents are excited about potential transformation. It is important to understand that many will experience this as destruction of something they hold dear, such as personal power, status, daily routines, and/or relationships. Cobus de Swardt, Managing Director for Transparency International, was a leader in South Africa's anti-apartheid movement, and shared with me a particularly moving story about empathy when he was imprisoned.

> I don't think you can engage in violence with someone you truly love... and so I ask 'what does this mean?' That if there's a true bond with these people (in prison), I won't get raped...so I'll have to really work to act on this bond.

> You can't act out that you have a bond with somebody...if you think that they're a total jerk, racist, then this will fail. I had to overcome something within myself. You have to seek out the common humanity with someone who you dislike, you might disrespect and have very negative feelings towards...you can't 'act out' that you have positive feelings. You need to truly believe it. For me that was my own biggest achievement because I had to overcome all my own prejudices. The process to social justice is in many ways more challenging to overcoming your own prejudices than the big social justice issues you fight on a big stage.[184]

Personal system awareness. Transformation intimately involves building ties across traditional boundaries (jurisdictions, disciplines, issues, social, political, and spiritual, etc.) and seeing connections that are often not evident to others. Change agents tend to see connections much more easily than others. Much of the work is about making visible interdependence through personal experiences and use of tools, like mapping.

System awareness also has to do with understanding that you are part of the system, rather than someone outside the system acting on it. There is often a moment at which a change agent's language shifts from asking questions and talking about "you," to talking about "we" and "us." It is a shift to realize that we are part of both the challenge and opportunity, because we have entered the system. This shift implies shared commitment and peer accountability.

The Change Maker Role

Often I think of myself as a community organizer: developing relationships and capacity amongst diverse people connected to an issue, helping them realize their personal, distinct organizational, and collective goals. There are three terms that continually arise around the role of a change agent. Each has a distinct value and place.

---

184 Corbus de Swardt, Personal communication. 2010.

Leader. Commonly, people working for transformation call for an end to leadership, as it is traditionally construed as reflecting a "hero" status. But, rather than simply dismissing tradition, I believe what is needed is a dramatic shift from that model, as both exalted and dominant, while still retaining the capacity to be a hero. Too often 'leadership' is expressed as taking away power from others, centralizing authority, and implementing top-down solutions that simply do not generally effectively address complex challenges. Nevertheless, there is an important role for heroic leadership in transformation. Reflect upon Nelson Mandela's decision to open up conversations with the apartheid government, without consulting his colleagues. He believed that the notion would be too difficult for colleagues to accept, and that it was better that he expose just himself to potential criticism. This is the "courage" quality of traditional leadership, expressed with respect for others, but coupled with the willingness to move into a possibility fraught with potential dangers.

Leadership is commonly derided for its command-and-control approach. Indeed, this is not a dynamic that works well as a dominant one in transformation processes. However, many people working for change must be ambidextrous. Many spend time working with a transformation project or network with a collaborative ethos, but they may spend most of their time in a more traditional organization (e.g., a corporation, government, or NGO) that functions best with something like a command hierarchy. Moreover, there are many change organizations leading change initiatives that are themselves hierarchical, such as the "Secretariats" of Global Action Networks. There is a need to recognize the roles of hierarchy and networks, and to support people in shifting their behavior as they move between them.

Steward. For me, this is the most important role in day-to-day transformation work. This concept was brought home by Peter Block's 1993 book *Choosing Service Over Self-Interest*. Block writes:

> Stewardship focuses our attention on aspects...that have been most difficult to change, namely the distribution of power, purpose, and rewards...Stewardship is to hold something in trust for another. Stewardship is...the choice to preside over the orderly distribution of power. This means giving people at the bottom and the boundaries of the organization choice over how to serve a customer, a citizen, a community. It is the willingness to be accountable for the well-being of the larger organization by operating in service, rather than in control, of those around us. Stated simply, it is accountability without control or compliance.[185]

I often make the term an active verb that is explicitly collaborative: *co-stewarding*. This is particularly useful in describing the approach at the beginning of an initiative that requires continually supporting the emergence of a network

---

185 Block, Peter. 1993. *Stewardship: Choosing Service Over Self-Interest*. San Francisco, CA, USA: Berrett-Koehler. pp xix-xx

and community to take on a powerful role vis-a-vis an issue. For example, with the Global Finance Initiative, I identified individuals who would have the commitment and capacity to take the Initiative forward, as they shaped it. My assumption was that I would play a much less critical role in its future or even step out of it altogether. I was holding space, waiting for the emergence of a leadership group that would have system legitimacy — a positive profile, relationships, and knowledge — that could undertake action towards the goal of integrating sustainability into global finance logic. This led to the identification of a "stewardship team," which described an initial group who stepped into the role of supporting Initiative development.

This approach recognizes that at the early stages of developing a change initiative, no appropriate "formal" authority structure usually exists. Instead, one key goal is to build relationships across current divides. The stewarding approach also builds on recognition that defining formal structures early on is usually both energy draining and a waste of time, compared with actually experimenting and doing things. From the experience of actually doing things, a more formal structure can evolve. However, in change initiatives, even the concept of a "Board of Directors" is usually inappropriate compared with something like a "Council of Stewards."

The "stewarding" concept can guide anyone working on transformation. For example, interviewers are not simply getting information; they are creating an intervention and opportunity to steward the emergence of new ideas and commitments by those being interviewed.

Facilitator. This term is usually associated with a specific role in a meeting, but the underlying logic is key in many transformation-work exchanges. Facilitating is the capacity to support meaningful exchanges that, at their best, create generative action. The goal is to support others in expressing themselves clearly and authentically.

Being in meetings with skillful facilitators is a true joy. They have impressive repertoires of tools to support people to become individually and collectively clear about purpose, differences, and actions (some of these are referred to in Chapter 8).

Reflector. This role is about both personal introspection, and reflecting back to others their communication. In this work, the people who have had the greatest impact upon me are the ones who can act reflectively, rather than always valuing either action or reflection, above all else. For participants in a *Leadership and Change* executive management program that I co-founded at Boston College, nothing was as hard as reflecting. Business emphasizes action; academia, and many NGOs, focus on discussion and reflection. A change maker integrates the two.

Along with this comes the quality of simple curiosity, and asking questions about oneself, others in your orbit, and the broader world. Often, I find myself jumping to conclusions, at least mentally, only to discover that asking a question, rather than advocating dialogue, becomes generative rather than a debate.

One source of resistance to personal reflection is that it involves making yourself vulnerable. Creating change requires continually learning about how to improve. It is a practice and a process. Recognize, but don't get hung up on past shortcomings; each moment creates a new opportunity. Remember to practice with joy, and to strive to be the change.

Chapter 11

Summary Guiding Questions

Chapter Summary

Reflection is key to large systems change. Therefore, summary lessons are presented in the form of questions to ask yourself on your pathways toward large systems change through societal change systems.

This book is about large systems change (LSC) through societal change systems (SCSs). The lessons offered are therefore about how to approach LSC challenges through SCS development. Nevertheless, they do not simply apply to those working specifically on SCS development. They are also relevant for people working on many change initiatives (on any issue) that fall within SCSs.

1. **Work with SCS awareness.** Even when you are undertaking a large change initiative, remember that you are not the change system. You are only a part of it. Thinking about the systemic change matrix of Chapter 6: *Which of your SCS's functions and sub-systems are you working in? Are there ways to improve your connection and role with the entire SCS for greater collective impact?*

2. **Be transformation focused.** As Chapter 2 explained, transformation involves engaging with experiments, change-as-reform, and incremental change. However, remember that you are working within the SCS for large systems change in depth and breadth, not simply producing more of the same. Creation and innovation are central. *How might you further invigorate commitment and excitement energy that comes with this spirit of creation?*

3. **Create an early adopters community:** Enormous energy can be spent, and frustration felt, trying to convince or win the support of players who simply oppose change. Look for your core support amongst those who have fire in

their bellies and are committed to change. Having power (in terms of position and access to resources) is extremely valuable, but fire is critical. Think of your work as a pebble creating ripples in the pond, rather than trying to reach beyond the ripples. If you're taking a Co-creating Change strategy, create a stewardship group amongst diverse stakeholders. Those working with a Forcing Change strategy will want a narrower group. Whatever your issue, you are a community organizer. Build a team with others ready to take up the battle. You need a community to support you in tough transformation work. *Are you paying too much attention to your opponents? Do you have a good early adopters support group?*

4. **Build capacity to work across differences:** LSC creates connections across divisions and brings together those who have weak ties or are even in opposition. This includes bridging differences in goals, beliefs, competencies, and life experiences. Remember the primary message of the Societal Learning and Change Matrix of Chapter 6: organizations and people are different, even in what they look at to make sense of the world. Differences are the source of generative energy for transformation, which requires diverse resources and competencies. The imperative to build bridges across differences is most obvious with the Co-creating Change strategy. However, even those using the Forcing Change strategy need to keep in mind the whole societal change system for their issue, and consider how to connect with those who employ other strategies.

   Working across differences is not an unequivocal imperative, however. Some people are simply committed to oppressing others, such as the leaders of the Islamic State. Some organizations' interests are opposed to the change you seek, such as tobacco companies in the fight against lung cancer. They are, however, still part of the societal change systems and usually require Forcing Change strategies (at least until they are significantly weakened). *To achieve the desired transformation, are there ways that your own personal beliefs and qualities, or those reflected in your change initiative, are limiting your ability to effectively work across differences? Can these be shifted positively, without losing the essence of your role in the SCS?*

5. **Match the tools to the task:** To be an effective change maker means understanding, at least in broad strokes, the tools needed for a particular task. Chapter 2 emphasizes that different types of change (transformation, reform and incremental) require different tools (visioning, mediating, and negotiating). Chapter 9 describes a more detailed palette of available options. They come from a wide range of traditions that continue to develop new approaches, but are fragmented. *Are you using the appropriate tools for your particular change work? How can you access ones that are important for your work and that you may not yet be using?*

6. **Hold complexity, learning and emergence as the *core* dynamics:** LSC involves inventing and innovating. Issues appear intractable and wicked because we haven't yet figured out how to handle them. While technology

often plays an important role in formulating an effective response, deeper transformation questions are about how to invent new ways to act together. Learning is key from two perspectives: the process perspective, because we still have much to learn about the "how to do LSC," and the content perspective, because issues require new capabilities. *Do you have a sufficiently robust learning system? Is there something you want to experiment with? How can you investigate it?*

7. **Recognize a role for complicated and engineered:** To realize LSC, experiments that produce inventions must become a part of society at large. This requires reform and incremental efforts, *within* the new logic. Take the German energy transition (highlighted in Chapter 3), for example. In that case, prosumers (those producing and consuming electricity) became a huge new factor – so significant that complicated changes in the electrical production and delivery systems were required. *When should your SCS issue incorporate complicated approaches, as described in Chapters 2 and 4? How do you ensure that this approach does not overwhelm the need for context sensitivity and complex approaches?*

8. **Develop change process understanding:** Keep in mind the big picture of LSC. It usually takes years. Where are you in that process? Once you have a sense of history and possible outcomes, put your particular change activity into the perspectives presented in Chapter 8. *Where are you in terms of developing a particular change initiative?*

9. **Keep in mind geographic levels:** In LSC, the local and global are not like Russian matryoshka dolls, neatly fitting inside one another, nor are they a hierarchy. Each has its own particular dynamics and logics. However, they do influence each other and inhibit or support action in each other. *Is there a level that is inhibiting or providing new opportunities to advance your change work? How can you respond with an SCS perspective?*

10. **Emphasize** *organizing* **rather than** *organization.* Particularly in the inventing, emergence and experimenting modes, avoid focusing significant attention on organizational form, structures, and procedures. This will sap energy and inhibit invention. Remember that LSC invention involves bridging divides and transcending differences. This also requires inventing new organizing methods. Support interactions between people to creatively work together, and let lessons about organization arise out of this. *Do you have a good balance between organizing and organization?*

11. **Let highest aspirations and potential lead:** Be audacious and humble, or we will never realize our full potential. *Is your initiative supporting people to move towards their highest aspirations and potential in a flourishing future?*

Works Referenced

Ackoff, Russell L. 1971. "Towards a system of systems concepts." *Management Science* 17(11):661-71.

Ackoff, Russell L. 1997. "Systems, messes and interactive planning." *The Societal Engagement of Social Science* 3(1997):417-38.

Alexander, Neville. 2002. *An Ordinary Country: Issues in the Transition from Apartheid to Democracy in South Africa*. Scottsville, South Africa: University of Natal Press.

Allee, Verna. 2015. *Value Networks and the True Nature of Collaboration*: Meghan-Kiffer Press

anonymous. undated. "Awesome Gay Memes." http://likes.com/misc/pro-gay-marriage-memes: likes.com.

Argyris, Chris. 1976. "Single-Loop and Double-Loop Models in Research on Decision Making." *Administrative Science Quarterly* 21(3):363-76.

Armstrong, Patrick. Undated. "Great Bear Rainforest Lessons Learned 1995-2009": Moresby Consulting.

Biggs, Reinette, Maja Schlüter, and Michael L Schoon. 2015. Principles for Building Resilience: Sustaining Ecosystem Services in Social-Ecological Systems: Cambridge University Press.

BMWI. 2015. "Public Dialogue." http://www.bmwi.de/EN/Topics/Energy/Grids-and-grid-expansion/public-dialogue.html: Federal Ministry for Economic Affairs and Energy.

Bond, Patrick. 2014. *Elite transition: From apartheid to neoliberalism in South Africa*. London, UK: Pluto Press. Location 1089/9634.

Bradbury, Hilary. 2015. "Introduction: How to Situate and Define Action Research." Pp. 1-12 in *The Sage Handbook of Action Research*, edited by Hilary Bradbury. Boston: Sage.

Bradbury, Hilary. 2015. "The Integrating (Feminine) Reach of Action Research: A Nonet for Epistemological Voice." Pp. 573-82 in *The Sage Handbook of Action Research*, edited by Hilary Bradbury. Los Angeles, USA: Sage.

Brinton, Crane. 1938. *The anatomy of revolution*. New York, USA: Vintage Books.

Brouwer, H., Woodhill, J., with, Hemmati, M., Verhoosel, K., & Vugt, S. v. (2015). *The MSP Guide: How to design and facilitate multi-stakeholder partnerships*. Wageningen, The Netherlands: University of Wageningen.

Bruns, Elke, Dörte Ohlhorst, Bernd Wenzel, and Johann Köppel. 2010. *Renewable Energies in Germany's Electricity Market: A biography of the innovation process*: Springer Science & Business Media.

Bunker, Barbara, and Billie Alban. 1996. *Large Group Interventions : Engaging the Whole System for Rapid Change*. San Francisco, CA, USA: Jossey-Bass.

Burns, Danny. 2007. *Systemic action research: A strategy for whole system change*: Policy Press.

Centre, Crowdfunding. 2016. "2016: The State of the Crowdfunding Nation Global Report." http://thecrowdfundingcentre.com/index. php?page=login - report|page/report/?: Crowdfundingcentre.com.

Churchman, C. West. 1967. "Guest Editorial: Wicked Problems." *Management Science* 14(4):B141-B42.

Cognitive Edge. 2014. "Using Sensemaker to Understand Girls' Lives: Lessons Learnt From GirlHub ": Cognitive Edge.

Congress Alliance. 1955. "The Freedom Charter." http://www.anc.org.za/show. php?id=72: African National Congress.

Creed, WE Douglas, Rich DeJordy, and Jaco Lok. 2010. "Being the change: Resolving institutional contradiction through identity work." *Academy of Management Journal* 53(6):1336-64.

Dawkins, Richard. 1976. *The Selfish Gene*. New York, USA: Oxford University Press.

Diamond, Jared. 2005. *Collapse: How societies choose to fail or succeed*: Penguin.

Dowskin, E. (2016) *Regulator Warns Tech Companies of Big Data Bias*. Wall Street Journal, Jan. 7. on.wsj.com/1JxIBsf

Droesch, Kristen. undated. "The 15 Gay Marriage Memes You NEED To See." http://www.yourtango.com/2013188239/top-fifteen-gay-marriage-memes: Your Tango: Love Your Best.

Duhl, Len, and Trevor Hancock. 1988. "Promoting Health in the Urban Context." in *Healthy Cities Paper No. 1*, edited by FADL. Copenhagen, Denmark: WHO Healthy Cities Project Office.

Frank, Nathaniel. 2012. "How Gay Marriage Finally Won at the Polls." http://slate.me/1moCuLZ: slate.com.

Friedman, Thomas L. 2016. "Social Media: Destroyer or Creator?" Pp. A23 in *New York Times*. New York, NY, USA: New York Times Company.

Future Search Network. 2015. "Historical Roots and Theoretical Basis." https://www.futuresearch.net/method/whatis/history.cfm: Future Search Network.

Gallup. 2015. "Gay and Lesbian Rights." Gallup.

Geels, Frank W. 2005. "Processes and patterns in transitions and system innovations: refining the co-evolutionary multi-level perspective." *Technological Forecasting and Social Change* 72(6):681-96.

Geels, Frank W. 2010. "Ontologies, socio-technical transitions (to sustainability), and the multi-level perspective." *Research Policy* 39:495-510.

Gibson, James L. 2004. "Does Truth Lead to Reconciliation? Testing the Causal Assumptions of the South African Truth and Reconciliation Process." *American Journal of Political Science* 48(2):201-17.

GIZ. 2015. "Leadership for Global Responsibility (GC21)." http://bit. ly/1o6MpqX: MOOC List.

Greater Good Science Center. "What Is Forgiveness?". http://greatergood. berkeley.edu/topic/forgiveness/definition: Greater Good Science Center, University of Berkeley.

Greenpeace Energy eG. 2015. "Was Strom wirklich kostet." http://www.foes. de/pdf/2015-01-Was-Strom-wirklich-kostet-kurz.pdf: Greenpeace Germany.

Grin, John, Jan Rotmans, and Johan Schot. 2010. *Transitions to sustainable development: new directions in the study of long term transformative change*: Routledge.

Gumede, William Mervin. 2007. *Thabo Mbeki and the Battle for the Soul of the ANC*: Zebra.

Hake, Jürgen-Friedrich, Wolfgang Fischer, Sandra Venghaus, and Christoph Weckenbrock. 2015. "The German Energiewende – History and status quo." *Energy* 92, Part 3:532-46.

Hamilton, H. (undated) *The Sustainable Food Lab Interview with Hal Hamilton/ Interviewer: L. News.* http://www.sustainablefoodlab.org/images/PDF/ LIM_interview_with_HH_Issue_112.pdf.

Hassan, Zaid. 2014. *The Social Labs Revolution: A New Approach to Solving our Most Complex Challenges*. San Francisco, CA, USA: Berrett-Hoehler.

Holling, C. S., L. Gunderson, and D. Ludwig. 2002. "In Quest of a Theory of Adaptive Change." in *Panarchy: Understanding Transformations in Human and Natural Systems*, edited by L.H. Gunderson and C.S. Holling. Washington, DC: Island Press.

Holman, Peggy, and Tom Devane (Eds.). 2007. *The Change Handbook: The Definitive Resource on Today's Best Methods for Engaging Whole Systems*. San Francisco, CA, USA: Berrett-Koehler.

IDRC. 2010. "Outcome Mapping." Ottawa, Ontario, Canada: International Development and Research Centre.

Ikeda, Daisaku. 2007. "Civil Society Peace Forum at New York's Cooper Union Focuses on Abolishing Nuclear Weapons ". http://www.joseitoda.org/ reports/070908c.html: Soka Gakkai

Isaacs, William. 1999. *Dialogue and the art of thinking together*. New York, NY: Currency Doubleday.

Jennings, Charles. 2011. "Social & Workplace Learning through the 70:20:10 Lens." http://charles-jennings.blogspot.nl/2011/08/social-workplace-learning-through.html: Charles Jennings.

Kahane, Adam. 2010. *Power and love: A theory and practice of social change*: Berrett-Koehler Publishers.

Kania, John, and Mark Kramer. 2011. "Collective Impact." *Stanford Social Innovation Review* Winter:36-41.

Kania, John, and Mark Krarner. 2013. "Embracing Emergence: How Collective Impact Addresses Complexity." Blog Entry: Stanford Social Innovation Review.

Keim, Daniel, Florian Mansmann, Jorn Schneidewind, and Hartmut Ziegler. 2006. "Challenges in visual data analysis." Pp. 9-16 in *Information Visualization, 2006. IV 2006. Tenth International Conference on*: IEEE.

Kim, Daniel. 1992. *The Toolbox Reprint Series: Systems Archetypes I*. Waltham, MA: Pegasus Communications, Inc.

Klarman, Michael J. 2013. "How Marriage Came to Be." *Harvard Magazine* (March-April):30-35.

Kuenkel, Petra. 2008. *Mind and Heart*: BoD–Books on Demand.

Kuenkel, Petra. 2015. "Navigating Change in Complex Multi-Actor Settings: A Practice Approach to Better Collaboration." *Journal of Corporate Citizenship* 2015(58):119-36.

Kuenkel, Petra. 2016. *The Art of Leading Collectively: Co-Creating a Sustainable, Socially Just Future.* . White River Junction, VT, USA:: Chelsea Green Publishing.

Kuhn, Thomas. 1962. *The Structure of Scientific Revolutions*. Chicago, IL: The University of Chicago Press.

Lauber, Volkmar, and Moritz Buschmann. 2013. "Germany: Challenges of a Full Transition to Renewable Energy." Pp. 295-313 in *Renewable Energy Governance*: Springer.

Leap, Dennis. 2013. "The Shrewd Strategy Behind Same-Sex 'Marriage.'" in *The Trumpet*: Philadelphia Church of God.

Lissack, Michael R. 2003. "The Redefinition of Memes: Ascribing Meaning to an Empty Cliché." *Emergence* 5(3):48-65.

Loorbach, Derk. 2010. "Transition management for sustainable development: a prescriptive, complexity-based governance framework." *Governance* 23(1):161-83.

———. 2014. "To Transition! Governance Panarchy in the New Transformation." Rotterdam: Faculty of Social Sciences, Erasmus University.

Malia, Martin. 2008. *History's Locomotives: Revolutions and the Making of the Modern World*. New Haven, CT, USA: Yale University Press.

Marais, Hein. 2001. *South Africa: Limits to change: The political economy of transition*: Palgrave Macmillan.

Markshal K. Kirk, and Erastes Pill. 1987. "The Overhauling Of Straight America: Waging Peace, Part Two." *Guide Magazine* (November):7-14.

Marx, Karl. 1859/1973. "A Contribution to the Critique of Political Economy." in *Dynamics of Social Change: A Reader in Marxist Social Science*, edited by H. & Goldway Selsam, D. New York: International Publishers.

McLeod Grant, Heather. 2010. "Transformer: How to build a network to change a system A Case Study of the RE-AMP Energy Network." San Francisco, CA, USA: Monitor Institute.

Meadows, D.H., D.L. Meadows, J. Randers, and W.W. Berhens. 1972. *The Limits to Growth*. New York: Universe Books, republished by Productivity Press, Portland, OR.

Meadows, Donnella. 1999. "Leverage Points: Places to Intervene in a System." Harland, VT, USA: The Sustainability Institute.

Midgley, Gerald, Robert Y Cavana, John Brocklesby, Jeff L Foote, David RR Wood, and Annabel Ahuriri-Driscoll. 2013. "Towards a new framework for evaluating systemic problem structuring methods." *European Journal of Operational Research* 229(1):143-54.

Millennium Ecosystem Assessment. 2005. *Millennium Ecosystem Assessment Findings*: Millennium Ecosystem Assessment.

Moore, Michele-Lee, Darcy Riddell, and Dana Vocisano. 2015. "Scaling Out, Scaling Up, Scaling Deep: Strategies of Non-profits in Advancing Systemic Social Innovation." *Journal of Corporate Citizenship* 2015(58):67-84.

Ndebele, Njabulo Simakahle. 1999. *Of lions and rabbits: Thoughts on democracy and reconciliation*.

OECD. 2013. "OECD Economic Surveys: SOUTH AFRICA." Paris, France: OECD.

Olsen, Stephen, and Glenn Page. 2008. "Applying the Orders of Outcomes to NOS Initiatives in Gulf Of California, Mexico." Noroeste Sustentable, Walton Family Foundation.

Pang, John, Chris Vlahoplus, John Sterling, and Bob Gibson. 2014. "Germany's Energiewende." *Public Utilities Fortnightly* 152(11):14.

Patton, Michael Quinn. 2010. *Developmental Evaluation: Applying Complexity Concepts to Enhance Innovation and Use*. New York, NY, USA: Guilford Press.

Pawson, Ray. 2013. *The science of evaluation: a realist manifesto*: Sage.

Pew Research Center. 2015. "Section 2: Knowing Gays and Lesbians, Religious Conflicts, Beliefs about Homosexuality." http://www.people-press. org/2015/06/08/section-2-knowing-gays-and-lesbians-religious-conflicts-beliefs-about-homosexuality/: People-press.org.

Raelin, Joseph. 2003. *Creating Leaderful Organizations: How to bring out leadership in everyone*. San Francisco, CA, USA: Berrett-Koehler.

Reinicke, Wolfgang H. 1999-2000. "The Other World Wide Web: Global Public Policy Networks." *Foreign Policy* (Winter):44-57.

Reinicke, Wolfgang H., and Francis M. Deng. 2000. "Critical Choices: The United Nations, networks, and the future of global governance." Toronto, Canada: International Development Research Council.

Rischard, Jean-Francois. 2002. *High Noon: 20 Global Problems, 20 Years to Solve Them*. New York, NY, USA: Basic Books.

Ritchie-Dunham, James L. . 2014. *Ecosynomics: The Science of Abundance*. Amherst, MA, USA: Vibrancy Publishing (ecosynomics.com).

Ritichie-Dunham, J., & Rabbino, H. (2001). *Managing from Clarity: Identifying, Aligning and Leveraging Strategic Resources*. Chichester, UK: John Wiley & Sons, Ltd.

Rockstrom, Johan, Will Steffen, Kevin Noone, Asa Persson, F. Stuart Chapin, Eric F. Lambin, Timothy M. Lenton, Marten Scheffer, Carl Folke, Hans Joachim Schellnhuber, Bjorn Nykvist, Cynthia A. de Wit, Terry Hughes, Sander van der Leeuw, Henning Rodhe, Sverker Sorlin, Peter K. Snyder, Robert Costanza, Uno Svedin, Malin Falkenmark, Louise Karlberg, Robert W. Corell, Victoria J. Fabry, James Hansen, Brian Walker, Diana Liverman, Katherine Richardson, Paul Crutzen, and Jonathan A. Foley. 2009. "A safe operating space for humanity." *Nature* 461(7263):472-75.

Scharmer, C Otto. 2009. *Theory U: Learning from the future as it emerges*: Berrett-Koehler Publishers.

Scharmer, Otto, and Katrin Kaufer. 2013. *Leading from the Emerging Future: From Ego-System to Eco-System Economies*. San Francisco, CA, USA: Berrett-Koehler Publishers, Inc.

Schmid, Eva, Brigitte Knopf, and Anna Pechan. 2016. "Putting an energy system transformation into practice: The case of the German Energiewende." *Energy Research & Social Science* 11:263-75.

Schumpeter, Joseph Alois. 1939. *Business cycles*: Cambridge Univ Press.

Schweizer, Pia-Johanna, Ortwin Renn, Wolfgang Köck, Jana Bovet, Christina Benighaus, Oliver Scheel, and Regina Schröter. 2014. "Public participation for infrastructure planning in the context of the German "Energiewende"." *Utilities Policy*.

Seagal, Sandra, and David Horne. 2000. *Human Dynamics: A new framework for understanding people and realizing the potential in our organizations*. Waltham, MA USA: Pegasus Communications.

Senge, Peter M. 1990. *The Fifth Discipline: The Art and Practice of the Learning Organization*. New York: Doubleday.

Senge, Peter, Richard Ross, Bryan Smith, Charlotte Roberts, and Art Kleiner. 1994. *The Fifth Discipline Fieldbook*. New York, NY: Currency Doubleday.

Simonsen, Sturle Hauge, Reinette (Oonsie) Biggs, Maja Schlüter, Michael Schoon, Erin Bohensky, Georgina Cundill, Vasilis Dakos, Tim Daw, Karen Kotschy, Anne Leitch, Allyson Quinlan, Garry Peterson, and Fredrik Moberg. Circa 2015. "Applying resilience thinking: Seven principles for building resilience in social-ecological systems." Stockholm Resilience Centre. http://bit.ly/R4A6uI

Skocpol, Theda. 1979. *States and social revolutions: A comparative analysis of France, Russia and China*: Cambridge University Press.

Snowden, B. (2015). The Family of My Dreams. Living Buddhism. Santa Monica, CA, USA, Soka Gakkai International. 19: 22-23.

Snowden, David J., and Mary E. Boone. 2007. "A Leader's Framework for Decision Making." *Harvard Business Review* 85(11):68-76.

Snyder, William M., and Etienne Wenger. 2004. "Our World as a Learning System: a Communities-of-Practice Approach." Pp. 35-58 in *Creating a learning culture: strategy, technology, and practice*, edited by Marcia L. Conner and James G. Clawson: The Press Syndicate of the University of Cambridge.

Sokka Gaki International. 2015. "Human Revolution." http://www.sgi.org/about-us/buddhism-in-daily-life/human-revolution.html: Soka Gakkai International.

Sokka Gaki International. 2015. "Shakabuku." http://www.sgilibrary.org/search_dict.php?id=1974: Soka Gakki International.

Sustainable Food Lab. Circa 2006. "SFL Phase II (version 4)." Sustainable Food Lab.

Tapscott, Don. 2014. "Introducing Global Solution Networks: Understanding the New Multi-Stakeholder Models for Global Cooperation, Problem Solving and Governance." *Innovations* 9(1-2):3-46.

Technology, Parliamentary Office of Science &. 2014. "Big Data: An Overview." in *Postnote*. London, UK: Houses of Parliament.

Tennesen, Michael. 2015. *The Next Species: The Future of Evolution in the Aftermath of Man*: Simon and Schuster.

Torjman, Lisa. 2012. "Labs: Designing the Future." MaRS Solutions Lab.

Tosey, Paul, Max Visser, and Mark NK Saunders. 2012. "The origins and conceptualizations of 'triple-loop' learning: A critical review." *Management Learning* 43(3):291-307.

Transparency International. 2015. "Our History - In the Beginning." https://www.transparency.org/whoweare/history/: Transparency International.

Trist, Eric. 1983. "Referent Organizations and the Development of Inter-Organizational Domains." *Human Relations* 36(3):269-84.

UNEP. 2015. "The Financial System We Need - The UNEP Inquiry Report - Aligning the financial system with sustainable development." UNEP.

Verbruggen, Aviel, Rosaria Di Nucci, Manfred Fischedick, Reinhard Haas, Frede Hvelplund, Volkmar Lauber, Arturo Lorenzoni, Lutz Mez, Lars J Nilsson, and Pablo del Rio Gonzalez. 2015. "Europe's electricity regime: restoration or thorough transition." *International Journal of Sustainable Energy Planning and Management* 5:57-68.

Waddell, Steve, Heinz Greijn, Koen Faber, Jonas Haertle, and Annalisa Mauro. 2013. "Inter-organizational Learning: A new frontier." *Capacity.org* January(46):3-6.

Waddell, Steve, Sandra Waddock, Sarah Cornell, Domenico Dentoni, Milla McLachlan, and Greta Meszoely. 2015. "Large Systems Change: An Emerging Field of Transformation and Transitions." *Journal of Corporate Citizenship* (58):5-30.

Waddell, Steve. 2002. "Core Competencies: A Key Force in Business-Government-Civil Society Collaborations." *Journal of Corporate Citizenship* (7):43-56.

Waddell, Steve. 2005. *Societal Learning and Change: How Governments, Business and Civil Society are Creating Solutions to Complex Multi-Stakeholder Problems*. Sheffield, UK: Greenleaf Publishing.

Waddell, Steve. 2011. *Global Action Networks: Creating our future together*. Bocconi University on Management. Hampshire, UK: Palgrave-Macmillan.

Waddell, Steve. 2012. "Design Guidelines to Address Global Challenges: The Case of Global Action Networks." *Journal of Organization Design* 1(3):1-19.

Waddock, Sandra, Greta M. Meszoely, Steve Waddell, and Domenico Dentoni. 2015. "The complexity of wicked problems in large scale change." *Journal of Organizational Change Management* 28(6):993-1012.

Waddock, Sandra. 2015. "Reflections: Intellectual Shamans, Sensemaking, and Memes in Large System Change." *Journal of Change Management*.

Waxman, Olivia B. 2015. "Here Are Today's Best Marriage Equality Memes." in *Time*. http://time.com/3938004/us-supreme-court-gay-same-sex-marriage-memes/.

WBCSD. "Vision 2050: The new agenda for business." Geneva, Switzerland: World Business Council for Sustainable Development.

Weisbord, Marvin, and Sandra Janoff. 2010. *Future Search: Getting the Whole System in the Room for Vision, Commitment, and Action*. San Francisco, CA: Berrett-Koehler.

Weisbord, Marvin, and Sandra Janoff. 2010. *Future Search: Getting the Whole System in the Room for Vision, Commitment, and Action*. San Francisco, CA: Berrett-Koehler.

Wenger, Etienne C., and William M. Snyder. 2000. "Communities of Practice: The Organizational Frontier." *Harvard Business Review* (January - February):139-45.

Wenger, Etienne, Richard McDermott, and William M. Snyder. 2002. *Cultivating Communities of Practice*. Boston, MA, USA: Harvard Business School Press.

Westley, Frances, Nino Antadze, Darcy J. Riddell, Kirsten Robinson, and Sean Geobey. 2014. "Five configurations for scaling up social innovation: case examples of nonprofit organizations from Canada." *The Journal of Applied Behavioral Science* 50(3):234-60.

Westley, Frances, Per Olsson, Carl Folke, Thomas Homer-Dixon, Harrie Vredenburg, Derk Loorbach, John Thompson, Måns Nilsson, Eric Lambin, and Jan Sendzimir. 2011. "Tipping toward sustainability: emerging pathways of transformation." *AMBIO* 40(7):762-80.

Westley, Frances, Sam Laban, Cherul Rose, Katharine McGowan, Kirsten Robinson, Ola Tjornbo, and Mark Tovey. Circa 2015. "Social Innovation Lab Guide." Waterloo, Ontario, Canada: Waterloo Institute for Social Innovation and Resilience.

WHO. 1994. "Action for Health in Cities." Copenhagen, Denmark: World Health Organiation - Regional Office for Europe.

Wilber, Ken. 1996. *A Brief History of Everything*. Dublin, Ireland: Gill & Macmillan Ltd.

Wilkinson, Angela, and Esther Eidinow. 2008. "Evolving practices in environmental scenarios: A new scenario typology." *Environmental Research Letters* 3(Oct-Dec).

Wilkinson, Angela. 2009. "Scenarios Practices: In Search of Theory." *Journal of Futures Studies* 13(3):107-14.

Wkipedia. 2014. "Ecosystem." http://en.wikipedia.org/wiki/Ecosystem.

Wkipedia. 2016. "Crowdfunding." https://en.wikipedia.org/wiki/Crowdfunding - Types: Wikipedia.

Wolsink, Maarten, and Sylvia Breukers. 2010. "Contrasting the core beliefs regarding the effective implementation of wind power. An international study of stakeholder perspectives." *Journal of environmental planning and management* 53(5):535-58.

Wolsink, Maarten. 2010. "Contested environmental policy infrastructure: Socio-political acceptance of renewable energy, water, and waste facilities." *Environmental Impact Assessment Review* 30(5):302-11.

Index

CPSIA information can be obtained
at www.ICGtesting.com
Printed in the USA
BVOW11s0735110416

443479BV00005B/13/P